A YEAR OF

Powerful Prayer

A YEAR OF

Powerful Prayer

Getting Answers
for Your
Life Every Day

365 DAILY READINGS

**DESERET
BOOK**

SALT LAKE CITY, UTAH

© 2013 Deseret Book Company

DESERET BOOK is a registered trademark of Deseret Book Company.

Visit us at DeseretBook.com

Library of Congress Cataloging-in-Publication Data

A year of powerful prayer : getting answers for your life every day.
    pages cm
  Includes bibliographical references.
  Summary: A daily devotional book on the power of prayer.
  ISBN 978-1-60907-363-3 (hardbound : alk. paper)
  1. Prayer—The Church of Jesus Christ of Latter-day Saints. 2. Devotional calendars—The Church of Jesus Christ of Latter-day Saints.
  BX8656.Y43 2013
  248.3'2—dc23   2012043329

Printed in the United States of America
Worzalla Publishing Co., Stevens Point, WI

10   9   8   7   6   5   4   3   2   1

Contents

GOD IS CLOSER THAN WE THINK

JESUS SET THE EXAMPLE FOR US

IMPROVING THE QUALITY OF OUR PRAYERS

WHAT IS REQUIRED?

LET THE SPIRIT GUIDE

PREPARE FOR OPPOSITION

LEARNING TO LISTEN

UNEXPECTED ANSWERS

PRAYER IN ADVERSITY

"Not My Will, but Thine"

The Lord's Timetable

PRAYERS FOR HOME AND FAMILY

How Prayer Helps Us

Sources for the quotations in this book can be found online at
www.deseretbook.com/pdf/A_Year_of_Powerful_Prayer-Sources.pdf

"Let Him Ask of God"

Let Him Ask of God

"If any of you lack wisdom, *let him ask of God,* that giveth to all men liberally, and upbraideth not; and it shall be given him" (James 1:5; emphasis added).

These five words in the epistle of James changed the world. Joseph Smith's first prayer is traceable to this verse of scripture and the powerful impression that it left on his soul. The consequences of that teenage prayer led many thousands to cross oceans and continents in an attempt to build Zion. But this verse was not written for Joseph Smith alone. The message of James 1:5 for the rest of us is that God is approachable, generous, and willing to answer our prayers. An additional implication is that if we don't ask of God, He won't give liberally. Later in the epistle, James writes, "Ye have not, because ye ask not" (James 4:2). In the same spirit, Elder Jeffrey R. Holland taught, "God is anxiously waiting for the chance to answer your prayers and fulfill your dreams, just as He always has. But He can't if you don't pray, and He can't if you don't dream. In short, He can't if you don't believe" (*Broken Things to Mend* [Salt Lake City: Deseret Book, 2008], 85).

—*John Bytheway*

The Divine Law of Prayer

In prayer, man asks and Deity answers. Those who do not ask receive no answer. "Ask, and it shall be given you," Jesus said; "seek, and ye shall find; knock, and it shall be opened unto you." Why? Because the promise is: "Every one that asketh receiveth; and he that seeketh findeth; and to him that knocketh it shall be opened." Such is the divine law.

—Bruce R. McConkie

Only through Prayer

Why should we pray? We should pray because prayer is indispensable to the accomplishment of the real purpose of our lives. We are children of God. As such, we have the potentiality to rise to his perfection. The Savior himself inspired us with this aspiration when he said, "I would that ye should be perfect even as I, or your Father who is in heaven is perfect." (3 Nephi 12:48.)

No one shall ever reach such perfection unless he is guided to it by Him who is perfect. And guidance from Him is to be had only through prayer. In our upward climb, this mortal experience through which we are now passing is a necessary step. To obtain perfection, we had to leave our pre-earth home and come to earth. During the transfer, a veil was drawn over our spiritual eyes, and the memory of our pre-earth experiences was suspended. In the Garden of Eden, God endowed us with moral agency and, as it were, left us here on our own between the forces of good and evil to be proved—to see if, walking by faith, we would rise to our high potentiality by doing "all things whatsoever the Lord [our] God shall command [us]." (Abraham 3:25.)

—*Marion G. Romney*

God Has Made Himself Available to All His Children

It is comforting to know that no one is required to walk life's paths alone. Each of us should find great satisfaction and strength in knowing that we do not need to face our challenges, undertake our assignments, or resist temptations through our own un-aided efforts. No scriptural invitation is given more frequently than the divine encouragement to ask, to seek, to knock. God has made himself available to all his children. He has offered his Beloved Son in willing sacrifice to make possible a forgiveness of sins and the

LET HIM ASK OF GOD" 5

immortality of the soul. And he has sent his Spirit, the Holy Ghost, to comfort, remind, reveal, teach, confirm, sanctify, and seal. Indeed, consider the sweet implications of the following scriptural promise: "I will go before your face. I will be on your right hand and on your left, and my Spirit shall be in your hearts, and mine angels round about you, to bear you up" (D&C 84:88).

—*Robert L. Millet*

DAY 5

Prayer Has Changed the World

Prayer is man's means of communicating with his Heavenly Father, the Almighty, Creator of heaven and earth. Only the deceived and the fool refuse to pray. An urgent need today is for more prayer—secret, individual prayer; family prayer; prayer in organizations, associations, and meetings generally, and in schools, and in government bodies. People of all nations need more prayer. We need to be on our knees. (*God, Family, Country,* p. 114.)

Prayer has literally changed the development of man. It has brought him out of the morass of indecision and discouragement into the sunlight born of faith through works and love and trust. Fervent prayer on the part of a young fourteen-year-old boy in New York State in 1820 started a chain of events which is literally changing the lives of millions of people today. The direct result of this prayer has brought a positive understanding of the being of God the Father and His Son, Jesus Christ. It has caused the uncovering of ancient histories which contain divine truths that if obeyed will lead directly to the eventual exaltation of man and to a situation of happiness and joy that words cannot describe.

—*Ezra Taft Benson*

Pray Continually

We would say to the brethren, seek to know God in your closets, call upon him in the fields. Follow the directions of the Book of Mormon, and pray over, and for your families, your cattle, your flocks, your herds, your corn, and all things that you possess; ask the blessing of God upon all your labors, and everything that you engage in. Be virtuous and pure; be men of integrity and truth; keep the commandments of God; and then you will be able more perfectly to understand the difference between right and wrong—between the things of God and the things of men; and your path will be like that of the just, which shineth brighter and brighter unto the perfect day.

—*Joseph Smith*

Prayer Is the Key

Prayer is the key that unlocks the door to communion with Deity. "Behold," said the Lord, "I stand at the door, and knock: if any man hear my voice, and open the door, I will come in to him, and will sup with him, and he with me." (Revelation 3:20.)

A similar promise, as Jesus gave it to the Nephites, is: "Whatsoever ye shall ask the Father in my name, *which is right,* believing that ye shall receive, behold it shall be given unto you." (3 Nephi 18:20; emphasis added.)

To us of this last dispensation, the promise is thus stated: "Whatsoever ye ask the Father in my name it shall be given unto you, *that is expedient for you.*" (D&C 88:64; emphasis added.)

The sacred records are replete with proof that such promises are fulfilled.

Prayer brought forgiveness of sins to Enos. (See Enos 1:4–5.) The prayers of Alma Senior sent an angel to bring his son Alma to repentance. (See Mosiah 27:14.) Prayer brought the Father and the Son to visit the Prophet Joseph Smith. (See Joseph Smith—History 1:14–17.) Prayer brought the seagulls from the lake to help save the crops of the pioneers.

Not every prayer brings a spectacular response, but every sincere and earnest prayer is heard and responded to by the Spirit of the Lord.

—*Marion G. Romney*

Prayer Changes Lives

Prayer has changed many lives. It has had an effect on our lives, both yours and mine. Prayer is that which brings us in close communion with God. It is the very beginning of our relationship with God. It has existed from the beginning, for an angel spoke to Adam in the Garden of Eden and said to him, "Wherefore, thou shalt do all that thou doest in the name of the Son, and thou shalt repent and call upon God in the name of the Son forevermore"

—*Howard W. Hunter*

What Prayer Is

Once we dwelt in our Father's presence, saw his face, and knew his will. We spoke to him, heard his voice, and received counsel and direction from him. Such was our status as spirit children in the pre-earth life. We then walked by sight.

Now we are far removed from the divine presence; we no longer see his face and hear his voice as we then did. We now walk by faith. But we need his counsel and direction as much as or more than we needed it when we mingled with all the seraphic hosts of heaven before the world was. In his infinite wisdom, knowing our needs, a gracious Father has provided prayer as the means of continuing to communicate with him. As I have written elsewhere: "To pray is to speak with God, either vocally or by forming the thoughts involved in the mind. Prayers may properly include expressions of praise, thanksgiving, and adoration; they are the solemn occasions during which the children of God petition their Eternal Father for those things, both temporal and spiritual, which they feel are needed to sustain them in all the varied tests of the mortal probation. Prayers are occasions of confession—occasions when in humility and contrition, having broken hearts and contrite spirits, the saints confess their sins to Deity and implore him to grant his cleansing forgiveness." (*Mormon Doctrine,* 2d ed. [Salt Lake City: Bookcraft, 1966], 581.)

—*Bruce R. McConkie*

DAY 10

Why Pray?

Why do we pray? First, we believe our heavenly Father is a Man of Holiness (Moses 6:57), a glorified and exalted Being to be sure, but a resurrected and redeemed Man who is literally the Father of our spirits. He knows us, one by one, and has infinite love and tender regard for each one of us. He has a physical body, parts, and passions. He feels. He yearns. He pains and sorrows for our struggles and our wanderings. He delights in our successes. He responds to petitions and pleadings. He is neither untouchable nor unapproachable. Thus our prayers allow us to express to God our needs, our challenges, our deepest feelings and desires, and to ask sincerely for his help. The more prayerful we become, the more dependent we are upon God, and thus the more trusting and reliant upon spiritual powers beyond our own. Prayer thus builds our spiritual strength by pointing us beyond our limited resources to him who has all power. In short, we pray to better understand who we are and who God is. We pray to better understand what we can do on our own and what we can do only with divine assistance.

Second, prayer allows us to communicate with Deity, to open ourselves to conversation with divinity. If indeed the quality of our lives is largely a product of the kinds of associations we enjoy, then we may rest assured that individuals who spend much time in prayer will in time blossom in personality, rise above pettiness, littleness of soul, and mortal jealousies and fears. We cannot have contact with influences that are degrading without being affected adversely, almost as though the degrading words and deeds become a part of us. On the other hand, if we regularly call upon God, pour out our soul in prayer, and yearn for genuine communion with Deity, we cannot help but be elevated and transformed by the association. The very powers of God, coming to us through his Holy Spirit, make us into men and women of purpose, of purity, and of power. In short, we pray in order to receive an infusion of power, to draw strength from an omnipotent Being.

—*Robert L. Millet*

God Commands Us to Pray

The importance of prayer is emphasized by the fact that the most oft-repeated command given by God to men is to pray.

The first commandment God gave Adam and Eve was "that they should worship the Lord their God."

And later "an angel of the Lord appeared unto Adam, saying: . . .

"Thou shalt do all that thou doest in the name of the Son, and thou shalt repent and call upon God in the name of the Son forevermore." (Moses 5:5–6, 8.)

The Lord took occasion to personally instruct the brother of Jared as to the importance of prayer. When he, with the Jaredite colony, reached the great sea, "the Lord came . . . unto [him]. . . . And for the space of three hours did the Lord talk with [him] and chastened him because he remembered not to call upon the name of the Lord.

"And the brother of Jared repented of the evil which he had done, and did call upon the name of the Lord.

" . . . And the Lord said unto him: I will forgive thee and thy brethren . . . but thou shalt not sin any more, for ye shall remember that my Spirit will not always strive with man; wherefore, if ye will sin until ye are fully ripe ye shall be cut off from the presence of the Lord." (Ether 2:13–15; italics added.)

Amulek admonished the backsliding Nephites in these words:

"May God grant unto you, my brethren, that ye may begin to exercise your faith unto repentance, that ye begin to call upon his holy name, that he would have mercy upon you;

" . . . cry unto him for mercy; for he is mighty to save.

" . . . humble yourselves, and continue in prayer unto him." (Alma 34:17–27).

—*Marion G. Romney*

DAY 12

Prayer Opens the Door

Prayer may be gibberish and nonsense to the carnal mind, but to the saints of God it is the avenue of communication with the Unseen. To the unbelieving and rebellious it may seem as an act of senseless piety born of mental instability, but to those who have tasted its fruits it becomes an anchor to the soul through all the storms of life.

Prayer is of God—not the vain repetitions of the heathen, not the rhetoric of the prayer books, not the insincere lispings of lustful men, but that prayer which is born of knowledge, which is nurtured by faith in Christ, which is offered in spirit and in truth.

Prayer opens the door to peace in this life and eternal life in the world to come. Prayer is essential to salvation. Unless and until we make it a living part of us so that we speak to our Father and have his voice answer, by the power of his spirit, we are yet in our sins.

—*Bruce R. McConkie*

Prayer Is an Opportunity

For the unconverted, prayer may seem a burden or at best a duty. But for the seasoned Saint, one who has begun to grow up in the Lord and mature in the gifts and fruit of the Spirit (1 Corinthians 12–14; Galatians 5:22–25), prayer is a blessed opportunity, a consummate privilege, a remarkable honor for a finite, fallen creature to be allowed and even commanded to communicate with an infinite, pure, and glorified Being.

—*Robert L. Millet*

Why We Pray

The Key to the Lord's Blessings

The Lord truly wants to bless us in all aspects of our lives—our temporal needs, our goals, our relationships, our spiritual desires, and everything else. The key to receiving these blessings is to ask in prayer. Those who ask in faith and then obey the direction he gives them will receive the blessings. Of course, if we choose not to obey the Lord, we receive no promise, as a result of our disobedience.

I think many of us have a tendency to have our morning or evening prayers, and maybe even pray a few other times in a day, but not really pray. I'd ask you this question: When you face a new challenge in your day, what's the first thing that comes to your mind? Where does your heart run first? I hope it's to the Lord. That will be the case if you're trying to pray without ceasing. If you're not, I would say you're "winging it" on your own. You're trying to work through the day's many problems with the hope that your prayer in the morning covered it all.

It is most helpful when you move into any new circumstance, or when you are trying to assist others, that you have a prayer in your heart. "How should I deal with this? What should I do? Are there any special concerns that I ought to know about? Heavenly Father, help me. Help me."

Unfortunately, many of us don't ask. So we go off on our own and don't obtain the help we could have received with the problems we face each day.

Once again I bear humble witness that if we ask, as the scriptures say over and over again, we will receive. Again I bear witness that not one single, sincere prayer has been offered since the beginning of time that the Lord didn't respond to. Not one. Our problem is we don't ask.

—*Gene R. Cook*

DAY 15

Ask, Seek, Knock

"*Ask,* and it shall be given you; *seek,* and ye shall find; *knock,* and it shall be opened unto you" (Matthew 7:7).

There is almost an ascending order in those three commands. *Asking* is primarily a verbal action. *Seeking* implies a higher level of involvement—when we seek we begin to do something; the word implies an earnestness that commits both the mind and the heart, the intellect and the emotions. Finally, *knocking* suggests some actual physical action. The implication is also that once the door is open, we will move through it, for that was the purpose in our knocking. The Lord drew on that latter imagery in one of the letters to the seven churches in Asia included in the book of Revelation. He said: "Behold, I stand at the door, and knock: if any man hear my voice, and open the door, I will come in to him, and will sup with him, and he with me" (Revelation 3:20).

—*Gerald N. Lund*

We Have to Ask

The scriptures are literal when they encourage us to "pray oft unto the Lord' (1 Nephi 18:3), pray always (Ephesians 6:18), "pray without ceasing" (1 Thessalonians 5:17), "let your hearts be . . . drawn out in prayer unto him continually" (Alma 34:27), "give ourselves continually to prayer" (Acts 6:4), and to "pray every where" (1 Timothy 2:8). Why? Because praying constantly allows us to have an on-going conversation with the Lord. When we pray frequently throughout the day and address specific needs, we open the door to receive more frequent and specific answers.

The Bible Dictionary explains, "Prayer is the act by which the will of the Father and the will of the child are brought into correspondence with each other. The object of prayer is not to change the will of God, but to secure for ourselves and for others the blessings *that God is already willing to grant, but that are made conditional on our asking for them.*" (Bible Dictionary, s.v. "prayer"; emphasis added.)

Frequent prayer gives us an opportunity to ask for blessings at all hours of the day—especially during those moments when we find ourselves running on empty. There are blessings that God is already willing to grant if we just take the time to ask. Elder David A. Bednar said, "Morning and evening prayers—and *all* of the prayers in between—are not unrelated, discreet events; rather, they are linked together each day and across days, weeks, months, and even years. This is in part how we fulfill the scriptural admonition to 'pray always.' Such meaningful prayers are instrumental in obtaining the highest blessings God holds in store for his faithful children." (David A. Bednar, "Pray Always," *Ensign,* November 2008, 42; emphasis added.)

—*Emily Freeman*

DAY 17

Praying with Real Intent

The most basic truth about the universe is that a magnificent, kindly Being upholds all things. And the most basic truth about us is that each of us is his own child, treasured in his sight. . . .

During our premortal sojourn with God, we spoke to him freely, and he never failed to answer. Now in the mortal test, we do not see him for a little season, and we feel that we do not know him as well. But his interest in us has not diminished one whit. His eyes are still upon us. It is still our privilege to speak with him, and he still promises to answer.

Of course, there can be no communing with him, or with anyone for that matter, unless we are genuine. Prayer is genuine or it isn't prayer. A good parent welcomes every conversation from a sincere child. Otherwise the conversation isn't real. A good teacher welcomes any question as long as the student really wants to hear the answer. Otherwise it isn't really a question.

We are genuine with God when we trust not only that he is "up there somewhere" but also that he is our friend and that he is always right. This is our courtesy, our faith in the Father—giving him credit for what he really is.

And it is only honest to pray with "real intent"—the intention to do his will as soon as he replies (Moroni 10:4). We lean forward, ready to obey. In fact, we already know many of the things he would have us do. If our intent is real, we are already doing those things, even before the next answer comes.

Those who pray genuinely discover again and again that he answers prayers.

—*Wayne E. Brickey*

Ask in Faith

My brethren and sisters, let us remember and call upon God and implore His blessings and His favor upon us. Let us do it nevertheless in wisdom and in righteousness, and when we pray we should call upon Him in a consistent and reasonable way. We should not ask the Lord for that which is unnecessary or which would not be beneficial to us. We should ask for that which we need, and we should ask "in faith, nothing wavering[, for] he that wavereth," as the Apostle said, "is like the wave of the sea, driven by the wind and tossed. For let not that man think that he shall receive anything of the Lord." But when we ask of God for blessings let us ask in the faith of the Gospel, in that faith that He has promised to give to them who believe in Him and obey His commandments.

—*Joseph F. Smith*

DAY 19

Praying for Revelation

Let all persons be fervent in prayer, until they know the things of God for themselves and become certain that they are walking in the path that leads to everlasting life; then will envy, the child of ignorance, vanish and there will be no disposition in any man to place himself above another; for such a feeling meets no countenance in the order of heaven. Jesus Christ never wanted to be different from his Father. They were and are one. If a people are led by the revelations of Jesus Christ, and they are cognizant of the fact through their faithfulness, there is no fear but they will be one in Jesus Christ, and see eye to eye.

—*Brigham Young*

Prayer and Growth

One can pray and yet not really pray. Prayers can be routinized and made very superficial. When this happens, there is very little communication and very little growth. Yet, given the times in which we live, improving our prayers should be one of our deepest desires if we are genuinely serious about growing spiritually.

Prayer may not be a hard doctrine, but it can be a very deep and soul-satisfying experience. It is the means by which we can draw close to our Heavenly Father and understand better His deep doctrines.

Certainly, in hard times, prayer is no less needed. It is sobering to remember that we have been told that in the final days of this dispensation the righteous will pray almost unceasingly to the Lord for Him to hasten His coming—so bad will be the circumstances on the earth. However, even apart from such stressful circumstances, praying is a part of that triad of things we must do: *serving, studying,* and *praying* in order to find joy and happiness and to grow closer to the Lord.

—*Neal A. Maxwell*

Is Prayer a Crutch?

It is said that prayer is a crutch. After all, mature people are supposed to stand on their own two feet; they don't have to pray. Prayer is a form of wishful thinking, a kind of wanting pie in the sky. Well, as to that, first of all there is nothing wrong with crutches for people who need them. There is nothing wrong with escalators and elevators. But speaking of crutches, agnosticism is a kind of crutch. It is a perennial postponement of decision, and it assumes that postponement is safer than commitment. Atheism is a pair of iron braces. It claims to know more than can be known. Someone has said that atheists don't find God for the same reason that bank robbers don't find policemen. They work very hard to avoid Him. But throughout the Doctrine and Covenants is the admonition, "Seek and ye shall find." The implication is, don't seek and you likely won't find.

—*Truman G. Madsen*

DAY 22

Every Breath a Prayer

I do not know any other way for the Latter-day Saints than for every breath to be virtually a prayer for God to guide and direct his people, and that he will never suffer us to possess anything that will be an injury to us. I am satisfied that this should be the feeling of every Latter-day Saint in the world. If you are making a bargain, if you are talking in the house, visiting in the social party, going forth in the dance, every breath should virtually be a prayer that God will preserve us from sin and from the effects of sin.

—*Brigham Young*

DAY 23

Live as You Pray

There is an old saying to this effect. "If you can't pray about a thing, don't do it," which is intended to tie our prayers and acts together. And true it is that our deeds, in large measure, are children of our prayers. Having prayed, we act; our proper petitions have the effect of charting a righteous course of conduct for us. The boy who prays earnestly and devoutly and in faith that he may go on a mission, will then prepare himself for his mission. The young people who pray always, in faith, to marry in the temple, and then act accordingly, are never satisfied with worldly marriage. So intertwined are prayer and works that having recited the law of prayer in detail, Amulek then concludes:

"After ye have done all these things, if ye turn away the needy, and the naked, and visit not the sick and afflicted, and impart of your substance, if ye have, to those who stand in need—I say unto you, if ye do not any of these things, behold, your prayer is vain, and availeth you nothing, and ye are as hypocrites who do deny the faith." (Alma 34:28.)

—*Bruce R. McConkie*

DAY 24

When the Time Comes, Pray

It matters not whether you or I feel like praying, when the time comes to pray, pray. If we do not feel like it, we should pray till we do. And if there is a heavy storm coming on and our hay is likely to be wet, let it come. You will find that those who wait till the Spirit bids them pray, will never pray much on this earth. Such people would come to meeting and look at each other and then when they had stayed as long as they felt inclined, address their brethren with—"Good-bye, I am going home," and then leave. But when the time comes to have prayers, let them be made, and there will be no danger.

—*Brigham Young*

DAY 25

Pray to Him in All Your Doings

He [the Lord] has counseled us to pray over our flocks and fields, to cry unto Him for all of His support, to counsel with Him in *all* our doings so that He can direct us for good, to pour out our souls in our closets and in our wilderness, to have our "hearts be full, drawn out in prayer unto him *continually* for [our] welfare" (Alma 34:27, emphasis added; see also Alma 34:18–26; 37:36–37). "All our doings" sounds fairly all-inclusive. "Continually" doesn't make much allowance for items the Lord doesn't care about.

—*Sheri Dew*

Pray in Distress and Comfort

When we become frightened, when we become anxious about the future, and certainly when our lives are in danger, we turn to the Creator for help and guidance. What joy and comfort it is to know that there is One to whom we can turn in time of need.

. . . But what of those times when all is going well, when the decisions we make seem to be the right ones, when there appears little need for help? Are we as likely then to turn to Him? . . .

When life is going smoothly, it is easy to forget Him from whom all blessings flow. In this jet-age world, there are many of us who feel the need for constant prayer, but who don't take the time. And if we don't take the time—or worse, if we don't find the need for prayer when all is well, perhaps in times of trouble we may feel so out of touch, so out of practice, such a stranger in the art of communicating with the Lord, that we'll lack the faith, indeed, even the knowledge of how to pray." . . . Pray always, and be believing," it is written, "and all things shall work together for your good. . . ."

Prayer should not be an emergency measure to be used as we would a spare tire when we have a flat, but rather to be used as a steering wheel in guiding our destiny.

Gibran wrote, "You pray in your distress and in your need; would that you might pray also in the fullness of your joy and in your days of abundance."

—*J. Spencer Kinard*

Consistency in Prayer Can Begin Today

Consistency in prayer is an important factor in sustaining hope in this life. We're not saying that consistency in prayer is only to prepare us for times of crisis. . . . Even in the good times, we need daily inspiration, daily direction, daily comfort, and daily protection. That is one of the wonderful things about prayer. It too is daily. We can pray day or night, standing or kneeling, aloud or in our minds.

What about people who have neglected their prayers, perhaps even for many years? Is there no hope for them? While there are consequences for our slothfulness, it doesn't mean that we are completely cut off from God's help. Even though the Lord sharply rebuked those early Saints for not turning to Him earlier, He immediately added this: "Notwithstanding their sins, my bowels are filled with compassion toward them. I will not utterly cast them off; and in the day of wrath I will remember mercy" (D&C 101:9).

What a marvelous example of God's mercy and his long-suffering. There will be consequences for our neglect. But if we turn back to Him, we can immediately begin to see the Lord's influence in our lives. Of course, it will take time to . . . make our prayers a well-trodden path to the Lord, but consistency in prayer can begin today. This very moment. That is one of the blessings of prayer. And whether we are just starting, or our path is a well-beaten one, the promise is there: "Pray always, and be believing, and all things shall work together for your good" (D&C 90:24).

—Gerald N. Lund

DAY 28

Pray Anytime, Anywhere

Our Father in Heaven has promised us peace in times of trial and has provided a way for us to come to Him in our need. He has given us the privilege and power of prayer. He has told us to "pray always" and has promised He will pour out His Spirit upon us (D&C 19:38).

Thankfully, we can call upon Him anytime, anywhere. We can speak to Him in the quiet thoughts of our mind and from the deepest feelings of our heart. It has been said, "prayer is made up of heart throbs and the righteous yearnings of the soul" (James E. Talmage, *Jesus the Christ* [Salt Lake City: Deseret Book, 1977], 238). Our Heavenly Father has told us He knows our thoughts and the intents of our hearts (D&C 6:16).

—Rex D. Pinegar

If It's Important to You

Sometimes I've wondered if the things I pray about are too trivial or too unimportant when compared with everything else going on in the world. At least I *used* to think that until I had my own children. Now I think differently. If something is important to my five-year-old, it's important to me, no matter what other problems are on my mind.

In the Book of Mormon, the poor among the Zoramites were laboring under the false impression that they could only pray a memorized prayer from atop the Rameumptom. Amulek taught them that not only could they pray wherever they happened to be but also that they could pray for just about anything they needed:

Yea, cry unto him for mercy; for he is mighty to save. Yea, humble yourselves, and continue in prayer unto him. Cry unto him when ye are in your fields, yea, over all your flocks. Cry unto him in your houses, yea, over all your household, both morning, mid-day, and evening. Yea, cry unto him against the power of your enemies.

Yea, cry unto him against the devil, who is an enemy to all righteousness. Cry unto him over the crops of your fields, that ye may prosper in them. Cry over the flocks of your fields, that they may increase. But this is not all; ye must pour out your souls in your closets, and your secret places, and in your wilderness. . . . (Alma 34:18–26)

How can we apply this scripture to our day? I suspect that most people . . . do not have fields, crops, and flocks. But I'm fairly sure they have jobs, mortgages, and bills. I'll bet they also have challenges, trials, and problems. And if these things matter to them, they must also matter to their perfect Father in Heaven, who delights to bless. So, to paraphrase Amulek, cry unto him over your job, that you may prosper in it. Cry over your assets, that they may increase so you can provide for your loved ones, support the missionary fund, increase your fast offerings, and help the sick and afflicted (Jacob 2:19). Pray for all of these things because if they're important to you, they're important to God.

—*John Bytheway*

DAY 30

Being Savior-Centered

The Savior calls us to do two things—to come to him, and to open the door to our hearts and let him come to us. The Apostle Paul, struggling for words to express how complete our access is, says: "For I am persuaded, that neither death, nor life, nor angels, nor principalities, nor powers, nor things present, nor things to come, nor height, nor depth, nor any other creature, shall be able to separate us from the love of God, which is in Christ Jesus our Lord." (Romans 8:38–39.)

Think of the power and joy that come into our lives when we face our days and our nights with Jesus beside us. We can deal with adversity because Christ has been there before us, experiencing all that we experience, and being with us in our trials. We can make wise choices and set good priorities, knowing that our "no" is as important as our "yes" when he is with us. If we will let him, he will accompany us daily and hourly instead of being stuck in the back room, waiting patiently until we can snatch a few minutes to dash back and be with him. We can be free of guilt because he does not condemn us. On the contrary, he is our advocate. He stands ready, knocking and calling, ready to respond to the three-second prayer of our heart as well as to the longer pleadings on our knees. He is ready to heal us and make us whole. He desires our happiness and promises us his joy.

May we be Savior-centered, knowing that we are beloved of him.

—*Chieko N. Okazaki*

DAY 31

Pray Always

"Pray always." (2 Nephi 32:9.) So it is written—meaning: Pray regularly, consistently, day in and day out; and also, live with the spirit of prayer always in your heart, so that your thoughts, words, and acts are always such as will please Him who is Eternal. Amulek speaks of praying "both morning, mid-day, and evening," and says we should pour out our souls to the Lord in our closets, in our secret places, and in the wilderness. (Alma 34:17–29.) Jesus commanded us to hold both personal and family prayer: "Watch and pray always," he said; and also, "Pray in your families unto the Father always in my name, that your wives and your children may be blessed." (3 Nephi 18:15,21.)

The practice of the Church in our day is to have family prayer twice daily, plus our daily personal prayers, plus a blessing on our food at mealtimes (except in those public or other circumstances where it would be ostentatious or inappropriate to do so), plus proper prayers in our meetings.

—*Bruce R. McConkie*

DAY 32

The Glorious Thing about Prayer

Prayer is a direct personal relationship in which we acknowledge our Father in heaven, and must be sincere, expressing simply in our own words our feelings of gratitude and asking for the guidance and blessings of which we stand in need.

First, as the Lord said, the door must be shut against the distractions of the world so that we may concentrate on what we are saying to our Father in heaven. . . . What a glorious thing it is to realize and to know that we can go to our Heavenly Father without appointment, pour out our souls to him in all simplicity and faith, knowing that he is there and can and will hear and answer our prayers. We know that he is a living God who dwells in heaven, that we are his spirit children, and that his Son Jesus Christ has instructed us, regardless of who we are, to call upon God and to acknowledge him as our Father.

—*N. Eldon Tanner*

DAY 33

We Are Always Worthy to Pray

There may be things that we are unworthy to do at times in our life, but there is one thing we are *never* unworthy to do, and that is pray. I have a testimony about this. The Prophet Joseph Smith not only taught it, but exemplified it. You *go* to the Lord regardless of the condition of your soul, and He will respond. He *never* closes the door against you. You may close it against Him, but if so that is your initiative, not His. We should call upon Him when we need Him most, and that's usually when we feel least worthy, and then He can respond.

In the modern prophet Joseph Smith we have an example of living, breathing prayer—the kind that changes life. His early successes with prayer were the foundation of a pattern that brought him progressively closer to God. If prayer had no other function than to help us concentrate on the deepest concerns of our life— even to reveal ourselves to ourselves—it would be worth doing. But beyond that the prophet illustrates for all time that prayer isn't just subjective, it isn't just self-hypnosis. Rather, it is a plan and pattern whereby we do in fact break through the veil and receive at the living hand of the living God through His Christ.

—*Truman G. Madsen*

DAY 34

When Should We *Not* Feel Comfortable?

God has a great desire to share what He knows with His children. His entire work and glory is focused on helping us achieve immortality and eternal life. He not only invites us to come unto Him, but He commands us to do so. This is made very clear in the scriptures. In fact, one of the most frequently repeated commandments in all of scripture is one where we are told to "ask" of God so that we may "receive"! There are more than *forty* references where that counsel is given! That kind of repetition says much about what the Lord wants us to do. Through asking, we exercise our agency and initiate the contact. Surely with more than forty invitations, we may feel completely comfortable in approaching the Father and asking Him for things in prayer. In fact, we have been commanded to do this so often, we should not feel comfortable until we are doing so on a regular basis.

—*Gerald N. Lund*

God Is Closer Than We Think

Prayer Brings about Daily Miracles

The hymn reminds us, "Prayer can change the night to day." What changes night to day for you? For me, it's prayer. It brings about daily miracles.

Think of the line in the Lord's Prayer, "Give us this day our daily bread." Why does the prayer say the bread of "this day" and not the bread of "tomorrow"? Could it be because God wants us to come to him tomorrow likewise? If we already had tomorrow's bread, is it possible that we would fail to ask Heavenly Father for it? One writer points out, "Our greatest misery is really not want and pain, but distance from God. [Thus,] our extra loaf would really be a curse instead of a blessing; like the extra manna in the wilderness, it would only rot in our hands." Daily prayer, even hourly prayer, is the bread that nourishes our souls.

—*Chieko N. Okazaki*

A Divine Tutorial

As we feel the power of Christ's love pulling us toward Him, we anticipate the joy of His promise: "Be faithful and diligent . . . , and I will encircle thee in the arms of my love" (D&C 6:20).

The Lord reflected that affection in the way He addressed Joseph Smith. During Joseph's early years, Christ called him "my *servant* Joseph" (for example, D&C 1:17; emphasis added). But after Joseph had traveled long paths marked by consecration and hardship, the Lord said, "From henceforth I shall call you *friends*" (D&C 84:77; emphasis added).

What is the difference between a servant and a friend? The Lord had earlier said, "The *servant* knoweth not what his lord doeth: but I have called you *friends;* for all things that I have heard of my Father I have made known unto you" (John 15:15; emphasis added).

The Lord's "friends" thus feel His increased confidence in them—enough confidence that He is now willing to tutor them in the most personal ways. But they also discover that His tutorial asks more of them, not less. It is both possible and likely that the closer we come to Christ, the more we will be aware of what we yet need to do. He said, "*If* men come unto me I will show unto them their weakness. . . . if they humble themselves before me, . . . then will I make weak things become strong unto them" (Ether 12:27; emphasis added).

So if we are becoming more aware of our weaknesses, that

doesn't mean we are drifting away from Him; it may well mean that we are drawing closer. Like a good coach, a good tutor will always help his students see and correct their mistakes. When we understand that, correction is motivating, not discouraging. For because of the Atonement, we can learn from our mistakes without being condemned by them.

—*Bruce C. Hafen*

Gaining Spirituality through Prayer

How do you gain spirituality? First, pray. Prayer is a private interview with the Father of our spirits. It is intense conversation in which we have the opportunity both to acknowledge his blessings to us and to ask for his help with our daily problems. But sometimes we get too caught up in asking and forget to acknowledge; or we become so impressed with our own importance that we forget to pray altogether. We know from the scriptures that the Lord is displeased when we do not remember to pray. While the people of Jared were dwelling in tents on the seashore in the wilderness prior to coming to the Promised Land, they began to forget the Lord. The Lord chastised the brother of Jared, perhaps because he had ceased to pray with the fervor and frequency with which he had prayed in the past. The Book of Mormon account tells us: "And

GOD IS CLOSER THAN WE THINK   41

it came to pass at the end of four years that the Lord came again unto the brother of Jared, and stood in a cloud and talked with him. And for the space of three hours did the Lord talk with the brother of Jared, and chastened him because he remembered not to call upon the name of the Lord." (Ether 2:14.)

Make prayer a constant and vital part of your life. Your spirit can come to depend on the sustenance and strength it receives from the Lord through prayer just as much as your physical body depends on the sustenance and strength it derives from food.

—*Vaughn J. Featherstone*

DAY 38

Miraculous Communication with God

We live in a world filled with unparalleled means of communication. We have television, radio, fax machines, telephones, and computer modems—each sending communication signals at a speed of over 186,000 miles per second. At this rate, my voice, transmitted over the air waves, can travel completely around the world before the same sound waves would reach the rear of this Tabernacle. As astonishing as this technology may be, the most miraculous and dependable communication has been with us since the beginning of time:

More things are wrought by prayer
Than this world dreams of. Wherefore, let thy voice
Rise like a fountain for me night and day.

So wrote Alfred Lord Tennyson.

Yes, the greatest miracle of all communication is the power of prayer. It's a privilege God has given each of us to communicate directly with Him. And, because of His great love for us, He has set no limitation as to when, where, and what we should pray about. As the Apostle Paul wrote, "In every thing by prayer and supplication with thanksgiving let your requests be made known unto God."

Exercising our privilege to pray is an essential ingredient to finding joy and happiness in today's world. Dr. Alexis Carrel has written, "Only in prayer do we achieve that complete and harmonious assembly of body, mind and spirit which gives the frail human its unshakable strength."

Although not every prayer receives a dramatic answer, every simple plea is heard and quietly responded to. Sincere and humble prayer can guide us to a path that leads to peace in this life and eternal life in the world to come.

Yes, we live in a world that offers the technology to quickly communicate information as never before, but the most important line of communication is still between ourselves and God. And, because of His love for us, He promises that line will never be busy.

—*Lloyd D. Newell*

Praying for Eternal Things

Christ's promise to us forever is that we don't have to do it alone. So let's keep our focus on the right motives, let's just try to look to him for life, let us try to lay up for ourselves treasures in heaven rather than on earth. . . .

The secret, of course, is to pray earnestly that we will have enough energy just to do the truly essential things—the spiritual things, the eternal things. Then we can pray equally fervently that we will have peace regarding the nonessential things—even if some of those nonessentials seem to be Church-related too. There are many, many nonessential things to let go of if we are going to allow ourselves adequate time and freedom to embrace God. But it is worth it. For when we embrace him, he will embrace us! And to do it we must, at least in some areas of our lives, stop being too temporally focused and so telestially preoccupied.

—*Patricia T. Holland*

Finding God

We are here to learn the lesson, also, that we are here to do the will of the Father. And how do we discover His will? How do we find Him? Pascal gave us a line: "You would not seek me had you not found me." God is closer than we know, more truly concerned for us than we understand. And the best in us is better than we know and reaches out and up, seeking Him.

We worry about our faith: does He really exist? We worry about our worthiness: could He love me? We remember our sins: is He really willing to "rescue a soul so rebellious and proud as mine"? (*Hymns,* 1985, no. 193.) We want to find Him. We would like to yield to His will. But how do we do that? How do we qualify for the relationship that we so earnestly desire?

We do this through prayer, of course, and through studying the scriptures. I believe we can find Him best by learning to know the Christ, who seems nearer, who was "made flesh and dwelt among us," and of whom Paul wrote that "God was in Christ, reconciling the world unto himself." (2 Corinthians 5:19.) God was making Himself known through His Son. "If," Paul declared to the Romans, "when we were enemies [that is, apart from God], we were reconciled to God by the death of his Son, [how] much more, being reconciled [brought back into unison with Him], we shall be saved by his life." (Romans 5:10.)

—*Marion D. Hanks*

The Passport to Spiritual Power

The Lord has not promised us freedom from adversity of affliction. Instead he has given us an avenue of communication known as prayer, whereby we may humble ourselves and seek his help and divine guidance, so that we could establish a house of prayer. I have previously said that they who reach down into the depths of life where, in the stillness, the voice of God has been heard, have the stabilizing power which carried them poised and serene through the hurricane of difficulties. . . .

There is a great need in the world today for prayer which can keep us in touch with God and keep open the channels of communication. None of us should get so busy in our lives that we cannot contemplate with prayer. Prayer is the passport to spiritual power.

—*Spencer W. Kimball*

Faith in Prayer

I have more faith in prayer before the Lord than almost any other principle on earth. If we have no faith in prayer to God, we have not much in either Him or the gospel. We should pray unto the Lord, asking Him for what we want. . . .

I think sometimes that we do not fully comprehend the power that we have with God in knowing how to approach him acceptably. All that these men holding the priesthood, and all that our sisters need do, is to live near God, and call upon him, pouring out their soul's desires in behalf of Israel, and their power will be felt, and their confidence in God will be strengthened. But the blessings of heaven can only be obtained and controlled upon the principles of righteousness.

Brethren and sisters, you should live by faith, realizing every day that all power rests with God, and that it is through him that we are able to live in peace and enjoy plenty; that it is through him the wrath of our enemies is turned aside from time to time, and that it will be through him that the remainder of their wrath will be restrained. You should enter your secret closets and call upon the name of the Lord. Many of you have learned how to pray; then fail not to let your prayers ascend up into the ears of the God of Sabaoth; and he will hear you.

—*Wilford Woodruff*

Pray Mightily

There is scarcely a more profound and glorious promise in all holy writ than is contained in these words of the Lord to his great latter-day prophet: "It shall come to pass that every soul who forsaketh his sins and cometh unto me, and calleth on my name, and obeyeth my voice, and keepeth my commandments, shall see my face and know that I am." (D&C 93:1.) Come unto Christ; forsake your sins; pray mightily; keep the commandments; live as becometh a true saint—all this in full measure—and the Lord will unveil his face to you as he has done in days past to others who pursued the same course in their day.

—*Bruce R. McConkie*

True Followers Pray

C. S. Lewis said that "the trouble is that relying on God has to begin all over again every day as if nothing had yet been done" (*The Quotable Lewis,* 156). This means making worship a central part of life. True Followers pray. They have some kind of regular pattern of scripture study. They don't "find time" to go to the temple, they set it as a priority first and work other things around it. They welcome the opportunity to fast as a regular way of humbling themselves, putting God first, seeking answers to prayers, and strengthening their connection to the Lord. They do these things not to check them off some kind of forced obedience checklist, but because they have learned to find answers and peace in the temple, in the scriptures, and through prayer and fasting—and these elements of devotion are woven into the fabric of their daily life rather than something done on Sunday or sporadically as needed. Righteous acts help define who they are.

True Followers diligently seek to know the Lord and His doctrine, to understand His will for them, to know how to handle the latest challenge or even the latest triumph, to find answers to questions or dilemmas, even doctrines, that confuse or trouble them. They do this not to comply with some unwritten code of behavior, but because they really do want to follow Jesus Christ. They want to understand His gospel, particularly how it applies to them. They want to have their lamps filled with testimony and faith so they're ready when the Bridegroom comes, but also so they're ready when doubt or conflict or trial descend, usually without warning (see Matthew 25:1–13).

—*Sheri Dew*

What Is Required of Us?

The Lord will guide us if we live right.

The thing that all of us should strive for is to so live, keeping the commandments of the Lord, that He can answer our prayers, the prayers of our loved ones, the prayers of the General Authorities, for us. . . . If we will live worthy, then the Lord will guide us—by a personal appearance, or by His actual voice, or by His voice coming into our mind, or be impressions upon our heart and our soul. And oh, how grateful we ought to be if the Lord sends us a dream in which are revealed to us the beauties of the eternity or a warning and direction for our special comfort. Yes, if we so live, the Lord will guide us for our salvation and for our benefit.

—*Harold B. Lee*

We Will Find Him If We Call Out to Him

Pray; talk to the Lord; reach upward; bare your soul to Him. Pray for those you love, and for those you hate. Pray for your enemies. Pray for forgiveness. Tell Him what you dare not speak aloud to anyone else. Pray for yourself. One morning on the deck of our cabin in the mountains we knelt in morning prayer with a wonderful couple who are our dear friends. One of them led us in prayer, and as he did, my soul was enlarged and my understanding enlightened when he said, "If we have offended thee, in any way, we ask thy pardon. Help us to live consistent with the covenants we have made." He prayed other things, but these two ideas were burned into my heart. In what ways do I offend the Lord? Do I live each day consistent with the covenants I have made with my Heavenly Father? Am I truly grateful?

—*Ann N. Madsen*

Seek the Lord's Blessings in All Things

We are told that with none is the Lord angry, except those who do not acknowledge his hand in all things. Seek for his blessing upon everything you engage in. If you have a farm, dedicate it to God, and pray that his blessing may be upon it. If you build a house, dedicate it to God; also your garden, your cattle and sheep, and all that you possess, and pray that his blessing may rest upon you and upon everything that pertains to you.

—*John Taylor*

Based on Righteousness

We are entitled and expected to pray for all things properly needed, whether temporal or spiritual. We do not have the right of unlimited petition; our requests must be based on righteousness. "Ye ask, and receive not, because ye ask amiss, that ye may consume it upon your lusts." (James 4:3.)

Amulek speaks of crops and herds, of fields and flocks, as well as mercy and salvation, when he lists those things for which we should pray. (See Alma 34:17–29.) The Lord's Prayer speaks of "our daily bread" (see Matthew 6:11), and James urges us to ask for wisdom (see James 1:5), which in principle means we should seek all of the attributes of godliness. Our revelation says, "Ye are commanded in all things to ask of God." (D&C 46:7.) Nephi says, "ye must not perform any thing unto the Lord save in the first place ye shall pray unto the Father in the name of Christ, that he will consecrate thy performance unto thee, that thy performance may be for the welfare of thy soul." (2 Nephi 32:9.) And the Lord's promise to all the faithful is: "If thou shalt ask, thou shalt receive revelation upon revelation, knowledge upon knowledge, that thou mayest know the mysteries and peaceable things—that which bringeth joy, that which bringeth life eternal." (D&C 42:61.)

—*Bruce R. McConkie*

Staying on the Lord's Side

When I have been tempted sometimes to do a certain thing, I have asked myself, "Which side of the line am I on?" If I determined to be on the safe side, the Lord's side, I would do the right thing every time. So when temptation comes, think prayerfully about your problem, and the influence of the Lord will aid you to decide wisely. There is safety for us only on the Lord's side of the line.

—*George Albert Smith*

Devout Communication with God

Our modern times seem to suggest that prayerful devotion and reverence for holiness is unreasonable or undesirable, or both. And yet, skeptical "modern" men have need for prayer. If prayer is only a spasmodic cry at the time of crisis, then it is utterly selfish, and we come to think of God as a repairman or a service agency to help us only in our emergencies. We should remember the Most High day and night—always—not only at times when all other assistance has failed and we desperately need help. If there is any element in human life on which we have a record of miraculous success and inestimable worth to the human soul, it is prayerful, reverential, devout communication with our Heavenly Father.

—*Howard W. Hunter*

Anxious to Fill Our Souls

Sometimes we think we can do it by ourselves, that it will make us strong to struggle through a problem alone. Or sometimes we think that no one will help us, no one can understand us. The Savior can and will do both. James 1:5 is that wonderful scripture that gave the boy Joseph Smith courage to go out into the Sacred Grove. Let's paraphrase it so that it applies to us more directly: "When we lack wisdom, we should ask God. God will give us wisdom generously, without scolding or finding fault. Wisdom *will be given* to us." I think that God is waiting for us to ask him. He wants to give to us and give generously, and he will not scold or reproach us. He doesn't say, "Can't you figure this out on your own?" or "You, again! Didn't I just see you this morning?" No, he's anxious to fill our souls with his goodness and his love. Our questions are just as important to us as Joseph Smith's question was to him. And who knows, maybe the Lord has an answer for us that turns out to be as important to the world as Joseph Smith's answer was to us today!

—*Chieko N. Okazaki*

DAY 52

Prayer Deepens Your Relationship with God

To be in control of your life, to be a success regardless of your situation . . . , I recommend you come to know your Father in Heaven. Come to love Him. Always remember that He loves you and will give you guidance and support if you will but give Him the chance. Include Him in your decision making. Include Him in your heartaches and heartbreaks. Include Him when you take inventory of your personal worth. "For behold, this life is the time for men to prepare to meet God; yea, behold the day of this life is the day for men [and women] to perform their labors." (Alma 34:32.)

As you strive to become a quality person, commune daily with your Heavenly Father who knows you best of all. He knows your talents, your strengths, and your weaknesses. You are here on the earth at this time to develop and refine these characteristics. I promise you He will help you. He is aware of your needs. He is aware of your unanswered prayers.

—*Marvin J. Ashton*

Spiritual Hygiene

To have the sweet aroma of peace—the taste of eternal life—in our homes takes some doing. We might call it "spiritual hygiene." . . . Like the physical body, the spirit has to be in good health to face the rigors and threats around it. Stamina depends on regular hygiene. The gospel prescribes nutrients, labors, and even regular rest. We can think of these hygienic things by reviewing the counsel we have received and the covenants we have made.

The most crucial hygiene is daily prayer. To hold in place all else we do, we must stay connected with the great Father. He sent us on our family mission, and it is to him that we hope to return with everyone intact. . . . Prayer sets the stage for other essentials of spiritual health.

—*Wayne E. Brickey*

Morning Prayer

In my own life, I can see many things that need to be pruned. Although morning prayer is a priority for me, one day I recognized that I had gotten in the habit of getting up in the morning and turning on the computer to see if I had received any e-mails. Often, after I read the e-mails, something else on the computer would catch my eye, usually something I had no intention of reading. That would lead me to other interesting sites and soon I would be pushed for time, rushing to get dressed and leave for an appointment, never once giving any thought to prayer. One day it hit me: Was it more important for me to check my e-mail than to check in with my Heavenly Father?

Morning prayer was and is one of my highest priorities. What had happened? It was something that happens to all of us from time to time. I had unconsciously let myself slip into a bad habit. I had allowed myself to let something of comparatively little importance take the place of something of critical importance.

It wasn't that I read or looked at anything inappropriate on the computer. It was simply that I became distracted from my priority, from something that I valued, something that I knew made a real difference in how the rest of my day went. It seemed to have happened so gradually that I was totally unaware of the change. Once I recognized this pattern, however, I knew I needed to do some pruning immediately! . . . I knelt by my bed in prayer, seeking forgiveness and asking for strength from the Master Gardener to live with increased integrity.

—*Carolyn J. Rasmus*

Staying Connected

We live in a connected world. When I was growing up, the only telephone in the house was on the kitchen wall attached to a cord. Today, in every country of the world, men and women, boys and girls, ride subways and jeepneys and bicycles, with cell phones in hand, many of them sophisticated enough to send and receive calls, text messages, e-mail, and downloads any hour of the night or day. We want to be connected and go to extraordinary lengths and expense to be so.

Do we make even a fraction as much effort at connecting and staying connected with the heavens—with immersing ourselves in the Word of God and experiencing for ourselves its power, with seeking to learn the language of revelation and how to hear the voice of the Lord? The ultimate connection is conversing with our Father, in the name of Jesus Christ, through the ministering of the Holy Ghost. And that connection comes as a result of diligently, earnestly, steadily seeking the reward for which is great: "For he that diligently seeketh shall find; and the mysteries of God shall be unfolded unto them, by the power of the Holy Ghost" (1 Nephi 10:19).

—*Sheri Dew*

We Can Use the Power of God

Although through the Spirit of Christ we can be given all the help, strength, and comfort necessary, to gain this spiritual help for ourselves certain things are expected: that we are righteous, that we obey the precepts and commands of the gospel, and that we seek help from the Lord on our knees in prayer. Access to the Spirit is not granted by office held in the Church, or by wealth, by status, by gender or color. It is available to those who truly desire it and are willing to humbly do as they are commanded.

Thus, all the power of God is at our disposal to be used in our behalf when we need it, dependent only upon our righteousness, our spirituality, our desire to bow to God's command.

—Donna Lee Bowen Barnes

We Pray Because We Need Help

We don't pray because we're worthy. We pray because we need help. We don't take the sacrament because we are perfect, but because we are willing to be perfected. We don't go to the temple because we've made it, but because God is making us better there.

We are not earning a treasure in heaven, but learning to treasure heavenly things.

—*Brad Wilcox*

A Process for Exercising Faith, Part One

Believe. The first thing to remember is the simple word *believe.* By that I mean to have faith, to not doubt, to not have fear. Jesus said you must believe first, then you would see the blessing:

"I say unto you, What things soever ye desire, when ye pray, believe that ye receive them, and ye shall have them." (Mark 11:24.)

When you start praying you've got to believe as if your request has already been granted. That's the kind of belief the Lord is talking about. Of course, our belief and our faith are in Jesus Christ, who has both the power to grant blessings and the desire to do so. We must always center this belief in Christ, knowing that he will do what is best for us and trusting that our prayers will be answered according to his will.

Repent. The next thing to remember is to repent. Part of repentance is to "sacrifice, to pay the price." We need to find out what we need to change in our lives, what we need to do differently, and then we need to do it. . . .

Pray. The third key to remember is to pray as if everything depends on God. By trusting in him, by relying on his strength and power, we receive strength and power unto ourselves to see us through to the end.

Work. The fourth principle is to work as if everything depends on us. . . . The Lord reveals his will many times in half steps. He does this so that we will be pressed into exercising faith in order to receive the next step. We might think of this principle as walking to the edge of the light. We must do all in our power, walking to the edge of the light we have and maybe a little way into the dark, and then the lights of revelation will turn on again. But until we walk to the edge of the light and do all in our power to perform, we will often not be ready to receive more from the Lord.

—*Gene R. Cook*

A Process for Exercising Faith, Part Two

Prepare for intense trials. Number five is to prepare for intense trials of your faith. Remember that when you begin to truly seek answers to prayer, there will be forces that will do all in their power to stop you. So don't be surprised when opposition comes; in fact, you should expect it from the beginning. Then, when difficulties really descend upon you and you reach your blest moment, you have the opportunity to discover how much faith you really do have.

Will you stand tall and strong in the face of all adversity? Will you still believe? Will you continue to press forward? Will you pay the price until you've receive the blessing from the Lord (or until he tells you it's no longer his will that you seek it)? Do these things and you will endure the trials well, and you'll be that much closer to receiving the blessings you seek.

Expect to see the arm of the Lord revealed. Number six is to expect to see the arm of the Lord revealed on your behalf. Because you've done the things the Lord required, you now have full reason to believe that the Lord will intervene and assist you.

I like the way these ideas encapsulize what is required in receiving answers to prayer. Remember them, ponder them when you're trying to obtain an answer, and evaluate yourself:

Do I really believe? Do I have faith in the Lord and his promises?

Am I repentant of my sins?

Do I pray as if all depends on the Lord?

Do I work as if everything depends on me?

Am I prepared to endure intense trials of my faith?

After I've done all these things, do I honestly expect to see the arm of the Lord revealed on my behalf?

When you are in the midst of the battle and need extra assistance, remember the Lord's requirements and his promises, and you'll be able to move ahead more surely.

—*Gene R. Cook*

Jesus Set the
Example for Us

Jesus Set the Example for Us

Jesus understood and taught the importance of prayer. But more than that, he lived the concept. He prayed continually to the Father for direction and strength, because his greatest desire was to do the Father's will.

. . . The lesson for us is clear. We need to be prayerful. The importance of prayer was expressed by the prophet Nephi near the end of his ministry: "I say unto you that ye must pray always, and not faint; that ye must not perform any thing unto the Lord save in the first place ye shall pray unto the Father in the name of Christ, that he will consecrate thy performance unto thee, that thy performance may be for the welfare of thy soul" (2 Ne. 32:9).

—*Joseph B. Wirthlin*

Jesus Is the Ultimate Example

"Jesus valued prayer enough to spend many hours at the task," Christian scholar Philip Yancey wrote. "If I had to answer the question 'Why pray?' in one sentence, it would be, 'because Jesus did.'

He bridged the chasm between God and human beings. While on earth he became vulnerable, as we are vulnerable, rejected, as we are rejected, and tested, as we are tested. In every case his response was prayer."

Jesus Christ is truly the Light we hold up to one another and to all the world (3 Nephi 18:24). Mere mortals are but dim reflections of that light, mere lamps as compared to the light of the Son. In prayer, as in all facets of our lives, we look to our Model and Master: "And as I have prayed among you even so shall ye pray in my church. . . . Behold I am the light; I have set an example for you" (3 Nephi 18:16).

We seek to follow and emulate the praying Savior.

—*Robert L. Millet*

DAY 62

The Savior Taught Us How to Pray

Let's consider for a moment how to pray. The Savior told us how when he said:

"After this manner therefore pray ye: Our Father which art in heaven, Hallowed be thy name.

"Thy kingdom come. Thy will be done in earth, as it is in heaven.

"Give us this day our daily bread.

"And forgive us our debts, as we forgive our debtors.

"And lead us not into temptation, but deliver us from evil: For thine is the kingdom, and the power, and the glory, for ever. Amen." (Matt. 6:9–13.)

This sample prayer envisions appreciation, simplicity, and the avoidance of vain repetitions. Our prayers should simply be our soul's sincere desire.

—*Franklin D. Richards*

The Savior's Example of Prayer

Sincere prayer aligns our will with our Father's. Christ's prayer in the Garden of Gethsemane is the perfect example of a completely selfless utterance. Even while taking upon Himself the sins of all mankind and undergoing physical and spiritual pain beyond our comprehension, Christ prayed, "O my Father, if it be possible, let this cup pass from me: nevertheless not as I will, but as thou wilt." (Matthew 26:39.) The Lord's quiet conversation is a humbling demonstration of what it means to really pray. By all outward appearances, He seemed to be alone, engaging in a soul-weary monologue. But "for those who have eyes to see and ears to hear," He was involved in a perfectly selfless dialogue with God. His "self-talk" was so selfless that He became one with the Father. "Not as I

JESUS SET THE EXAMPLE FOR US 67

will, but as thou wilt" is a perfect demonstration of what it means to take the "self" out of "self-talk" and to become empowered by a recognition of divine worth.

—*Lloyd D. Newell*

DAY 64

How Jesus Prayed

Jesus sometimes began his day by rising early and finding a solitary place to pray. "And in the morning, rising up a great while before day, he went out, and departed into a solitary place, and there prayed" (Mark 1:35). During his three-year mission, he repeatedly and deliberately set aside hours of solitude during which he prayed to Heavenly Father and rejuvenated his spirit:

"And when it was day, he departed and went into a desert place" (Luke 4:42). "And he withdrew himself into the wilderness, and prayed" (Luke 5:16). "He went out into a mountain to pray, and continued all night in prayer to God" (Luke 6:12). Other examples are found in Matthew 14:23; 17:1; 26:36; Luke 9:18; and John 6:15.

Although Jesus was incessantly pressed upon by multitudes and many times forced to go without food and sleep, in key moments he would find solitude and commune with his Father in preparation for more spiritual labor. He also prepared the leaders of his Church: "He took Peter and John and James, and went up into a mountain to pray" (Luke 9:28). Even during the agony of Gethsemane, Jesus admonished his Apostles, "Rise and pray, lest ye enter into temptation" (Luke 22:46). Actually, that is one of the grand purposes of prayer: we cannot succumb to temptation while we are engaged in sincere communication with our Father, so prayer is key to avoid ruining ourselves with sin.

—*D. Kelly Ogden*

DAY 65

"Lord What Wilt Thou Have Me Do?"

Perhaps even more important than trying to speculate as to what Jesus would do in a given situation is to endeavor to determine what Jesus would have *you* do. Of course in order to give intelligent answers to such questions, one must have intimate acquaintance with the life of the Master and the account of his ministry and an understanding of the applications he made to the lessons he taught. History, either religious or secular, is valuable to us; for by learning how others adjusted in the past to given situations, we ourselves form patterns of conduct that will guide us to act similarly under similar circumstances.

—*Harold B. Lee*

For Our Benefit

How do we come to the Father? Listen to the words of the Savior:

"And when thou prayest, thou shalt not be as the hypocrites are: for they love to pray standing in the synagogues and in the corners of the streets, that they may be seen of men. Verily I say unto you, They have their reward.

"But thou, when thou prayest, enter into thy closet, and when thou hast shut thy door, pray to thy Father which is in secret; and thy Father which seeth in secret shall reward thee openly.

"But when ye pray, use not vain repetitions, as the heathen do: for they think that they shall be heard for their much speaking.

"Be not ye therefore like unto them: for your Father knoweth what things ye have need of, before ye ask him" (Matthew 6:5–8).

The Pharisees prayed publicly in the synagogues and in the streets. They prayed with vain repetition and much speaking. The Lord withdrew from the crowds and went to solitary places to pray. He taught us to come to the Father with the faith of a child, with humility and a believing heart. Even so, the Savior acknowledges that Heavenly Father already knows our needs and our hearts. So why do we pray?

Prayer is for our benefit. When we kneel down and bow our heads, and ask God for blessings that we need, we are acknowledging our dependence on Him for everything that we enjoy.

We recognize Heavenly Father as the giver of all, as the source of power, light, life, and strength. Over and over the scriptures repeat these words of the Savior: "Ask, and it shall be given you; seek, and ye shall find; knock, and it shall be opened unto you" (Matthew 7:7). . . .

We can and we must ask, knock, and seek for a variety of blessings. But in those moments of pouring out our souls and asking with full hearts, we must remember one very important principle. It is taught in the Lord's prayer with these words, "Thy will be done in earth, as it is in heaven" (Matthew 6:10). . . .

Is it possible that sometimes when we pray we are like a hungry child asking only for candy? In our prayers do we say, "Heavenly Father, this is the blessing I want," when what we really need and what He would give us are the rich experiences that will nourish our souls, increase our growth, and keep us on the path that will bring us home to Him? Many times the answers to our prayers are those refining experiences that we may not recognize as blessings.

—*Margaret Lifferth*

DAY 67

Following Christ's Example

We learn from Christ's prayer in Gethsemane . . . that he prayed, "Nevertheless not my will, but thine, be done." (Luke 22:42.) What a lesson for those of us who desire to be Christlike. Christ desired to do the Father's will. Even in the premortal life we have record of Christ, the Beloved Son, saying, "Father, thy will be done, and the glory be thine forever." (Moses 4:2.)

On numerous occasions Christ told us, "I seek not mine own will, but the will of the Father which hath sent me." (John 5:30; see also 3 Nephi 27:13; D&C 19:24.) He who exemplified by his life his desire to do the Father's will taught us, "Not every one that saith unto me, Lord, Lord, shall enter into the kingdom of heaven; but he that doeth the will of my Father which is in heaven." (Matthew 7:21; see also 3 Nephi 14:21.) Like Christ, other prophets have prayed, "Thy will, O Lord, be done, and not mine." (Jacob 7:14; Alma 14:13.)

Often it is shortsightedness that causes us to question if God hears our prayers, or to believe that our prayers are unanswered. We lack the perspective of our Heavenly Father. Knowing only our mortal existence, we often fail to see things in an eternal perspective.

Following his address at the Sermon on the Mount (and the similar discourse given to the Nephites), the Savior taught the disciples how to pray and concluded by giving them an example that has come to be known as the Lord's prayer. (See Matthew 6 and 3 Nephi 13.) In both instances, the disciples were instructed to pray to their Father "who art in heaven" and to pray that "thy will be done in earth, as it is in heaven." (Matthew 6:9–10; 3 Nephi 9:10.)

In Christ's instructions concerning how we are to pray, he indicates that our "Father knoweth what things [we] have need of, before [we] ask him." (Matthew 6:8; 3 Nephi 13:8.) Why then do we pray at all? I believe it is because as we go through the process of using words to express ideas, we are forced to clarify our thinking and, in most instances, come to a new and clearer understanding.

—*Carolyn J. Rasmus*

Hallowed Be Thy Name

Jesus looked up throughout the course of his ministry. He prayed constantly and sought faithfully the divine direction of his Father in heaven. Furthermore, he acknowledged that the work and the will he came to fulfill was his Father's, not his own. He, more than any other in this world's history, was willing to humble himself, to bow down, and to give honor and glory to the Most High.

Reverence and adoration were frequently declared in prayer by the Master and were beautifully expressed in the Sermon on the Mount when he gave this counsel: "After this manner therefore pray ye: Our Father which art in heaven, Hallowed be thy name." (Matt. 6:9.)

. . . Jesus was careful to place the petition "Hallowed be thy name" at the very forefront of his prayer. Unless that reverent, prayerful, honorable attitude toward God is uppermost in our hearts, we are not fully prepared to pray. If our first thought is of ourselves and not of God, we are not praying as Jesus taught. It was his supreme hope that our Father's name and station would be kept beautiful and holy. Living always with an eye single to the glory of God, he urged men everywhere to so speak, and act, and live, that others seeing their good works might glorify their Father in heaven.

The reverence of the Savior for our Father and the understanding of his love made the whole world hopeful and holy.

—*Howard W. Hunter*

DAY 69

The Lord Prayed for Others

Jesus said, "Peace I leave with you, my peace I give unto you: not as the world giveth, give I unto you. Let not your heart be troubled, neither let it be afraid" (John 14:27).

Moments later he says, "These things I have spoken unto you, that in me ye might have peace. In the world ye shall have tribulation: but be of good cheer; I have overcome the world" (John 16:33).

They depart for Gethsemane where he prays prior to his solitary moments with the Father. He is now minutes from the full atoning weight. It is already starting to descend upon him. We know this because he tells his disciples as he arrives at the garden of Gethsemane that he is heavy and amazed. Christ himself is astonished at the agony of suffering that is beginning to settle upon him as his understanding of human misery becomes intense. He now prays. Who does he pray for?

"I have manifested thy name unto the men which thou gavest me out of the world: . . . I pray for them: I pray not for the world, but for them which thou hast given me; for they are thine. . . . And now I am no more in the world, but these are in the world, and I come to thee. Holy Father, keep through thine own name those whom thou hast given me, that they may be one, as we are. . . . I pray not that thou shouldest take them out of the world, but that thou shouldest keep them from the evil. . . . And for their sakes I sanctify myself. . . . Father, I will that they also, whom thou hast given me, be with me where I am; . . . I have declared unto them thy name, and will declare it: that the love wherewith thou hast loved me may be in them, and I in them" (John 17:6, 9, 11, 15, 19, 24, 26).

That's a magnificently beautiful prayer, but it's not for himself. He's not saying, "Father, help me, strengthen me, I'm going to go through this awful agony." He is praying for others. He looked outward throughout that prayer.

—*S. Michael Wilcox*

Uniting Our Souls with Heaven

There is a definition in the LDS Bible Dictionary that is important to note as we try to understand the avenue to God that is ours: "Prayer is the act by which the will of the Father and the will of the child are brought into correspondence with each other. The object of prayer is not to change the will of God, but to secure for ourselves and for others blessings that God is already willing to grant, but that are made conditional on our asking for them. Blessings require some work or effort on our part before we can obtain them. Prayer is a form of work, and is an appointed means for obtaining the highest of all blessings" (pp. 752–53).

We know God lives and hears our prayers. Perhaps we don't always realize this wonder in our lives because often we are looking for some other blessing than that which we have at hand. The privilege of sacred prayer is to draw close to God. He already knows the desires of our hearts, but a change must occur within us; having been passive we become active through prayer. Prayer is, indeed, a boon for us. For a choice lift, sing again the old-fashioned heart-warming lines:

> *There is an hour of peace and rest,*
> *Unmarred by earthly care;*
> *'Tis when before the Lord I go,*
> *And kneel in secret prayer.*

May my heart be turned to pray,
Pray in secret day by day,
That this boon to mortals giv'n
May unite my soul with heav'n.
(Hans Henry Petersen, "Secret Prayer,"
Hymns, *no. 144)*

Being united with heaven is what gladness is really all about. When this condition exists, regardless of the terrifying or stressful details of life, everything will ultimately be happy and fine.

—*Elaine Cannon*

There Is Power in Prayer

Prayer will bring solace and comfort. It has healed sickness, comforted those distressed, and has continued the faithful in paths of righteousness. The value of a man is evidenced in part by the dust on his knees. His willingness to believe in and accept a being greater than himself as evidenced by his prayer has increased his moral stature, refined his understanding, and has brought him along the road of his eternal development. Our great example in prayer is our Lord and Master Jesus Christ who knew that only through constant supplication and obedience would God the Father manifest His will and release the power for its attainment through man. Truly there is power in prayer.

—*Ezra Taft Benson*

Prayers of Gratitude

Men pray for different reasons. Many are driven to their knees out of fear, and then only do they pray. Others go to the Lord when in dire need of immediate direction for which they know of no other place to go. Nations are called by their governments in case of a national tragedy, drought, or plague, famine or war, to call upon God for his blessings, or his protection, and for his direction. Some people ask to be healed, others to be strengthened. They ask for the blessings of the Lord to attend their families, their loved ones, and themselves in all their righteous endeavors. This, I am sure, is all good in the sight of the Lord.

It is most important, however, that we take time to express our gratitude to our Father in heaven for the many blessings we receive.

As we express our appreciation for our many blessings, we become more conscious of what the Lord has done for us, and thereby we become more appreciative. We all know what it means to hear or receive an expression of gratitude for anything we might have done. Our forefathers set aside a day of thanksgiving. I fear that some of us even forget that day.

I wonder if we are sometimes guilty of not expressing to the Lord our gratitude, even as the lepers who were healed.

—N. Eldon Tanner

DAY 73

Acknowledge Our Gratitude

Let us attend to our prayers. Do not forget that the Lord Almighty has said, "I will be inquired of by you," and, "he that seeketh me early shall find me." The Lord has made it obligatory upon us to seek after Him, to have prayerful hearts, and spirits, that we may supplicate the Lord, if for nothing more, than to acknowledge to Him that we feel we are His children, and believe in His word and in the promises that He has made to us. While He may have blest us with all the temporal blessings that are necessary for our happiness and well-being, and we need not ask Him for food, for clothing, nor for houses, or where to lay our heads,—we can at the same time acknowledge to the Lord our gratitude that He has so overruled all things, so provided for us and opened our way, that we have been able to obtain all these things and surround ourselves with the temporal blessings of life. Surely the Lord has been very merciful and very providential to us, up to this time, with reference to all these things.

—*Joseph F. Smith*

Criteria for Christlike Prayers

It should not surprise us as we grow if we are sometimes less than fully comprehending of prayer. The Lord's disciples said to him, "Lord, teach us to pray." (Luke 11:1.) Jesus then gave a marvelous model of what prayer could be. Yet even this model did not suffice for the needs of Gethsemane. Nor was it as sublime as His prayers given in the special circumstances after His resurrection when Jesus prayed among the surviving Nephites. (3 Nephi 17:15–18.) The point is obviously not to detract from the tutoring nature of the wonderful Lord's prayer, but to underscore how prayers will reflect circumstance; no single prayer will suffice for all circumstances!

There are no Christlike prayers, however, that do not include, as did the Lord's Prayer, deep expressions of gratitude and appreciation to our Father in heaven along with a submittal to Him.

—*Neal A. Maxwell*

Gratitude in Prayer

Joseph [Smith] prayed in extremity but he also prayed in great gratitude. And here is another insight. He taught the Saints that they should practice virtue and holiness, but that they should give thanks unto God in the Spirit for whatsoever blessing they were blessed with. In my own life, years have gone by, I'm sure, when I have offered prayers yet never spent an entire prayer simply to thank the Lord. My prayers have always had an element of asking, asking, asking. But Joseph taught the Saints that if they would learn to be thankful in all things—simply be thankful—they would be made glorious, and their prayers would take on a deeper, richer spirit.

The sin of ingratitude is one of the things that prevent us from as rich a prayer life as he had. He seemed to have an innate and deep capacity for gratitude, even for the slightest favor, from the Lord as from his fellowmen. And I have wept at times while reading that in his journal he sometimes wrote a kind of prayer for a brother. 'Bless Brother So-and-So, Father, who gave me $1.35 today to help with such-and-such a project.' Even the smallest favor called forth his warmth and gratitude.

—*Truman G. Madsen*

God-Centered Prayers

As Alma continued his itinerant teaching, he came to the Zoramites, a people who had broken away from the Nephites. They were a self-righteous people and their prayers were self-centered rather than God-centered: "Again we thank thee, O God, that we are a chosen and a holy people. . . . We thank thee, O God, for we are a chosen people unto thee, while others shall perish." (Alma 31:18–28.)

What followed this kind of praying was, unfortunately, all too natural: "Now after the people had all offered up thanks after this manner, they returned to their homes, never speaking of their God again until they had assembled themselves together again to the holy stand, to offer up thanks after their manner." (Alma 31:23.) Alma was grieved because of this shallow and selfish emphasis in Zoramite praying. It took his own earnest praying to give him the strength and will to continue his labors.

Although LDS prayers are not as self-righteous as the Zoramite praying was, I have felt for a long time that my praying has been too much a recital of my own needs and desired blessings. I believe our prayers should be more God centered. They should be expressions of our love, gratitude, and adoration for him. One of the most memorable prayers of my life was one given at a Thanksgiving worship service by a student who began by saying, "Father, we usually come to thee asking for blessings; today we come only to thank thee." He proceeded to enumerate the things for which he was grateful.

That prayer has stayed with me for thirty years, turning my thoughts often to the Lord in gratitude. He knows our needs. But we must reach out to him in humility and with love. A God-centered prayer will keep him in our minds and hearts more truly than a self-centered prayer. We must remember, however, that there is a time and place to pray for personal needs.

—*Lowell L. Bennion*

A Prayer of Thanksgiving

Each of us has many needs. We have personal and family responsibilities for which we need guidance. There are problems to address and challenges to face. There are sins to repent of and temptations to resist. We all need God's blessings in our lives. Yet despite all of the myriad of reasons we can petition our Father in Heaven in prayer, we would be well served to periodically pray a prayer of thanksgiving—no requests, no petitions, no pleadings, just heartfelt expressions of gratitude. It is not so much that God needs to hear it (even though I am sure He is pleased) as it is that I need to say it. I am blessed and refocused when I do so. I can sense a difference in myself when I give thanks for simple things—things that I don't often remember to thank Him for, such as indoor plumbing, hot water for my shower, good food to eat, clothes to wear, clean water to drink, a comfortable home, good friends, ears to hear good music and the laughter of my grandchildren, eyes to both read good books and see majestic mountains.

When I have counted my blessings in writing and offered prayers exclusively for the purpose of giving thanks, I have quickly discovered that I have far more reason to say "I thank thee" than "I ask thee." It is a humbling realization, but a strengthening one. A recognition that we are all "unprofitable servants" (see Mosiah 2:21) because of God's goodness, as humbling as it is, actually enriches our relationship with Deity, forges greater faith, and spiritually empowers us.

—*Brent L. Top*

DAY 78

Expressing Gratitude
in Prayer Brings Blessings

Most of the time we think of prayer only when we want something; but when we start by expressing gratitude for the things we already have, we begin to see our lives in a new way.

I experience this as the Primary general president. My calling is to care not only for the children in our church, but for the children in all of the world. This is a tremendous responsibility, and at first

I could feel only the burden of it. But I seek for the Lord's help constantly. . . .

Then, just the other morning, I thought, "I have been asking for so much. This morning I am not going to ask for one thing. I'm just going to be grateful." I knelt and thanked the Lord for my good health, for my understanding husband, for our children, for our missionary son, for the privilege of serving, for the board members and staff who assist me, for stake and ward members throughout the world who are serving, and especially for the teachers who give and care so much. I thanked him for the children everywhere. I thanked him for the prophet. And the list went on. My spirit soared. What an astounding experience to know that I have so much! It takes a grateful heart to experience that soaring, that realization of how much Heavenly Father loves you, how much he does for you.

—*Dwan J. Young*

DAY 79

See How Much the Lord Is Doing for You

The more humble and obedient we are, the more the Lord can give us the ability to see. When the Savior asked His disciples, "Having eyes, see ye not?" (Mark 8:18), He could have been saying to all of us, "Open your eyes. See who I really am and how much I have done and am doing for you. See who you really are and how much more you are needed to help others. Please follow me. Don't be like the unbelieving of whom I must say, 'their eyes they have closed,' but be believing so I can say, 'but blessed are your eyes, for they see'" (see Matthew 13:15–16). The Savior is always urging us to be more obedient so we can see more clearly—knowing that as we do, we will understand more and have more joy. . . .

God is the great Creator. He is the Giver of life and opportunity and hope. His hand is in all that is around us. I am confident that when we finally see things as they really are, we will bow in even deeper adoration for all the Lord has done for us. It will be so much more than we ever thought, we will want to say, "I had no idea! If only I had known!"

—*John H. Groberg*

DAY 80

Express Appreciation

Are you thankful for your blessings? Do you express your appreciation to the Lord? Do you seek him for guidance so that you might take the right path? Do you ask him for wisdom and for knowledge? Of course the older folks who are cramming for their final examinations need prayer in their lives, but you who still face the real problems of life need prayer and answers to prayer, for your peace of soul and mind and for your guidance.

—*Howard W. Hunter*

Improving the Quality of Our Prayers

Improve the Standard of Your Life

Sincere prayer is the heart of a happy and productive life. Prayer strengthens faith. Prayer is the preparation for miracles. Prayer opens the door to eternal happiness. . . .

As we learn to develop this two-way communication, the standard of our life will improve. We will see things more clearly; we will try harder to do better; we will see the real joy that can come through trials and testing. Although problems will still be with us, peace, contentment, and true happiness will be ours in abundance.

As you feel the need to confide in the Lord or to improve the quality of your visits with him—to pray, if you please—may I suggest a process to follow: go where you can be alone, where you can think, where you can kneel, where you can speak out loud to him. The bedroom, the bathroom, or a closet will do. Now, picture him in your mind's eye. Think to whom you are speaking. Control your thoughts—don't let them wander. Address him as your Father and your friend. Now tell him things you really feel to tell him—not trite phrases that have little meaning, but have a sincere, heartfelt conversation with him. Confide in him. Ask him for forgiveness. Plead with him. Enjoy him. Thank him. Express your love to him. Then listen for his answers. Listening is an essential part of praying. Answers from the Lord come quietly, ever so quietly. In fact, few hear his answers audibly with their ears. We must be listening carefully or we will never recognize them. Most answers from the

Lord are felt in our heart as a warm, comfortable expression, or they may come as thoughts to our mind. They come to those who are prepared and who are patient.

Yes, the trials will still be there; but with the companionship of the Spirit, our approach to trials will change frustrations and heart-aches to blessings.

Just for a moment, think with me. Forget the trials you now have. Remember back to those trials you had last year, five years ago, ten years ago. What did you gain? What did you learn? Aren't you better prepared now because of them?

I testify the Lord is ready and waiting to help us. For our own good we must take the first step, and this step is prayer.

—*H. Burke Peterson*

DAY 82

Prayers Require Effort by Both Man and God

The Lord knows that there are things we could do on our own if we so desired. (Although on a deeper level we can't do anything on our own, because we belong to him, the air we breathe belongs to him—everything about our lives is a gift from God.) But the Lord says, "I understand that you can do many things on your own, but if you want your actions to be for your spiritual well-being, you must pray and consecrate them unto me." Sometimes the purpose of such a prayer is simply to check in with Him, to tell him what you're planning to do, and to ask for his blessings. But at the same time, we should ask for instructions and guidance: Am I on the right course? Is there anything thou wouldst desire me to change about what I'm going to do? Is it all pleasing? Is there another approach that would be better?

There is always a danger in stressing so fervently these ideas about our being totally dependent upon the Lord. For some, it is all too easy to become fanatical; some feel that they should be on their knees praying all the time when instead they should be out working, having prayed already and continuing to pray in their hearts.

Some people expect the Lord to do all the work and reveal things to them that they haven't bothered to study out in their minds beforehand (see D&C 9). Some become extreme and perhaps say, rather pridefully, "I prayed through the entire night the last two nights; I didn't sleep at all," or "I fasted for three days straight." Or a young returned missionary might say, "I've been waiting for a wife now for five years. I've been praying and praying, but the Lord still hasn't sent her to me. I haven't done much dating, but I'm sure that when the Lord finds her, he will have her come and find me."

Others may be paralyzed into inaction, waiting for an answer from the heavens, when in actuality the Lord may be requiring them to move ahead, proceeding the best way they know how, before he will confirm their course. . . .

As we acknowledge our dependence on the Lord, we increase in our humility—and we enhance our ability to truly communicate with the Lord. Those who truly are humble will also do all in their power to do their part, knowing that answers to prayer are a mutual endeavor, requiring effort by both man and God.

—*Gene R. Cook*

Focus

Meaningful prayer is based on an understanding of our relationship with God. Consistent, fervent prayer is for our benefit; it is not how we change God's mind, but how we change our hearts. Prayer is action. It is one of the "works" required if we are to develop faith.

I believe that also means that effective, meaningful prayer takes real effort on our part. We have to work at it to do it properly.

I have come to know from my own experience that the cure for the shallow prayer is focus. Focus takes mental effort. It takes concentration. It takes a conscious act of will to stay focused on what we *should* be praying for, not just what we *want* to pray for. In other words, sometimes we may need to change our perception of prayer. Do we see prayer

- as an emergency exit, or as a place of refuge?
- as a mail-order house, or as an antidote to the infections of life?

- as a way to let people know how righteous we are, or as a confession of how far we fall short?
- as a desperate cry for deliverance, or as a longing cry for forgiveness?
- as a plea for help for ourselves, or as a plea to know who needs our help?

. . . This is what we mean by focus. There are prayers of faith, prayers of thanks, prayers of submission, prayers of convenience, prayers of anger and frustration and bitterness, prayers for help, prayers for enlightenment and understanding, prayers for direction, prayers for the promises, and prayers of duty. The focus of our prayers will directly influence what kind of prayers we offer and the blessings that come from them.

—*Gerald N. Lund*

DAY 84

Preparation Is Required

We should not expect to rush into the presence of Deity, mouth a few well-worn phrases, race away, and then feel satisfied with the marvelous spiritual experience we have just enjoyed. We prepare out of respect and love. We prepare because time is precious, and we want our limited moments to be taken up in weightier matters.

We prepare so that we might be in a position to drink in all the living water that a gracious Lord is willing to dispense.

—*Robert L. Millet*

Preparing Our Hearts and Minds

Preparation for prayer can help communication with the Lord become an experience full of meaning and full of love, and can help to bring about the realization of God's purposes, and of our appropriate purposes, in prayer.

Our *hearts* must be prepared for prayer, for the instruction is that we are to go to him with "all our hearts," with lowliness of heart, with sincerity of heart, with honest hearts, and with broken and contrite hearts.

If our hearts are really right and committed to the Lord, we will go to him with confidence, with, as the psalmist said, "expectation" in the Lord (Psalm 62:5), believing that we shall receive. The fullness of our blessings and the soul-satisfying answers to our prayers will come when we learn to "yield our hearts" unto the Lord:

"Nevertheless they did fast and pray oft, and did wax stronger and stronger in their humility, and firmer and firmer in the faith of Christ, unto the filling their souls with joy and consolation, yea, even to the purifying and the sanctification of their hearts, which sanctification cometh because of their yielding their hearts unto God." (Helaman 3:35.)

God expects us to come to him with our spirits in tune, ready to yield our hearts unto him. If we will do this, we have his promise, and we will receive the blessings.

Our *minds* also need to be prepared for prayer. Through search and study we can begin to learn what we need to know. And we must think—actively, consciously, quietly, reflectively, honestly, deeply think. Then we can in good conscience come to the Lord to seek wisdom, comfort, strength, grace, or courage. When we know our own needs, know what we have to be thankful for, know what our responsibility is to God and others, then, with our souls hungry and our desires strong and honest, we can approach the Lord with earnest questions, appropriate petitions, and grateful minds.

—*Marion D. Hanks*

Faith Is More Than a Positive Attitude

The most important thing we can do as we seek to communicate with our Heavenly Father is to have faith in Jesus Christ. If we have faith in Christ, we will have faith in our Father in Heaven, because Christ so clearly testified of him.

Some people think of faith as a positive attitude. That's only a small part of what faith really. Faith is the power that holds the worlds in place. Faith is the power by which God works. When we have faith, we have access to his power.

But remember that the commandment is not just to have faith in a general sense. We are to have faith in a person, faith in Jesus Christ. When we seek to understand that better, we'll understand why we are to end all of our prayers "in the name of Jesus Christ." When we pray in that manner, we're asking for the grace of the Lord Jesus Christ to intervene on our behalf. If we can keep our faith centered in him it will help us to have much more power than if we pray without such faith.

—*Gene R. Cook*

DAY 87

Accessing the Lord's Grace

How can you obtain access to this grace that we're talking about, so the heavens can help you? How do you fulfill the laws and the conditions for grace? The scriptures teach of some prerequisites.

First, have faith. As Paul wrote:

"Therefore being justified by faith, we have peace with God through our Lord Jesus Christ. By whom also we have access by faith into this grace."(Romans 5:1–2.)

If we truly have faith, casting out doubts and fears, we can receive grace, which can give us power unto the answering of our prayers.

Second, repent and do good works. As we read in Helaman:

"Therefore, blessed are they who will repent. . . . And may God grant, in his great fullness, that men might be brought unto repentance and good works, that they might be restored unto grace for grace, according to their works." (Helaman 12:23–24.)

A repentant heart and good works are the very conditions required to have grace given to us. When someone pleads fervently in prayer for a blessing, the answer may be conditioned on repentance from our own personal sins more than any other factor. (See D&C 101:7–8; Mosiah 11:23–24.)

Third, be humble. James said:

"He giveth more grace. Wherefore he saith, God resisteth the proud, but giveth grace unto the humble." (James 4:6.)

Humility seems to rest at the core of who we are in our hearts. If you'll humble yourself before God—and if your desire is in harmony with the will of the Lord—the grace will come, the power will come and intervene for you, and your prayer will be answered.

—*Gene R. Cook*

Praying to Gain Faith

Being faithful does not necessarily develop faith. The first principle of the gospel is faith in the Lord, Jesus Christ. To have faith in him is to know him, to know his doctrine, and to know that the course of our life is in harmony with and acceptable to him. It is relatively easy to be faithful, but faith is born out of study, fasting, prayer, meditation, sacrifice, service, and, finally, personal revelation. Glimpses of understanding come line upon line, precept upon precept. Our Father is anxious to feed us just as fast as we can handle it, but we regulate the richness and the volume of our spiritual diet. And we do this by the same method used by the sons of Mosiah: "They had waxed strong in the knowledge of the truth; . . . they had searched the scriptures diligently, that they might know the word of God. But this is not all; they had given themselves to much prayer, and fasting; therefore they had the spirit of prophecy, and the spirit of revelation, and when they taught, they taught with power and authority of God." (Alma 17:2–3.)

Faithfulness without faith, practices without principles, will leave us and our families seriously wanting as we move closer to that time spoken of by Heber C. Kimball when he said, "The time is coming when no man or woman will be able to endure on borrowed light. Each will have to be guided by the light within himself if you do not have it, you will not stand." (Quoted by Harold B. Lee, *Conference Report,* October 1955, p. 56.)

—*Ardeth G. Kapp*

The Faith of Enos

Some might say, "Well, maybe Enos just had more faith that the rest of us; most likely he was gifted that way—naturally religious."

Look more closely.

His words suggest that he was surprised to learn he had *any* faith. He knelt, mostly convinced of one thing: a weighty mountain of his own great need. That kind of mountain, incidentally, only faith can move. After many hours of pleading and receiving, he was in awe. "My guilt was swept away" (verse 6), he says. He did not doubt that it was gone. But marveling he cried out, "Lord, how is it done?" (Verse 7.)

Note the puzzling answer. "Because of thy faith in Christ, whom thou has never before heard nor seen." (verse 8.) It was true he had not seen Christ. But he had heard *of* him in the living words of his father.

But notice also that the instant he had a directing touch from the Lord, it brought a staggering inner influence. "My faith began to be unshaken in the Lord, . . ." (verse 11), he writes. Thus kneeling there, the mustard seed became a tree!

There is, in all of us, an eternity more of faith in God than we tap. Kneeling to reach our faith we may find we are reaching *with* it. That, Enos shows us, is another real facet of prayer.

Enos's response was total. He did not run away holding his ears. We have the hindsight (the record is clear) to know that Enos became a lifelong dynamo, that he was "wrought upon by the power of God" (verse 26) unto the end of his days and that he "rejoiced in it above that of the world" (verse 26).

That performance demonstrated the foresight of God. Surely the Lord knew the real Enos—that he had it in him to use divine power as the Lord himself would use it. That enabled the Lord to answer Enos without reserve. It must be a different problem for the Lord to answer cool, bargaining, curious, all-talk-and-no-listen prayers.

And isn't it true that, unlike Enos, we pray for God to change everything—except us?

We hear much today about an identity crisis—the ache that comes when one begins to ask in a lonely, anguished way, "Who am I? What do I really want?" A lot of fuzzy answers can be given. But what is needed is a change of question. If you are, as I happen to know, an embryonic Enos, then you can kneel in some forest or other and ask him from the center of you, "Whose am I?" And I testify that when you expose your hidden self and latent faith and when you honor the quiet voice with total response, you will make a double discovery—yourself and God.

That is what prayer is all about.

—*Truman G. Madsen*

Mental Wrestling through Prayer

This mental wrestling can take the form of prolonged prayer. It may be necessary to pray longer and harder sometimes in order to get the feeling that you have been heard. You remember the case of Enos and his day-long prayer. Of course, that was an extreme case involving a future prophet of God. If you ever get where you need to pray all day long, you will know it and the power will be given to you. It isn't the sort of thing you just set out to do because you would like to hear a voice like Enos did. Still, Enos's example is one you should ponder as you think of gaining the determination to think and communicate with God. There are lessons for everybody in the story of Enos.

—*Vaughn J. Featherstone*

The Hidden Self

So what was unique about Enos's prayer? . . .

It was a "wrestle which I had before God," a pouring of his real self into the cups of his words. But it was more than that. At one level we all indulge the daily clichés and more or less "mean" them,—"forgive us, help us to overcome our weaknesses." At a deeper level we voice actual present feelings, even when they are raw, ugly, miserable ones. "Father. I feel awful—I am racked with anxiety." But there is a deeper level, the inmost, which often defies words, even feeling-words. This level may be likened to what the scriptures call "groanings which cannot be uttered." Turned upward they became the most powerful prayer-thrust of all. There *is* a wordless center in us.

Such, we may be sure, was the tone of Enos's prayer through those long hours. He learned that when we break the veil to our deepest self, we also penetrate the veil of heaven.

—*Truman G. Madsen*

DAY 92

Persisting in Prayer

There was in a city a judge, which feared not God, neither regarded man:

And there was a widow in that city; and she came unto him, saying, Avenge me of mine adversary.

And he would not for a while: but afterward he said within himself, Though I fear not God, nor regard man;

> Yet because this widow troubleth me, I will
> avenge her, lest by her continual coming she weary
> me (Luke 18:2–5).

When children want something badly from their parents, we use various expressions—some of them slang terms—to describe what they do. We say, "They *pestered* me until I couldn't stand it anymore" or "They *bugged* me until I gave in" or "They *hounded* me until I said yes" or "I said yes just to *get them off my back*."

But is this what the parable is suggesting? Do we pester the Lord until He throws up His hands and gives in? Surely that is not how God works with us.

There is a deeper question triggered by this parable. In the Sermon on the Mount, the Savior taught that we are not to use vain repetitions in our prayers because "your Father knoweth what things ye have need of, before ye ask him" (Matthew 6:8). This is an important point to keep in mind. With His infinite knowledge of all things, we can never come to God in prayer and surprise Him. And if that is so, why would He request that we not only pray to Him but also that we persist in prayer? If He already knows what we need, why should we have to ask Him at all, let alone ask Him again and again?

Another name given to this parable is the parable of the importunate woman. The word comes from the verb *to importune*. This word conveys exactly the opposite meaning of *to faint*. To importune means "to press or beset with solicitations; demand with urgency or persistence." (*Random House Dictionary*, s.v., "importune.")

Jesus told His disciples that the parable is meant to teach us that we should importune the Lord.

The request that we importune God with great persistence cannot be to satisfy some petty whim of His. Nor can it be that He wants us to jump through some theological hoops in order to prove our submissiveness. That is completely counter to His nature and purposes for us. So the first conclusion we can draw is: The commandment to importune the Father is not for His benefit. *It is for ours.*

—*Gerald N. Lund*

DAY 93

Heartfelt Prayers

The Lord teaches in the Sermon on the Mount that our prayers should be heartfelt utterances and not mindless musings: "When ye pray, use not vain repetitions, as the heathen do. . . . Be not ye therefore like unto them: for your Father knoweth what things ye have need of, before ye ask him." (Matthew 6:7–8.) Because the "Father knoweth what things [we] have need of, before [we] ask him," perhaps prayer is more for *us* than for God. We are the ones who benefit most from bending our knees and humbling ourselves in the attitude of prayer. We are the beneficiaries of such spoken (or unspoken) gratitude, desire, repentance, and blessing. Just as positive self-talk helps to align our actions with a better outlook on ourselves and our lives, prayer goes several steps further and gives us a chance to contemplate life from God's divine perspective. As we turn to Him for direction, guidance, and support, we bless our lives with the vision of One who perfectly loves us, knows us, and desires everlasting joy for us.

—*Lloyd D. Newell*

DAY 94

Praying with Intensity

President Wilford Woodruff taught: "The inhabitants of the earth do not realize the effect and benefit of prayer. The Lord hears and answers the prayers of men, women and children. Prayer has more power, a great deal, to bring down the blessings of God, than almost any other thing." These words are true, and as we try them out, we will realize their truth.

How do we pray for the answers we seek? We need to pray with all the intensity of our hearts. There is no set formula. For some, that might be five minutes on their knees, and for others it might mean walking continually with a prayer in their hearts. Answers and relief and assurance and peace come in moments we least expect. These are blessed moments when we can connect with that which is holy.

—*Kristen M. Oaks*

To Importune

On a certain day the disciples asked Jesus how to pray. He not only gave them a model prayer but also taught them through a parable to seek God—as the friend at midnight—with "importunity" (Luke 11:8). The verb *importune* means "to request with urgency; to press with solicitation; to urge with frequent or unceasing application." (Webster, *American Dictionary,* "importune.")

Jesus' story relates how a guest dropped in on a man in the middle of the night, and the man, realizing he had no food to offer his guest at that hour, attempted to wake up his sleeping neighbor to borrow three loaves of bread. Though a friend, the neighbor was reluctant to arise at that hour but finally—because of the persistence of the would-be borrower—got up to answer the need.

The point of the parable is the importance of importuning—persisting in imploring for what we want from God. The parable is followed by the frequent injunction: "Knock, and it shall be opened unto you. . . . And to him that knocketh it shall be opened" (Luke 11:9–10). God wants us to pray, plead, implore, and *importune*—specifically, frequently, and sincerely. He wants us to plead with him in humility for what we need. In the Joseph Smith Translation, the parable of the friend at midnight begins with a simple but powerful promise: "*Your heavenly Father will not fail to give unto you whatsoever ye ask of him*" (JST, Luke 11:5; emphasis added). The message is,

"Don't give up or despair; keep asking." In this case the repetition is not vain repetition. As the Prophet Joseph Smith said, "Come to God [and] weary him until he blesses you." (Ehat and Cook, *Words of Joseph Smith,* 15.)

—*D. Kelly Ogden*

DAY 96

Pray as the Ancients Prayed

[Prayer] ought not to seem just a convenient and contrived miracle, for if we are to search for real light and eternal certainties, we have to pray as the ancients prayed. We are women now, not children, and are expected to pray with maturity. The words most often used to describe urgent, prayerful labor are *wrestle, plead, cry,* and *hunger.* In some sense, prayer may be the hardest work we will ever be engaged in, and perhaps it should be. It is pivotal protection against becoming so involved with worldly possessions and honors and status that we no longer desire to undertake the search for our soul.

—*Patricia T. Holland*

Yearning Prayer

They say it in one way or another, those who really know about prayer: Only yearning prayer gets through.

But there are three kinds of yearning.

We yearn when we mean what we say. But is that enough when we are asking the impossible, or when what we are asking is, if we could only see, not for our good?

We yearn when we care terribly. But is that enough when what we care for, however desperately, is a fist-shaking fixation that presumes God visions less of what is needed than we?

We yearn, finally, when we do not only mean and care intensively, but when at the core we are as anxious to listen as to ask. We yearn when we will to abide counsels already given and to respond to him and his way *in* his way.

So long as we are set in our uninspired desires, not moldable, we must break our hearts before we can pray from them. So need we wonder why the heavens are often like brass over our heads?

Humble prayer is the beginning of communion with the highest of personalities—God and his Son Jesus Christ—of higher ways of seeing and feeling, as it were, through their eyes.

Achieving this is a life-process, not a five-minute thing. But it is sometimes closer in youth than in maturity. Youth may keenly grasp the truth: that even at our best we are like the blind boy who walks with his friend. He does not believe, nor bluff, that he is self-sufficient. Instead, he responds to the slightest nudge. (If you would know the power of God, try, early in life, to become just this dependable in your dependence.)

As this happens, the whole thing becomes the instrument that vibrates upwardly. No special words are needed, no forced tone of voice, and no dramatic play-acting.

Then we being to recognize the "first-answers" to our prayers—the answers that always come before the others.

What are these?

They are subtle flashes that register within. And they are real. They center "in your mind and in your heart" (D&C 8:2) and are, therefore, a perfect blend of thought and feeling. They come with a serene flow of power that is light and warmth and liquid surety. They whisper a "Yes," or a "No," a "Wait," or a "Be still," a "Trust," or an "Act well thy part."

This is what a modern young prophet calls "breaking the ice" and "obtaining the Holy Spirit" which cause "the bosom to burn." He says that much emptying ourselves of unworthiness and much filling ourselves with concentration precedes it. He says we should strive to stay on our knees until it happens.

And how do you know that this burning is of God? Maybe it is just hope, guess, or wish.

You know by the quiet verdict of your own inner being. (And you know just as well when you don't know.) You know because the haunting "I doubt" and the painful "I fear" are swallowed up in living light. You arise this time, after many darkened times, tinctured with gratitude. With the glow comes a lingering love, a knowledge that forges resolve to do what must now be done, and a faith for next time.

Thus yearning prayer becomes burning prayer—burning-with-the-Spirit prayer.

Happy is the youth who prays for, and then until, and finally with, this subtle flame. For "he that asketh in Spirit shall receive in Spirit." (D&C 46:28.)

—Truman G. Madsen

DAY 98

A Process of Spiritual Growth

Importunity, as the Lord suggests it, initiates a tremendous process of spiritual growth. The very exercise of questioning, then seeking and humbling ourselves, and finally submitting our will to His, becomes spiritually enlivening and spiritually empowering. Knowing this, is it any wonder that sometimes the Lord withholds an answer from us for a time?

That is the principle taught in the parable of the unjust judge. We don't persist in prayer to change God's mind. We persist in prayer to change our hearts.

—Gerald N. Lund

Humility and Prayer

In the Doctrine and Covenants, the Lord directly connected humility to answered prayers when he said,

"Be thou humble; and the Lord thy God shall lead thee by the hand, and give thee answer to thy prayers." (D&C 112:10.)

When we're humble, we feel our dependency on the Lord. Because of this feeling of dependency, we reach out to him for help and guidance in many areas—and have open hearts and minds to receive it.

Some people argue that we shouldn't trouble the Lord about little things. In a way, that's a spirit of pride, a spirit of wanting to do things on one's own, rather than a desire to discover and do the Lord's will.

We hear much in the world about being self-sufficient and self-confident. We hear much about learning to do things on our own—after all, didn't the Lord bless us with good minds and the ability to think things through and reason them out on our own?

Yet that attitude takes us away from the spirit of humility and a reliance on the Lord. Certainly the Lord would have us do all that is in our power to do, but if we take the attitude of self-reliance to an extreme, we will begin to think that we can live our lives without his help.

Nephi addressed this very issue: Are there some things I ought not to pray about? Or should I pray about everything? If that's true, why don't we do it? Why is it we go on day after day, depending on our own strength? . . . Then he makes this significant statement:

"For if ye would hearken unto the Spirit which teacheth a man to pray ye would know that ye must pray; for the evil spirit teacheth not a man to pray, but teacheth him that he must not pray. (2 Nephi 32:8.)

The Lord wants us to grow and become strong and be able to do much good, but through it all he wants us to be dependent on the Spirit of the Lord for direction.

—Gene R. Cook

DAY 100

"You Can't Pray a Lie"

There are times when we need to sufficiently humble ourselves before the Lord. Mahonri Moriancumer, King Benjamin, Nephi, Abraham, and Moroni all practiced this principle. In fact, all of the prophets of all ages have practiced it.

Consider an introduction to prayer such as this: 'Our Father who art in heaven, I kneel before thee this day in deepest solemn gratitude. I realize I am as nothing, less than the dust of the earth, the least of all thy servants, the weakest of the weak. I humble myself before thee as dust and ashes, unworthy even to approach thee.'

I believe it pleases the Lord for us to come before him with this type of humility. It isn't false humility; we are not praying thus to impress others, for we are all alone with him. Therefore, we are not expecting others to say, "My, you are humble." We don't want that. We want him to know. We know and he knows, as Huckleberry Finn says, "You can't pray a lie." I think the Lord appreciates our humbling ourselves sufficiently before him. Then we express our gratitude, and then we implore him.

—*Vaughn J. Featherstone*

The Ultimate Expression of Humility

The condition of humility and meekness is closely connected to our ability to receive and recognize revelation. It is, of course, the opposite of pride. Often when the scriptures talk about a "softening" of the heart, they refer to a pushing aside of pride, a willingness to submit our will to the Lord's.

The ultimate expression of humility is to acknowledge God's divine perfections as being so infinitely superior to our own attributes that we, of our own free will, surrender our hearts to Him. As Abinadi noted, in the Savior we have the perfect model for humility, for "the will of the Son [was] swallowed up in the will of the Father" (Mosiah 15:7).

IMPROVING THE QUALITY OF OUR PRAYERS   113

Note how the Lord values this attribute and especially how often He links it directly to an increase in revelation:

- "Be thou humble; and the Lord thy God shall lead thee by the hand, and give thee answer to thy prayers" (D&C 112:10).
- "They did fast and pray oft, and did wax stronger and stronger in their humility, . . . yielding their hearts unto God" (Helaman 3:35).
- "Because of meekness and lowliness of heart cometh the visitation of the Holy Ghost" (Moroni 8:26).
- "Walk in the meekness of my Spirit, and you shall have peace in me" (D&C 19:23).

—Gerald N. Lund

DAY 102

Nothing Is Impossible with the Lord

It is easy to get discouraged. It is easy to quit, but you mustn't fail. You remember how Nephi went into an impossible situation and couldn't get the plates. His brothers couldn't. They couldn't buy them. They couldn't bribe them out of the hands of Laban. They couldn't force their way in, and their lives were hanging on a thread. In spite of all that, here comes one boy, unarmed, who walks into a city through a wall that was closed to him, through gates that couldn't be opened, into a garden that was impenetrable, into a vault that was locked, among soldiers that couldn't be bypassed, and comes out with his arms full of records to keep his posterity and others from perishing in unbelief. (See 1 Nephi 3–4.)

He did the impossible. But nothing is impossible to the Lord. Any time we have him on our side, when he has called us, given us a commandment, then, if our energy and our efforts and our planning and our prayers are equal to the size of the job, the job, of course, will be completed

—*Spencer W. Kimball*

DAY 103

Be Like Nephi: Desire the Things God Desires

Sanctification is a lifetime process. It is the means by which we, as partakers of the blessings of the sacred Atonement, are purified and come to love the things that may have been distasteful to us in our spiritual immaturity. By the purging and enabling power of the Spirit, God creates a clean heart and renews a right spirit within us (Psalm 51:10). We grow gradually into the spirit of revelation, begin to feel passionate about becoming a holy person, and thereby come to desire the things God desires. We can become like Nephi, son of Helaman, to whom the Lord God spoke the following sublime words: "Blessed are thou, Nephi, for those things which thou has done; for I have beheld how thou has with unwearyingness declared the word . . . And now, because thou hast done this. . . . , behold, I will bless thee forever; and I will make thee mighty in word and in deed, in faith and in works; yea, even that all things shall be done unto thee according to thy word, for thou shalt not ask that which is contrary to my will" (Helaman 10:4–5).

What trust! What honor! And what a blessing that we all seek. And yes, it is obtainable; it is within our reach.

—*Robert L. Millet*

DAY 104

Guided by Inspiration

Let every Saint, when he prays, ask God for the things he needs to enable him to promote righteousness on the earth. If you do not know what to ask for, let me tell you how to pray. When you pray in secret with your families, if you do not know anything to ask for, submit yourselves to your Father in Heaven and beseech him to guide you by the inspirations of the Holy Ghost, and to guide this people, and dictate the affairs of his Kingdom on the earth, and there leave it. Ask him to put you just where he wants you, and to tell you what he wants you to do, and feel that you are on hand to do it.

—*Brigham Young*

DAY 105

When the Heart Is Humble

Without humility, prayer loses much of its power in our lives. If our hearts are not humble, not only are we less likely to pray, but also we can end up praying for the wrong things. Or we may find ourselves praying out of habit or because "it's our duty." If we are not careful, our prayers may become shallow and filled with rote phrases that are repeated with no real depth of feeling. . . .

The Lord has said that "the spirit and the body are the soul of man" (D&C 88:15). With that definition in mind, note this prayer by Enos: "My soul hungered; and I kneeled down before my maker, and I cried unto him in mighty prayer and supplication for mine own soul" (Enos 1:4; see also Alma 34:26; 58:10; Mormon 3:12).

When the heart is humble, we become submissive, penitent, patient, trusting, open to instruction, and hungry for the things of the Spirit. When these qualities are present in our prayers, not only do we find greater power and receive more revelation, but our hearts are also filled with hope.

—*Gerald N. Lund*

Are We Too Content?

How many of you, my brethren and sisters, are seeking for these gifts that God has promised to bestow? How many of you, when you bow before your Heavenly Father in your family circle or in your secret places, contend for these gifts to be bestowed upon you? How many of you ask the Father, in the name of Jesus, to manifest Himself to you through these powers and these gifts? Or do you go along day by day like a door turning on its hinges, without having any feeling upon the subject, without exercising any faith whatever; content to be baptized and be members of the Church, and to rest there, thinking that your salvation is secure because you have done this? I say to you, in the name of the Lord, as one of His servants, that you have need to repent of this. You have need to repent of your hardness of heart, of your indifference, and of your carelessness. There is not that diligence, there is not that faith, there is not that seeking for the power of God that there should be among a people who have received the precious promises we have.

—*George Q. Cannon*

Prayers as Work

There is no aspect of the life of a true Latter-day Saint which does not involve working in some degree, either physically or mentally. It is equally evident that true prayer, the fervent, dedicated prayer that secures the needed answer, similarly represents a considerable effort. Read again the prayer experience of Enos in the Book of Mormon—notice that he did not merely get down on his knees and pray intently for five minutes, ten minutes, or even half an hour. He prayed all the day long and was still praying when night fell. Have you ever prayed with all of your heart and soul? Have you ever really needed something when it was as if you were confronted with a wall too high, too long and too deep to go over, around or under, but nevertheless you had to get to the other side? I have been in these circumstances a few times in my life, and I want to tell you that at such times you really learn how to plead with the Lord. And in doing so you make a tremendous mental and spiritual effort.

—Vaughn J. Featherstone

True, Powerful Prayer

Perhaps other lessons can be learned from the example of Enos's prayers. Note that he was alone and away from others and the normal pressures of day-to-day living as he meditated and prayed. . . . he took advantage of his situation while hunting to contemplate deeply on the messages of his father, Jacob. A certain amount of privacy and some undisturbed time for meditation is very valuable as we seek for deep personal communion with our Heavenly Father.

Also, seeds of gospel truth had been planted earlier in Enos' soul, and these were now ready to bear new, fresh fruit. Alma later wrote about this process . . . , and Moroni included the reading and pondering about the works of God as important preparation for prayer, as one seeks to receive the truthfulness and verification of God's word.

. . . The account of Enos and his mighty prayer demonstrates the importance of being taught gospel truths, the value of being alone as one meditates and prays, the necessity of prolonged and intense prayer, and, most important, the clear answers and profound peace that prayer can bring as God communicates with us through the Holy Ghost. Enos gives us a short but important lesson in some valuable characteristics of true, powerful prayer.

—Victor L. Ludlow

When You Confide in the Lord

As you feel the need to confide in the Lord or to improve the quality of your visits with him—to pray, if you please—may I suggest a process to follow: go where you can be alone, go where you can think, go where you can kneel, go where you can speak out loud to him. The bedroom, the bathroom, or the closet will do. Now, picture him in your mind's eye. Think to whom you are speaking, control your thoughts—don't let them wander, address him as your Father and your friend. Now tell him things you really feel to tell him—not trite phrases that have little meaning, but have a sincere, heartfelt conversation with him. Confide in him, ask him for forgiveness, plead with him, enjoy him, thank him, express your love to him, and then listen for his answers. Listening is an essential part of praying. Answers from the Lord come quietly—ever so quietly. In fact, few hear his answers audibly with their ears. We must be listening so carefully or we will never recognize them. Most answers from the Lord are felt in our heart as a warm comfortable expression, or they may come as thoughts to our mind. They come to those who are prepared and who are patient.

—*H. Burke Peterson*

What Is Required?

The Trouble with Most of Our Prayers

Believe in prayer and the power of prayer. Pray to the Lord with the expectation of answers. I suppose there is not a man or woman in this entire congregation today who doesn't pray. I hope that is so. The trouble with most of our prayers is that we give them as if we were picking up the telephone and ordering groceries—we place our order and hang up. We need to meditate, contemplate, think of what we are praying about and for and then speak to the Lord as one man speaketh to another. "Come now, and let us reason together, saith the Lord" (Isa. 1:18). That is the invitation. Believe in the power of prayer—it is real, it is wonderful, it is tremendous.

—*Gordon B. Hinckley*

Taking Time for Prayer

Often when I face difficulties, I need to turn off the phone, lock the door, kneel in earnest prayer, and then curl up in a chair and meditate, contemplate, search the scriptures, and cry out again and again in my heart, completely focusing my mind on the mind and will and presence of God until I can see a clear picture of him. I like to think of him with loving, outstretched arms. With such a loving image, I begin to feel my connection with him and a confirmation of his love. Sometimes I may have to work at this for hours, for a significant portion of the day, or for several days. . . .

I realize that life has to go on and that you will not be able to pursue this heavenly communication in a completely uninterrupted way, but if it is a high priority and a fundamental goal in your life, you will find ways, early or late, to be with God. If the key to your car or your mortgage payment check or a child were lost, would you take time to find them? Wouldn't finding them provide the peace you needed to then go about your day? If God is lost in your life and you are not going to be strong or stable without him, can you be focused and fixed enough to find him?

If you believed that your earthly father could comfort any heartache, heal any illness, solve any problem, or just be with you through the crucibles of life, wouldn't you call to him constantly? I am just childish enough to believe that our Father in Heaven can bless us in all those ways. The price to be paid for this kind of communion is time and your best powers of concentration, but by that investment you may offset untold hours, days, weeks, and months of struggle or sorrow or pain.

—*Patricia T. Holland*

Seek the Light for Answers to Prayers

Have you ever lain awake all night trying to solve a problem in your mind? Often these sleepless nights have led me to call on the Lord in prayer. When I can't sleep, I pray. Those dark, quiet hours allow uninterrupted time to counsel with the Lord. In Third Nephi we read, "Behold, I am . . . the light" (3 Nephi 15:9). In the darkest of hours, I have learned that the Savior really is a giver of light. When darkness surrounds us and seems to overtake us, we must do what Joseph Smith once did in a grove of trees—get down on our knees and pray.

. . . Maybe it's not the darkness of the night that is hindering your perception; maybe a sense of gloom is dimming your ability to see clearly. Try to shed some light on the situation. Turn to places and things that bring light. Morning hours, the scriptures, uplifting music, and time spent at the temple can help to illuminate your current circumstances. . . . If you can't see clearly now, wait for the light to come.

—*Emily Freeman*

Pray in Secret

Now, the Lord taught us to pray in secret. What happens to us when we pray in secret? First, our faith is put to the test. How foolish people would feel who pray alone and really do not believe in God. We can pray in public and people might think we believe, but praying alone takes faith. When we pray alone, there is no one to impress with our command of the language, with our beautiful phrases or eloquence. We simply talk with a loving, interested Father about what is troubling us most. We take problems that no one else, not another living soul, can help us with. We become like little children, feeling a dependence and need for someone wiser and with power and influence. We do not have to worry about embarrassment if our prayers are not answered the way we think they should be, because only we and God know for what we pray. When tears come, there is no embarrassment. We can be totally honest, knowing that we cannot lie to or deceive the Spirit or God. He knows us for our real worth. He knows who and what we really are, not what we seem to be. When we have personal problems or struggles, we can pray and know that these things are kept totally confidential. We can discuss our weaknesses, our sins, our frustrations, our needs, and know that He will listen and respond.

We can learn a great deal about a person by the way he or she prays in private. A hurried, get-it-done attitude in private prayer shows a lack of reverence for God and demonstrates that perhaps that person does pray to be heard of men.

The hymn recalls, "There is an hour of peace and rest, unmarred by earthly care; 'tis when before the Lord I go, and kneel in secret prayer." The last verse reminds us of the comfort we receive: "When thorns are strewn along my path, and foes my feet ensnare, my Savior to my aid will come, if sought in secret prayer." (Hans Peterson, "Secret Prayer," *Hymns,* no. 144.)

—*Vaughn J. Featherstone*

DAY 114

Sincere Prayer Helps the Spirit Flow

A fervent, sincere prayer is a two-way communication that will do much to bring the Spirit flowing like healing water to help with the trials, hardships, aches, and pains we all face. What is the quality of our secret prayers? As we pray, we should think of our Heavenly Father as being close by; full of knowledge, understanding, love, and compassion; the essence of power; and having great expectations of each of us.

—*James E. Faust*

Silent Prayers

Was the Prophet [Joseph Smith] effective in silent prayers, did he commend that or even command it? I note with interest eight different places where the Lord, through the Prophet, says, 'pray always.' That's a strong imperative. How can we? If 'pray always' means vocally, then none of us do it—none of us can. But if 'pray always' includes the kind of prayer that is from the heart and wordless, we're getting closer to a possibility. And if it means, even more profoundly, that we are to be in the spirit of prayer regardless of what we may be doing, then all of us can pray always.

The Prophet gave us a better rendering of a New Testament verse about prayer. It is Romans 8:26. The King James Version of the Bible has Paul saying (speaking of how the Spirit can assist us in prayer), 'The Spirit itself maketh intercession for us with *groanings* which cannot be uttered.' The Prophet's version is, 'The Spirit maketh intercession for us with *striving* which cannot be expressed' (Joseph Smith, *Teachings* [1938], 278). I think he is saying that when we have enough confidence in the discerning power of the Spirit, we stop worrying so much about the words we use and are concerned more simply to open up what is really deep in us—even things that we cannot find words for. Strivings are different than groanings—you can groan in discouragement and despondency and it can all be turned down instead of turned up, but strivings are upreaching. We can take our strivings—even those that we cannot express—and know that as we silently think and pour out our feelings, the Spirit will translate those and perfectly transmit them to the Lord. And in turn, the Spirit can respond from the Lord to us. A great confidence and a great freedom can come when we trust the Spirit for that.

—*Truman G. Madsen*

DAY 116

Pray When the Cup Is Bitter

One of the most important ways we can be pure before the Lord is to be scrupulously honest in our words and deeds.

The first person we need to be honest with is with the Lord. The Lord doesn't want just pretty prayers. He wants real prayers. Sometimes we think of those eloquent, gracious prayers in sacrament meeting and general conference as the models for our personal prayers. We try to organize our rough thoughts into smooth sentences and it seems hard. We know how to say, "I'm so grateful for our son who is on his mission," but we might not know how to say, "I'm so scared and so mad about our son who is on drugs." Heavenly Father wants to hear the scared and mad prayers just as much as he wants to hear the grateful prayers.

Sometimes it's very hard for us to be honest, especially with negative feelings and ideas. Elder Neal A. Maxwell asked a soul-searching question: "Can we partake of tiny, bitter cups without becoming bitter?" I think we can, with God's help, but not if we deny that the cup is bitter in the first place.

When Jesus was praying in the Garden of Gethsemane, he was honest about how hard the Atonement was going to be for him when he prayed that the cup might pass from him. He struggled with a "very heavy" burden of feelings, saying, "My soul is exceeding sorrowful unto death," and he prayed, "Father, all things are possible unto thee; take away this cup from me" (Mark 14:33–34, 36). He was honest about how much he *didn't* like what was happening; and I think it's because of his honesty that we so revere the love and humility revealed by the rest of his prayer: "Nevertheless not what I will, but what thou wilt" (Mark 14:36).

Can we be equally honest in our prayers? Remember, we're not going to shock our Father in Heaven. There isn't anything we can say that he hasn't already heard, nothing we can show him that he hasn't already seen. We may shock ourselves a little when we start being honest, but I think some very profound revelations come to us in those moments.

—*Chieko N. Okazaki*

His Love Is Unconditional

Why don't we just talk and share more with our Heavenly Father? Do you think maybe sometimes we don't really believe that God does hear and understand us and that He will actually answer us? Are we nervous about talking to Him? I'm convinced that our Heavenly Father doesn't sit somewhere up there watching for us to make mistakes, watching for our imperfections—He's not trying to catch us doing something wrong. He wants to catch us doing things that are right and good, and then He says, "Way to go! You're all right!"

Too many of us seem to think of God as being disappointed or disgusted with us. We prayed for a magic wand. He said no. There can be no hope from now on. No, I don't think that's how it is. He allows us to learn and progress. He is pleased with our progress, our increase in awareness, our desire to truly communicate with Him.

It's unfair to imagine that God has anything but unconditional love for us, His children. He wants us to succeed. He does listen, understand, and respond to all the yearnings of our souls and each prayer we offer. There is nothing you or I could do that would cause God to stop loving us. Nothing. His love is unconditional, and we work to have that same kind of love for others.

—*Mary Ellen Edmunds*

The Language of Prayer

In public prayer with the Saints in meetings and gatherings, we are counseled to maintain the "language of prayer." It helps avoid either the too frequent use of sacred names or a tone that may sound like contemptuous familiarity.

In private prayer, it seems to me, the language to be used is the one that best expresses our depths. And I believe the only irreverence, the only approach that causes the Lord to weep, occurs when we use words to conceal rather than to reveal our most intense feelings and needs. In the end, each of us must pray in the words and style and attitude that seems most authentic to us. At such time there is no such things as being "too familiar" but only the blasphemy of being too distant, of pretending that aches and confusion and doubts and strivings are not really there. The Lord cannot help us where we most need help until we spill it all out, however starkly. I know from experience that the Father does not make us offenders for our words. Was Christ hiding or measuring his words in the Garden?

—*Truman G. Madsen*

Learning to Talk with God

Now there is a lot of difference between saying a prayer and talking with God. There are a few whom I have heard pray who did talk with God, one of whom was the late President Charles A. Callis. I never heard him pray at the holy altars in the temple, I never heard him when we knelt together in prayer when we were out on difficult missions but what he seemed, as he talked, to be reaching right into the portals of our Father's holy dwelling place, and he talked with divine beings. Do not say prayers, do not read prayers, but learn to talk with God.

—*Harold B. Lee*

Being Honest with God

Prayer, therefore, that is too self-conscious of itself is not yet really praying. What is needed by us all are feelings of adoration that produce a mental posture of contemplation—and more meditation and less premeditation.

When we pray, we are not conveying any information to God

that He does not already have. Nor, when we confess our sins before Him, is it news to Him that we have misbehaved. It is vital, therefore, that we open our souls to Him and tell Him what our concerns are now, as well as acknowledge what we now are, for this is a part of the process of aligning ourselves with His will. We cannot, for the purposes of real prayer, hurriedly dress our words and attitudes in tuxedos when our shabby life is in rags. More than we realize, being honest with God in our prayers helps us to be more honest with ourselves.

—*Neal A. Maxwell*

DAY 121

Avoid Lengthy Prayers

How often do we hear people who wax eloquent in their prayers to the extent of preaching a complete sermon? The hearers tire and the effect is lost, and I sometimes wonder if perhaps the dial of the heavenly radio is not turned off when long and wordy prayers are sent heavenward. I feel sure that there is too much to do in heaven for the Lord and his servants to sit indefinitely listening to verbose praises and requests, for as we are told in Matthew, he knows, before we ask, our needs and desires. (See Matthew 6:8.)

—*Spencer W. Kimball*

Prayerful Saints

What a marvelous spiritual revival we would have if the Saints would pray sincerely and humbly to God—the One Being in all of eternity who is available to every soul who walks the earth, every moment of every day. None are exempt save it be by their conduct and choosing. Oh, how we ought to love and worship our God and His Son. Oh, what an answer to the trials, frustrations, and perplexities of life. Peace and blessings come to the contrite soul who approaches God with a broken heart.

This is also what the Savior taught in the parable of the two men who went up to the temple to pray, describing the publican as "standing afar off, [he] would not lift up so much as his eyes unto heaven, but smote upon his breast, saying, God be merciful to me a sinner."

The Lord described this man as going "down to his house justified." (Luke 18:13–14.)

Let us be most earnest, humble, sincere, forgiving, and filled with charity as we pray. Peace will come, answers will be given, promises will be fulfilled; and the soul will be satisfied. Prayer is the righteous soul's sincere desire.

—*Vaughn J. Featherstone*

Real and Honest Prayers

Heavenly Father doesn't want to hear only "nice" prayers. He wants to hear real prayers, honest prayers. How many times are our evening prayers just one more chore? Scoop up the evening paper and put it away, jot "celery salt" on the shopping list, collect that dirty sock for the hamper, brush your teeth, and drop to your knees. We all know how to say prayers. We know the polite formula of "we thank thee for the gospel, we ask thee to bless the missionaries . . ."

But who are we trying to kid? Jesus has just seen the stove where the spaghetti boiled over, and it was pretty obvious that wasn't the only thing that had ever boiled over on that stove. He heard what you muttered when you picked up that one sock, just as you've been doing for the past eight years. He caught that worry about the dentist bill that flashed across your mind when you were putting toothpaste on your brush. He doesn't want polite platitudes. He wants you! All of you! He wants to be the center of your total life—the worried you, the mad you, and the sad you as well as the inspired, happy, obedient, loving you.

—*Chieko N. Okazaki*

Purpose in Prayer

[Prayer] is the means by which I have continued opportunities to call upon and talk with my Heavenly Father, now that I am no longer in his presence. Because I believe that he is all-knowing and that he knows me better than I know myself—as earthly parents often know their children better than the children know themselves—I know that he will respond to me in ways that are best for me.

When we come to understand that prayer is our means of access to God our Father, we become increasingly more comfortable in calling upon him. When we know that our Father knows us and hears us and responds to us, we will be anxious to "commune" with him. (See Exodus 25:22.) It is then that we will put aside "vain repetitions" (3 Nephi 13:7) and "pour out our whole souls to God." (Mosiah 28:14.) Ultimately, we will be more anxious to listen than to rehearse our own litany of lists.

How often, in the hope of fulfilling the responsibility we feel to pray, do we simply go through the motions of prayer?

—*Carolyn J. Rasmus*

Sincere Repetition

When I pray it is usually repetitive. Every time I kneel down I pray for my wife, children, and grandchildren by name. I always pray for our beloved prophet and the other Brethren. I always pray faithfully for all of our missionaries, for their personal welfare, and for their protection from the evil one. I pray for our great country, and I pray that doors to other nations will be opened.

Of the last thousand prayers that I have offered, the above items would have been prayed for a thousand times. Repetition? Of course, but sincere repetition. The Lord is offended by vain repetition. Vain repetition, I think, is when we kneel down and say, "Our Heavenly Father," and then we say words that are repetitious and habitual, but our minds are on what we are going to do after we pray, or what we are going to do the next day, or what is going on in the other room while we are praying. Heavenly Father finds out that we really didn't want to talk to him.

—*Vaughn J. Featherstone*

What Is Vain Repetition?

I suppose we border on vain repetition when we allow our personal prayers to become rote or ritualistic or almost meaningless. When we rush through our evening prayers, for example, as though they are the final task to be performed before we climb into bed, the those prayers serve little or no function. We would be better off to take a few moments to offer a brief but sincere prayer. Our Lord and Savior knows firsthand what it feels like to be tired; he is no stranger to hunger, thirst, and fatigue (Mosiah 3:7).

But there is little reason to be rushed in our prayers. We just may need to plan our time—including how and when we will pray—a little better in the future.

—*Robert L. Millet*

An Open Conversation with God

We need to have an ongoing conversation with God that shares our whole hearts with him. That means we need to be honest about what we love and what we don't, where we succeed and where we fail, what we're feeling and what we're thinking. One of the most human things about us is the strength and power of our feelings—and some of those feelings are very negative. We feel grief so intensely that we think our hearts will break. We are consumed by a rage so fiery that our whole world seems angry. We feel discouraged. We feel depressed. We aren't always honest, always kind, always faithful. We aren't uniformly cheerful, compassionate, and courageous. And usually it's during those very moments that we choose not to pray, because we think that God doesn't want to see that part of us, respond to such turbulent emotions, or accept us in our negative moments.

I think that the scriptures teach a far different message.

—*Chieko N. Okazaki*

DAY 128

Prayer Can Cleanse Us

The secret to cleansing our spirit of whatever the impurity is not very complicated. It begins with [sincere, heartfelt] prayer every morning and ends with prayer every night. This is the most important step I know in the cleansing process. It may simply be a prayer for strength to turn from bad habits, or a prayer that sin will be distasteful to you

Meanwhile, remember that not all prayers are answered the

same day or even the next day. Sometimes it takes a long time. But with this step in place, I have seen hundreds of miracles take place. Without it, there is continued frustration, unhappiness, ineffectiveness, and despair.

—*H. Burke Peterson*

DAY 129

Don't Get Discouraged

The task is to draw close enough to the Lord that we progress to the point where we petition Him according to His will, not ours. "And this is the confidence that we have in him, that, if we ask any thing according to his will, he heareth us." (1 John 5:14.) In modern revelations the Lord has declared His willingness to grant us the requests contained in our petitions if what we ask for is expedient for us. (D&C 88:64–64.)

When we become sufficiently purified and cleansed from sin, we can ask what we will in the name of Jesus "and it shall be done." (D&C 50:29.) The Lord even promises us that when one reaches a certain spiritual condition, "it shall be given you what you shall ask." (D&C 50:30.)

Thus we clearly need to have the Spirit with us as we petition, because "in the Spirit" we will ask "according to the will of God; wherefore it is done even as he asketh." (D&C 46:30.)

If, meanwhile, in the face of such sublime ultimate promises, our prayers sometimes seem so very proximate, we should not be discouraged. So much can be done "in process of time" to improve our petitioning. Neither the pure City of Enoch nor pure prayers are arrived at in a day!

—*Neal A. Maxwell*

DAY 130

Prayer and Works Go Together

It is not, never has been, and never will be the design and purpose of the Lord—however much we seek him in prayer—to answer all our problems and concerns without struggle and effort on our part. This mortality is a probationary estate. In it we have our agency. We are being tested to see how we will respond in various situations; how we will decide issues; what course we will pursue while we are here walking, not by sight, but by faith. Hence, we are to solve our own problems and then to counsel with the Lord in prayer and receive a spiritual confirmation that our decisions are correct.

As he set forth in his work of translating the Book of Mormon, Joseph Smith did not simply ask the Lord what the characters on the plates meant; rather, he was required to study the matter out in his mind, make a decision of his own, and then ask the Lord if his conclusions were correct. (See D&C 8 and 9.) So it is with us in all that we are called upon to do. Prayer and works go together. If and when we have done all we can, then in consultation with the Lord, through mighty and effectual prayer, we have power to come up with the right conclusions.

—*Bruce R. McConkie*

DAY 131

Participation Required

Asking is not enough.

We have talked before of when Oliver Cowdery came to Harmony, Pennsylvania, and began acting as scribe for the Prophet. He also desired the gift of translation, which the Lord granted to him. But he failed. I what is now section 9 of the Doctrine and Covenants, the Lord told him why this happened.

The Lord said: "Behold, you have not understood; you have supposed that I would give it unto you, when you took no thought save it was to ask me" (D&C 9:7).

We may be tempted to be a little critical of Oliver and ask ourselves how he could have missed something that seems so obvious. However, many of us also make this mistake as we seek inspiration and revelation from the Lord. We think that asking is sufficient. What Oliver learned that day is a lesson for all of us. *Obtaining revelation is not a passive experience.* We don't just toss off a prayer, then sit back and wait for the answer to come. We must choose to actively participate in the revelatory process. Asking is how the process beings, but it is not how it ends.

—*Gerald N. Lund*

DAY 132

The Great Answerer

There can't be an answer without a question. Could there be "answers" in the back of a math book without any problems in the front? There must be a question.

And, generous as our Father is, he cannot do the asking and seeking for us. The one with the need is the one who has to try on the answer, just as the one with the hunger is the one who has to eat.

But once the question is asked or the request is made, and once we actually exert ourselves to go looking and trying things on, he answers. He doesn't hide from our requests. He isn't like that. He is generous. He asks us to ask. It is a command. He isn't reluctant to answer. Answering is what he does. He is the Great Answerer in the universe, "quick to hear the cries of his people and to answer their prayers."

But if he is generous and sees our need, why pray? Isn't He always aware, always watching? Yes, but when we pray, something wonderful happens.

Something wonderful happens when a baby begins to smile and coo. The connecting of eyes, the response to the parent's voice, the sweet effort to speak, these put the relationship on a new level. Prayer connects us to him who wishes to be more than a guardian. He seeks the bond of friendship.

When we open the conversation, when we invite him to us and plead for His attention, he is no longer waiting for personal contact between himself and his child. When we break the silence, the contact has begun.

—*Wayne E. Brickey*

DAY 133

Some Blessings Require Effort

Some [prayers] are simple expressions of appreciation and requests for a continuation of blessings on our loved ones and us. However, in times of great personal hurt or need, more may be required than mere asking. The Lord said, "You have supposed that I would give it unto you, when you took no thought save it was to ask me" (D&C 9:7). Blessings sought through prayer sometimes require work, effort, and diligence on our part.

—*James E. Faust*

Open the Scriptures

Sometimes we are tempted to ask the Lord for a solution when a serious study of the scriptures and the words of the living prophets would give us the answer we are seeking. We may not wish to expend the effort to find our answers that way, or we may, being equally mistaken, decide that we can simply ask the Lord and He will give us what we need, even if He has given it elsewhere. Either way, this violates the principle of spiritual self-reliance. We should not expect new revelation when the Lord has already taught us the doctrine or principle that provides the answer we seek.

Someone once expressed just how important the scriptures are to the process of revelation in this way. "If you wish to talk to the Lord, get down on your knees. If you want the Lord to talk to you, open the scriptures." Of course, the scriptures don't answer all the specific questions of our lives, but they are an essential element in the revelatory process.

—*Gerald N. Lund*

Daily Meditation

Strive in your homes, and teach others, to take some time of each day to have a quiet hour, meditation. Let there be study of the scriptures at least thirty minutes of each day. At an early morning hour, or at late night, as best suits your schedule, allow yourself an hour of prayerful meditation where you can tune in with God and discuss with Him problems that are too much for human understanding, too great for human strength.

—*Harold B. Lee*

Seek Revelation

Ask the Lord if the conclusions you have reached in your study are correct. Ask, and ye shall receive; knock, and it shall be opened unto you. If any of you lack wisdom, let him ask of God—in faith—and it shall be given. Pray in the approved manner—to the Father, in the name of Christ. The answer will come by the power of the Holy Ghost. "I will tell you in your mind and in your heart,"

saith the Lord, "by the Holy Ghost, which shall come upon you and which shall dwell in your heart. Now, behold, this is the spirit of revelation." (D&C 8:2–3.)

—*Bruce R. McConkie*

Gaining Wisdom through Prayer

The scripture that led to the opening of this dispensation was, "If any of you lack wisdom, let him ask of God" (James 1:5). There it is. There's the key to getting answers, direction, guidance, and wisdom. Since this is our dispensation, shouldn't we embrace that "opening" scripture as our guide to any and all questions we have?

I believe you will receive all the wisdom you are seeking to help you and your loved ones if you:

- Take your . . . questions to your Heavenly Father in prayer. Confide in Him the *one* question you most need answered through the scriptures *that* day.

- Ask for the Spirit to be with you as you read the word of the Lord. Plead for the Holy Ghost to be with you. Imagine Him being right there by you.

- Open your scriptures and read until you find the answer.

I believe you won't have to read very far because the rest of the scripture that opened this dispensation is true: '[God] giveth to all men liberally, and upbraideth not; and it shall be given him. But let him ask in faith, nothing wavering' (James 1:5–6).

—*Wendy Watson Nelson*

Prayer and Scripture Study

I read with a friend early in the day. Shirley and I read on the phone 15 to 20 minutes most weekday mornings, then launch into our day. We've been doing this for more than 30 years. We visit for a moment or two. We take turns praying for the Spirit to be part of our enterprise, and then we read aloud to each other. So many times we exclaim how a scripture answers today's pressing need. One morning she told me of one of her son's questions asked the night before. Then we read D&C 124:109–116, and each of his questions was answered. I wrote his name next to each verse that had his answer in it. Coincidence? No. Miracle? Yes. We shouldn't be surprised at how often such answers have come over these many years.

Pray each time you pick up these amazing books. Ask to understand, to see your daily problems as God sees them, and to be able to liken all scriptures to yourself as Nephi directed his people. The scriptures give us a panoramic perspective: an endless, wide-angle view. You will develop a template that will help with each day's decisions. You will come to know that miracles take time, but they happen.

—*Ann N. Madsen*

Expecting Sacrifice

I went to the temple one afternoon to seek guidance about my children. The calm, loving spirit of the temple seemed to magnify my natural love for my family, and I found myself offering a deeply sincere prayer filled with desire for my children. I told the Lord I was willing to offer any sacrifice if he would protect my children from Satan's power and bless them with his Spirit until they could come to his house and receive their own endowment. I do not think I offered a unique prayer. It is the uttered and unuttered prayer of every true Latter-day Saint parent, and I think most parents would give the Lord the sacrifice he required.

As I sat in the temple, an answer was given in which the required sacrifice was revealed to me. I thought the Lord would demand some great thing for the blessing I was asking. . . .

However, the Spirit simply whispered: "This is the sacrifice I ask of you. Be in this house *frequently, constantly,* and *consistently,* and the promised protection you seek, which this house has the power to bestow, will be extended to those you love." For that blessing alone I would be in the temple as often as I could.

At first I thought this counsel was unique to me, but I came to realize as I read and studied the scriptures that it is a promise with much broader application. I found this promise again and again in both the scriptures and in the words of our living prophets and apostles. It was not a special request and promise to me, but one that was extended to all the Saints in behalf of those they love.

—*S. Michael Wilcox*

What Is Required to Gain a Testimony?

I fear sometimes that we pay little attention to the seriousness of this life, and that we take it too much for granted until it is too late. I remember being on a train one day with a man who was born and reared in the Church. We were returning from California, and I made myself known to him. As we visited, I talked to him about the gospel of Jesus Christ. He told me that his people were members of the Church, but he didn't understand anything about it. And he said as we discussed the principles of the gospel, "These things interest me." We visited quite a long time, and when we finished, that good man, I believe he was a good man, said to me, "I would give all that I possess to have the assurance that you have of eternal life." I said, "My brother, you don't have to give all that you possess to have that assurance. All you have to do is to search the scriptures prayerfully. Go where they may be explained to you. Seek the truth, and the beauty of the truth will appeal to you, and perhaps without much of an effort on your part, and I am sure without giving away all your property, you can know as I know that God lives, that Jesus is the Christ, that Joseph Smith is a prophet of the living God, and that we are living eternal lives."

—*George Albert Smith*

DAY 141

"This Kind Cometh Not Out"

One day a father brought a child who was having seizures. The father begged the Savior to bless his son, saying that he had taken him to the disciples, but they couldn't heal him. Jesus blessed the child and immediately the boy was healed (see Matthew 17:14–18).

Afterward, the disciples, troubled by their inability to heal the child, asked Jesus, "Why could not we cast him out?" (Matthew 17:19). The Savior said that it was because they didn't have sufficient faith. But then He added a significant comment: "Howbeit [nevertheless], this kind goeth not out but by prayer and fasting" (Matthew 17:21).

Some challenges, some circumstances, and some conditions

are of such magnitude and are so serious that an extra measure of spiritual power is required to overcome them. The Savior suggests that in such cases prayer alone is insufficient. To it we can add fasting. There is something about fasting that generates greater spiritual power and deeper spiritual sensitivity. Perhaps it comes from deliberately and consciously putting the flesh in subjection to the spirit. One obvious benefit of fasting is that the pangs of hunger constantly remind us of the issue at hand. We find ourselves praying about it all day long, not just in the morning and evening.

In short, fasting is a way to intensify the process of importuning the Lord. It generates the power we need to finally bring down the powers of heaven in our behalf.

—*Gerald N. Lund*

DAY 142

Without Prayer, Fasting Is Not Complete

In the scriptures, fasting is almost always linked with prayer. Without prayer, fasting is not complete fasting: it's simply going hungry. If we want our fasting to be more than just going without eating, if we desire also the spiritual benefits of the fast, we must also lift our hearts, our minds, and our voices in communion with our Heavenly Father. Fasting, coupled with mighty prayer, is powerful. It can fill our minds with the revelations of the Spirit. It can strengthen us against times of temptation.

Fasting and prayer can help us develop courage and confidence. It can strengthen our character and build self-restraint and discipline. Often when we fast, our righteous prayers and petitions have greater power. Testimonies grow. We mature spiritually and emotionally and sanctify our souls. Each time we fast, we gain a little more control over our worldly appetites and passions.

—*Joseph B. Wirthlin*

DAY 143

Fasting Shows We Are Serious in Seeking a Blessing

Fasting feeds faith. Fasting brings joy. Fasting, linked with prayer, creates an attitude of gratitude. Fasting and prayer are, in fact, the same as rejoicing and prayer (D&C 59:13–15). When we fast and pray, we hunger and thirst after righteousness. Fasting and prayer work miracles, for they demonstrate to the Almighty that we are serious in seeking this particular blessing, serious enough to deny ourselves of that which pleases the eye and gladdens the heart, that which strengthens the body and enlivens the soul (D&C

59:18–19). Fasting is a sublime form of spiritual discipline, and the glorious outcome is dedicated and dynamic Christian discipleship.

—*Robert L. Millet*

Praying in Times of Trial

On one occasion when I was down visiting one of the stakes in Arizona, the president and bishops of that stake and other stakes in the area had met to discuss the intense drought that was prevailing in the area. It had been so dry for the previous two or three years that they had lost heavily on their crops. Their reservoirs were too low to afford sufficient irrigation, and they were destitute to the point of losing their farms. They held a day of fasting and prayer and supplicated the Lord to grant them rain, that their destitute circumstances might be alleviated. Then it commenced to rain, and I was there when the members of the presidency reminded the Saints that for the first time since the reservoirs had been built the dam was overflowing. The Lord had heard the prayers of these Saints.

—*Harold B. Lee*

The Lord Will Accept a Simple Prayer

The Lord can hear a simple prayer, offered in faith, in half a dozen words, and he will recognize fasting that may not continue more than twenty-four hours, just as readily and effectually as He will answer a prayer of a thousand words and fasting for a month. Now remember it. . . . The Lord will accept that which is good enough, with a good deal more pleasure and satisfaction than that which is too much and unnecessary. It is good to be earnest, good to be diligent, to persevere, and to be faithful all the time, but we may go to extremes in these things; when we do not need to.

—Joseph F. Smith

Fasting and Prayer Bring Blessings

Fasting and prayer will help us control our thoughts, feelings, passions, and appetites. We can bring these and our bodies under subjection of our spirits. We will experience added spirituality, strength, power, humility, and testimony. We will be able to get answers to our prayers and enjoy feelings of peace and comfort. Our guilt will be swept away as we truly repent. We will enjoy the companionship of the Spirit. We will experience an increase of love. Ill feelings will be removed from our souls. We will have added power to resist temptations and to overcome weaknesses. We will become free from undue worry. Our faith and hope will be increased. Feelings of doubt and discouragement will be dispelled.

—*L. Lionel Kendrick*

Fast Occasionally and Pray Often

We should all give some attention to the matter of fasting. We haven't really called on the Lord so that we can reach him intimately if we don't fast occasionally, and pray often. Many of our personal problems can be solved by so doing. Do you remember what the Savior said to his disciples who couldn't cast out the evil spirit, after they had asked why they couldn't do it when Jesus had done it so easily? He replied, "This kind goeth not out but by prayer and fasting." (Matt. 17:21.)

—*Marion G. Romney*

Fasting and Prayer

Fasting, with prayer, is much more than going without food. It is a small sacrifice; but if it comes with purpose and commitment, it is acceptable of the Lord. When we fast with a purpose in Him—or turn our faces to the Lord and yield our hearts to Him—there is a cleansing power in that sacrifice that engages and shapes the desires and commitments of the heart.

Here is an analogy: Imagine an automatic garage door that will not open. You look and find that the infrared light receptor is dirty and misaligned. The light signal, and thus the circuit, has been interrupted, so the door will not open. You clean the receptor, align it with the source of light, and the door works. Fasting and prayer are like cleaning and aligning our spiritual light receptors. Through fasting and prayer we open ourselves more fully to the ministry of the Holy Ghost and, thus, to receive light and truth in our search of the scriptures. If we keep those receptors clean and aligned, we may then say of our search for the things of heaven, as Alma said, "For, the Lord God hath made them manifest unto me by his Holy Spirit; and this is the spirit of revelation which is in me" (Alma 5:46).

As we fast and pray and invite the Holy Ghost into our search for truth, the Spirit will teach us what we need to know and do. We will receive guidance for our families and our callings in the work of the Lord. If we are consistent in our fasting and prayer, and if we always remember Him, the Holy Ghost may be our constant companion.

—*Kim Clark*

Your Prayers Are Personal

I think that Heavenly Father is pleased with all of our prayers, but I think he is especially pleased when we pray with our whole hearts, when we share ourselves completely without trying to make excuses or to make ourselves look good. Fasting is a way of peeling away things that are constant distractions so that we can temporarily concentrate on our spiritual relationships. Although fasting may bring physical discomfort, I have always loved to fast because it frees what seems like an enormous amount of time that goes into preparing, eating, and cleaning up after a meal. And having this time to pray, meditate, and read the scriptures is a wonderful gift.

Can we approach the Lord as a beloved friend? Can we hunger and thirst for the time that we can spend with our Heavenly Father? Can we go eagerly and with anticipation to our prayers? When we do, our faith will increase, because we will discover that prayer becomes easy and joyous, our hearts become stayed upon the

Lord in love, and the Holy Ghost will indeed become our constant companion. Does that sound impossible? I assure you, it is not. Our God is a God of miracles, and the greatest miracle is that of his love for us and trust in us.

—*Chieko N. Okazaki*

Let the Spirit Guide

"The Mind of Christ"

To grow to the point when we can utter inspired prayers (which we can do only insofar as we can align ourselves with the will of God and petition Him in faith and righteousness and appropriateness) is part of being proven.

The powers of heaven simply cannot be drawn upon except on the principles of righteousness—whether it is the powers of the priesthood or the powers relating to prayer also.

We clearly cannot have the Spirit in our prayers if our lives do not reflect reasonable righteousness. We should, therefore, using the criteria given by the Lord, want to avoid trying to cover up sins, gratifying our pride and advancing our vain ambitions, or exercising compulsion over others. We should want to live in such a way that our way of living reflects relationships with others that are filled with persuasion, long-suffering, gentleness, meekness, love unfeigned, kindness and pure knowledge. (D&C 121:36–41.) When we are developing and living in these ways, we can access the powers of heaven and petition with especial effectiveness, having done much to align ourselves with the will of our Father in heaven. It may be helpful in this regard for us to remember that we must finally come to have "the mind of Christ" and then we can pray as He did. (1 Corinthians 2:16.)

—Neal A. Maxwell

How Does He Communicate with You?

I remember a time in my twenties when I was desperate for guidance on a crucial decision. I had fasted and prayed and been to the temple many times, but the answer wasn't clear. In frustration, I told a friend that I just couldn't get an answer. His simple response took me by surprise: "Have you asked the Lord to teach you *how* He communicates with you?" I hadn't, but I began that day to pray that He would.

—*Sheri Dew*

The Holy Ghost and Prayer

Having spoken of the role of the Holy Ghost in leading us to all truth, Nephi turned his attention to the role of the third member of the Godhead in the matter of prayer. "If ye would hearken unto the Spirit which teacheth a man to pray," he said, "ye would know that ye must pray; for the evil spirit teacheth not a man to pray, but teacheth him that he must not pray." (2 Ne. 32:8.) It has ever been the purpose of the adversary to separate men from association with their God. By contrast, no servant of God has ever argued that the heavens are sealed or that the canon of scripture is full. No servant of God has ever suggested that the honest in heart should not seek divine direction in all things. . . .

The Holy Ghost will always lead a person *to* prayer and *in* prayer. That is, the Spirit teaches us to pray and also gives us direction in the things for which we should pray. To have the Holy Ghost is to have the promise, "It shall be given you what you shall ask" (D&C 50:30), and the promise that "he that asketh in the Spirit asketh according to the will of God; wherefore it is done even as he asketh" (D&C 46:30). The prayer of the Twelve in 3 Nephi is a classic illustration of this principle. Of this prayer we read: "They did not multiply many words, for it was given unto them what they should pray, and they were filled with desire." (3 Ne. 19:24.)

—*Joseph F. McConkie*

DAY 153

More Than Petitions

If we are willing to move beyond a casual relationship with God, willing to spend the time and exert the energy necessary to make of our prayer life something more than it is now, then great things await us. For one thing, in time and with experience, our prayers can become more than petitions, as important as it is to petition the Lord. Our prayers can become instructive, the means whereby God can reveal great and important things to us. The apostle Paul taught us that "the Spirit also helpeth our infirmities: for we know not what we should pray for as we ought: but the Spirit itself maketh intercession for us with [striving] which cannot be [expressed]." (Romans 8:26.) (Compare Joseph Smith, *Teachings of the Prophet Joseph Smith,* comp. Joseph Fielding Smith [Salt Lake City: Deseret Book, 1976], 278; 3 Nephi 19:24; D&C 46:30; 50:29–30; 63:65.) That is to say, if we are quiet and attentive, the Spirit of the Lord can, on some occasions, lead us to pray for things that were not on our personal agenda, things deep down, things that pertain more to our eternal needs than our temporal wants. At such times we find our words reaching beyond our thoughts, praying for people and circumstances and eventualities that surprise us.

—*Robert L. Millet*

DAY 154

Simple Prayers

There is no greater feeling than uttering a prayer and expressing gratitude to God and knowing that the thoughts and feelings and words are coming from Him. It is worth every effort to achieve such an assurance. When we come closer to God our prayers become very simple: basically a desire to more adequately express our appreciation, a desire for deeper understanding of God's will, and a desire for more strength to do His will forever.

—John H. Groberg

Praying with the Spirit

One might ask, "Why is it necessary that the Holy Ghost prompt us even in our prayers?" One reason is that only with the help of the Holy Ghost can we be lifted outside the narrow little theater of our own experience, outside our selfish concerns, and outside the confines of our tiny conceptual cells. It was Jacob who reminded us, and in such beautiful language, that the Spirit (which teaches us to pray) also "speaketh of things as they really are, and of things as they really will be." (Jacob 4:13.) The Spirit "searcheth the deep things of God" (1 Corinthians 2:10), and superficial prayer will not produce such probings.

God sees things as they really are and as they will become. We don't! In order to tap that precious perspective during our prayers, we must rely upon the promptings of the Holy Ghost. With access to that kind of knowledge, we would then pray for what we and others should have—*really* have. With the Spirit prompting us, we will not ask "amiss."

—Neal A. Maxwell

Seeking the Guidance of the Spirit

The adversary sometimes uses unbelievably sophisticated ways to disguise himself and his traps. But the Holy Ghost can identify every whiff of evil. So, what can we do to have the Spirit of the Lord with us? Let me offer four suggestions:

1. Increase the intensity and frequency with which we pray for the companionship of the Holy Ghost. Many women have found that by praying at crucial times for His companionship, profound changes occurred. What were the crucial times?

After praying in the morning for the Spirit to be with them throughout the day, as these women encountered any tempting, trying, or difficult situation they prayed in that very moment for the Spirit to be with them. They visualized the Holy Ghost being right there by them and then followed through on what they felt drawn to do, say, or feel. They experienced the guidance of the Spirit in ways they never had before.

2. Increase the earnestness and frequency of our pleadings to learn how He personally speaks to us. If you're not sure how it feels or sounds when He's talking to you, ask for Him to teach you how to recognize His promptings. He may not speak to you through a burning in your bosom. He may speak through the line of a hymn that comes to your mind, disquieting feelings that persist, flashes of ideas you've never considered before, or scriptural passages that seem written exclusively for you.

3. Decrease the time between receiving an instruction and acting on it. The Holy Ghost is eager to help us. Showing Him that we're grateful for His guidance by actually following through on His promptings will increase our ability to receive even more.

4. Toss out, turn off, quit purchasing, and stop participating in anything that would prevent His companionship. By the way, we can quickly tell which thoughts, feelings, behaviors, videos, Internet activities, TV offerings, books, magazines, clothes, and music need to be discarded—because the Spirit will flee in the presence of anything that offends Him. We can simply ask ourselves: Can the Spirit be with me when I watch, wear, do, hear, read, think, or feel the following? If the answer is "No," we know what to do. We need to create an environment in our homes, minds, and hearts where He will want to be. Where He *can* be!

—*Wendy Watson Nelson*

Latter-day Clarifications on Prayer

Those who lack, through no fault of their own, certain plain and precious things about the process of prayer are left through the Holy Bible to assume that if they ask in faith, it will be granted: "For every one that asketh receiveth; and he that seeketh findeth; and to him that knocketh it shall be opened." (Matthew 7:8.) "And

LET THE SPIRIT GUIDE 171

all things, whatsoever ye shall ask in prayer, believing, ye shall receive." (Matthew 21:22.)

For a more full understanding of prayer, these disclosing and refining verses are vital:

> Yea, I know that god will give liberally to him that asketh. Yea, my God will give me, if I ask not amiss . . . (2 Nephi 4:35.)

> And now, if God, who has created you, on whom you are dependent for your lives and for all that ye have and are, doth grant unto you whatsoever ye ask that is right, in faith, believing that ye shall receive, O then, how ye ought to impart of the substance that ye have one to another. (Mosiah 4:21.)

> And whatsoever ye shall ask the Father in my name, which is right, believing that ye shall receive, behold it shall be given unto you. (3 Nephi 18:20.)

The matured disciple can be even further blessed by having his very petitions inspired. Then yet another and an awesome dimension of prayer unfolds:

> And now, because thou hast done this with such unwearyingness, behold, I will bless thee forever; and I will make thee mighty in word and in deed, in faith and in works; yea, even that all things shall be done unto thee according to thy word, for

thou shalt not ask that which is contrary to my will. (Helaman 10:5.)

He that asketh in the Spirit asketh according to the will of God; wherefore it is done even as he asketh. (D&C 46:30.)

These are not minor clarifications and amplifications. . . . In fact, these additional scriptures lie at the very heart of understanding the vital doctrine of prayer, which comprises man's primary pattern of personal communication with God.

—*Neal A. Maxwell*

Pray for the Holy Ghost to Inspire Our Prayers

We are taught by the Savior in 3rd Nephi how to pray. In verse 9 of chapter 19 it states, "and they did pray for that which they most desired; and they desired that the Holy Ghost should be given unto them." The reason we pray for the Holy Ghost when we pray is that He will inspire us as to the things for which we should pray.

The Holy Ghost will never err in the things he inspires us to say and do. He is also perfect and abides with us as we prove worthy. There are resplendent blessings that come to us as we pray as guided by the Holy Ghost. These are the prayers that appeal to God in His loving kindness and goodness.

For the most part we should be guided by the Holy Ghost in our prayers. Then we will seldom pray for issues or things, guidance or direction, that are not pleasing to God.

—*Vaughn J. Featherstone*

"The Spirit Itself Maketh Intercession"

Another gift of the Holy Ghost, often less appreciated and less explored, is how He can bless us by guiding our very prayers. Have not all of us on occasion puzzled beforehand over how to frame our petitions? Hence, this candor and assurance:

"Likewise the Spirit also helpeth our infirmities: for we know not what we should pray for as we ought: but the Spirit itself maketh intercession for us with groanings [sighings] which cannot be uttered" (Romans 8:26).

How often we need this very help with our prayers, for although we know we should pray, we are not always certain as to that for which we should pray!

—*Neal A. Maxwell*

What Language Will the Lord Use?

What will be the language the Lord will use? Through the Prophet Joseph Smith, the Lord counseled Oliver Cowdery who wondered about an answer to his prayers:

"Verily, verily, I say unto you, if you desire a further witness, cast your mind upon the night that you cried unto me in your heart, that you might know concerning the truth of these things.

"Did I not speak peace to your mind concerning the matter? What greater witness can you have than from God?" (D&C 6:22–23.)

Sometime later, the Lord again instructed Oliver Cowdery through the Prophet Joseph Smith: "You must study it out in your mind; then you must ask me if it be right, and if it is right I will cause that your bosom shall burn within you; therefore, you shall feel that it is right.

"But if it be not right you shall have no such feelings, but you shall have a stupor of thought." (D&C 9:8–9.)

Learning the language of prayer is a joyous, lifetime experience. Sometimes ideas flood our mind as we listen after our prayers. Sometimes feelings press upon us. A spirit of calmness assures us that all will be well. But always, if we have been honest and earnest, we will experience a good feeling—a feeling of warmth for our Father in Heaven and a sense of his love for us.

—*Spencer W. Kimball*

How Can We Know What to Pray For?

Because the Comforter knows all things (D&C 42:17; Moses 6:61), he knows what lies deep down within us, those longings and hopes and desires, those needs that so often go unexpressed and thus unmet. That is, as the apostle Paul wrote, the Spirit helps us with our infirmities, for we generally do not know what things we ought to pray for. But "the Spirit maketh intercession for us with groanings which cannot be uttered'; (see Romans 8:26). "And he that searcheth the hearts knoweth what is the mind of the Spirit, because he maketh intercession for the saints according to the will of God" (Romans 8:27). This is known as prayer in the Spirit, and it empowers the Saints of the Most High to pray for those things the Lord would have us pray for, rather than praying amiss (James 4:3). In modern revelation we learn that "he that asketh in the Spirit asketh according to the will of God; wherefore it is done even as he asketh" (D&C 46:30). Similarly, "and if ye are purified and cleansed from all sin, ye shall ask whatsoever you will in the name of Jesus and it shall be done. But know this, it shall be given you what you shall ask" (D&C 50:29–30).

—*Robert L. Millet*

Asking for That "Which Is Right"

We must have the Spirit with us, so that the Holy Ghost can prompt us to pray for that which is right. Nephi advised us that the Spirit "teacheth a man to pray." (2 Nephi 32:8.) There is, therefore, a definite connection between our righteousness and our capacity to draw upon the Spirit so that we will ask for what we should ask for. The Lord told Joseph smith in 1831, "And if ye are purified and cleansed from all sin, ye shall ask whatsoever you will in the name of Jesus and it shall be done. But know this, it shall be *given* you what you shall ask." (D&C 50:29–30; emphasis added.)

Obviously this purposeful praying reflects a high order of spirituality. For those of us less far along in the path of prayer, these insights at first might seem quite discouraging, because while the promises are valid, we feel so distant from that point when "it shall be given you what you shall ask." Even so, we need to understand the significance of these scriptures if we are to move very far along the path of prayer by learning to pray for correct things as well as developing our faith. Only then will our prayers deserve to be characterized as "counsel[ing] with the Lord in all [our] doings." (Alma 37:37.)

—*Neal A. Maxwell*

Prayer Is Not a One-Way Conversation

Perfect prayer is offered to God the Eternal Father, in the name of his Only Begotten Son, by the power of the Holy Ghost. Most of us are well aware that God the Father is the ultimate object of our worship and that our prayers should be directed to him. And we know that we are to pray to Father in the name of the Son. But perhaps we are not quite so familiar with the idea that our prayers, in order to meet the divine standard, should be prompted, guided, and empowered by the Holy Spirit. In other words, as with all forms of divine communication, including sermons, gospel lessons, and so forth, prayers should be carried out under the direction of the third member of the Godhead.

Another way of putting this is to observe that prayer is not, and should not be, merely a product of our own thoughts and feelings. Prayer is intended to engender communion with Deity. Communion certainly entails more than monologue. It should in fact be a dialog, a true conversation with speaking, listening, digesting, learning.

—*Robert L. Millet*

God Hears and
Answers Prayers

God Hears and Answers Our Prayers

I know that you pray, and that is a wonderful thing. Sometimes you pray to the Lord with great earnestness for help, for companionship, for relief from your struggles. You wonder why your prayers are not answered as you would like them to be.

We have all had that experience. But we come to know as the years pass that our Father in Heaven does hear our prayers. His wisdom is greater than ours, and we come to know that He answers our prayers even though the answers at times are difficult to discern.

—*Gordon B. Hinckley*

Someone Is Always Listening

In all of His wisdom and foreknowledge, the Lord knew that we would need to do more than just talk to ourselves positively; we would need to "pray always." (Luke 21:36.) We would need to know that Someone would always be listening, that our petitions would always be heard, that we would not just be talking to ourselves, and that we could pray about anything and everything.

When we call upon our Heavenly Father, there will not be a busy signal. There is no call-waiting. There is never even a hold button, because He keeps His line open for us, never disconnecting us from His unconditional love and concern.

Tevye talked to himself and to God about everything from his lame horse to his empty pockets to his "lost" daughters. And I believe that God intends for us to do the same. He wants us to intimately involve Him in our lives. No matter how positive our attitude may be, we all need the validation of a listening and loving Ear—always and in "all" ways. Nothing is too small or too great for a sincere prayer directed to a loving Heavenly Father. Positive thinking without reliance on God, without prayer, becomes a selfish attempt to demonstrate our independence. Only when a positive attitude of humble dependence is coupled with faith in God (and voiced in prayer) can real inspiration and empowerment take place.

—*Lloyd D. Newell*

DAY 166

God Knows and Understands Us

It is God our Father, through the instrumentality of His Only Begotten Son, Jesus Christ, who has provided us with the iron rod, the tree of life, and the gospel, which are all part of His great plan of happiness for us. There comes trailing down from the preexistence, in the deep recesses of our soul, a dependence upon our loving Father. In our moments of agony, terror, death, and overwhelming burdens our inner soul cries out to Him. Somehow we feel that He and only He can bring peace to our overburdened souls. He never fails to answer in His perfect way and with His perfect love and with our eternal welfare as His focus. . . .

Our prayers will be heard and out of the depths of our suffering there will come sweet and tender whisperings that we are not alone; that somewhere in the realms of Heaven, He knows, He understands and He will bring us peace and healing.

Our prayers to Him should focus on our Father, the great Elohim, and we should acknowledge before His throne our absolute and total willingness to accept whatever befalls us, knowing that our eventual becoming like Him is through our submission and obedience to Him.

—*Vaughn J. Featherstone*

DAY 167

God Will Not Leave Us Alone

It's when we're in trouble, when we have special needs, that we seek with some intensity to obtain answers to our prayers. And when those answers don't seem to come, our need seems to increase.

It's natural in that situation to contemplate, "Where are you, Heavenly Father?" "Are you listening?"

We can answer those questions by remembering that God is constant. He operates by pre-established principles, not unwisely or by whim. We should also remember that he has promised to not leave us alone.

—Lindsay R. Curtis

Receiving Instructions from Home Base

It is difficult to understand why some cannot believe, or find it very hard to believe that God can hear and answer our prayers, and yet they believe that astronauts can leave the earth and travel in outer space at thousands of miles per hour and still be directed from home base; that they can keep in touch with home base and receive instructions and be led in their activities and then be brought back to a safe landing here upon the earth.

How can we question God's ability to hear and answer our prayers and direct us in all things if we will but keep in tune with him, and at the same time have no doubt that marvelous machines and men can be sent out from the earth to the moon and there be directed by mere man here upon the earth?

We are as astronauts, sent out by God to fill our missions here upon the earth. He wants us to succeed. He stands ready to answer our prayers and assures us a safe landing as we return if we will but keep in touch with him through prayer and do as we are bid.

As we pray, however, are we prepared to ask the Lord to bless us as we answer his call or acknowledge and serve him?

Are we prepared to ask the Lord to forgive us as we forgive one another?

We may well stop and analyze our own situation. Do we wait until we are in trouble and then run to the Lord? As we pray, do we give orders to the Lord by saying, "Bless this," and "Bless that," "Give us this," and "Give us that," "Do this," and "Do that"?

Or do we pray that we might be led to do that which is right, or be blessed with those things which are for our best good? We should always pray for the desire and strength and determination to do the will of our Heavenly Father, and always stand ready to do his bidding.

—*N. Eldon Tanner*

DAY 169

Prayer and Change

Perhaps the most important catalyst of change is the sincere prayer of the humble believer. No greater testimony is born of our inherent worth than the peaceful assurance that comes from asking God, in a moment of private petitioning, on bended knee, if He knows us personally and if He loves us unconditionally as His children.

I believe that God hears and answers our prayers and will bless us with the comforting assurance that *He knows and loves us.* Such prayer may not only give us the strength to take *action,* but it may also give us an *awareness*—and the ability to *accept* the awareness—that we are children of God.

—*Lloyd D. Newell*

DAY 170

Creating a Relationship with God

God has not always granted those things that we have wanted or even asked for desperately. But He frequently puts His divine signature on small events of the day. And His presence—the indescribably settling quality of His great love—more than recompenses for all tragedies and disappointments. He says, with these tender mercies, "I am here. I care about you. You are living your life with my approval. Everything will work together for your good. Trust me."

The miracle of prayer doesn't reside in the ability to manipulate situations and events, but in the miracle of creating a relationship with God.

Think about that carefully, would you? What does it do for you to have an assurance that the Lord is with you? . . .

Even thou we may not see from minute to minute that we are moving forward and making progress, I believe we will be able to one day look back at our lives and see that we were, in fact, doing just what we needed to be doing at just the right time in just the right place. We can trust that the Lord will work in and through us. Mormon expressed it beautifully: "And now, I do not know all things; but the Lord knoweth all things which are to come; wherefore, he worketh in me to do according to his will (Words of Mormon 1:7).

—Virginia H. Pearce

DAY 171

Teaching Children That God Hears and Answers Prayers

During the years when our children were growing up, I performed a small ritual as I lay in bed after family prayer. I would put the name of each child before the Lord so that I could analyze the unique challenges he or she faced. Then I would ask for the Lord's help in being his instrument to nurture and guide. It was such a tender task. I looked forward to it and to the mornings that followed when many of my queries were answered quietly during that clean-slate time of just-after-awakening.

One of my great concerns during those late-night reveries was how to teach each of our children to really pray—to open conduits to their Heavenly Father. I remember thinking that this would be the best insurance we could leave them if anything should happen to us before they were grown. And so I prayed that they would learn that God hears and answers prayers.

About this time, during a severe drought, when the Wasatch Mountains had never greened through spring and summer, President Spencer W. Kimball asked us as a church to fast for rain on an appointed day. Our family did. During family home evening, we heard the rain begin to fall on the metal roof of our patio. It was an electric moment. At first it was just a few drops, but soon it was a torrent. We all ran outside, and one of our children said, "Let's kneel down here with the rain falling on us to thank the Lord." Then we all put around small bottles to catch the water. I've kept mine since that day; it's full of "holy" water. Our children learned part of the lesson then; God indeed hears and answers prayers. Their dripping faces and soaking clothes and water bottles clutched in their damp hands were tangible proof.

—*Ann N. Madsen*

Does God Need Our Help in Deciding What We Need?

Since by definition, revelation is the communication of the mind and will of God to man, then clearly *revelation is always unidirectional.* Revelation always flows vertically from God to man, not the other way around. Man cannot ever reveal anything to God. We may have two-way communication with Him through prayer, but we never reveal anything to Him. The very idea that we could kneel in prayer and share something with God that He doesn't know or that would surprise Him is, of course, ludicrous. He already knows all things, including the thoughts and intents of our hearts (see, for example, Matthew 6:8; Acts 15:18; Alma 18:32; D&C 38:2), so we can never reveal anything to Him. And yet it seems to be the nature of us finite mortals to forget this basic and fundamental truth. Often we act as if God needs our "help" in deciding what we need or how to solve our problems.

—*Gerald N. Lund*

I Make a Logical Choice and Ask God If It Is Correct

"Lord, what shall I do?" The words seem to come so easily when I'm struggling with a problem or have a difficult decision ahead. I need to remember that the decision is up to me. I must make it logically and intelligently, then ask God if my choice is correct.

God has promised answers
Every time I pray,
Sometimes in a minute,
Sometimes in a day.
It might take a decade
Till I plainly see
I've received the answer
God has promised me.
God has promised answers
Coming in all forms,
Sunlight on my mountains,
Snowflakes during storms,
Just a nice warm feeling
When I do my part;
Listening in faith brings
Answers to my heart.

The nice warm feeling I speak about in my poem is what the Lord has promised in Doctrine and Covenants 9:8, "And if it is right I will cause that your bosom shall burn within you."

It's always been comforting to know that Heavenly Father will help me as I make important decisions; that he is always there and always listening.

—*Brad Wilcox*

DAY 174

Using Our Own Good Sense

Part of spiritual self-reliance is that even as we seek the Spirit's direction in our lives, we should be using our best judgment in working through our problems and challenges. We have already seen that the Lord is displeased when we take no thought but to ask (D&C 9:7). Part of the testing experience (and part of the process of gaining wisdom) is using our own good sense, coupled with a sensitivity to the Light of Christ, to try to work things out, sometimes without precise and specific direction from the Lord at every step.

The story of the brother of Jared presents an excellent example of this. When he approached the Lord with the problem of how to get light into the barges, the Lord didn't give him a specific answer. He said simply, "What will ye that I should do that ye may have light in your vessels?" (Ether 2:23). This is not to suggest that the Lord did not respond. The Lord did answer the brother of Jared, but His answer was that the brother of Jared should use his own good judgment in working out the problem. Once the brother of Jared had done so, then the Lord responded again in a marvelous way by touching the stones.

The Lord made it clear that He would help, but He gave the brother of Jared an opportunity to act for himself, to use his wisdom and judgment to find a solution (see Ether 3:1–5).

—*Gerald N. Lund*

DAY 175

Keep Moving Forward

Sometimes we may feel we are simply left on our own to do the best we can. I believe that if we were to wait until we recognized a clear answer every time we prayed, most of us would be waiting and wasting a good part of our lives.

Elder Richard G. Scott asks the question, "What do you do when you have prepared carefully, have prayed fervently, waited a reasonable time for a response, and still do not feel an answer?" He continues: "You may want to express thanks when that occurs, for it is an evidence of His trust. When you are living worthily and your choice is consistent with the Savior's teachings and you need to act, proceed with trust. . . . God will not let you proceed too far without a warning impression if you have made the wrong decision." (Richard G. Scott, "Using the Supernal Gift of Prayer," *Ensign,* May 2007, 10.)

President Gordon B. Hinckley had a personal motto that is quite practical. He taught it in many settings: "Things will work out. If you keep trying and praying and working, things will work out. They always do." (Sheri Dew, *Go Forward with Faith* [Salt Lake City: Deseret Book, 1996], 423.)

And so we have to pray and then keep moving forward, trusting that if it is a direction that will *not* be for our good, the Lord will help us know. Otherwise, we trust that the Lord is bound to own and honor the decisions we have made using our own best judgment. (See *Journal of Discourses,* 26 vols. [London: Latter-day Saints' Book Depot, 1854–56], 3:205, in which Brigham Young taught: "If I ask Him to give me wisdom concerning any requirement in life, or in regard to my own course, or that of my friends, my family, my children, or those that I preside over, and get no answer from Him, and then do the very best that my judgment will teach me, He is bound to own and honor that transaction, and He will do so to all intents and purposes.")

—*Virginia H. Pearce*

Do All That Is in Your Power; Let the Lord Do the Rest

There is another way to express this principle. Pray as though everything depends on the Lord, then work as though everything depends on you. . . .

When we obtain blessings from the Lord, it's not just because of the work we do. The work doesn't necessarily bring the blessing, but it does show our true desire, which enables the Lord to bless us.

Here is the principle, then: We must do all that is in our power, and then let the Lord do the rest. That suggests we need to find out what the Lord requires, then do it.

One thing I've learned over the years is that you need to count the cost up front. You need to clearly decide what you will do before you go after the blessing. What sacrifices and offerings does the Lord require? What are you willing to give? If you don't receive the blessing you seek, what are you going to do? Will you harden your heart? Will you become angry with the Lord? Will you say prayers don't work, or will you say, "Heavenly Father, I don't know why it didn't work. I gave it all I could and it still hasn't worked, but I know that it's not thy fault. Either it's not thy will or I have fallen short."

In my experience, the problem usually lies in ourselves. Often we have not sacrificed enough (i.e., paid the price) and thus the heavens cannot respond. But if you are willing to pay the price, the Lord will whisper to you and tell you some specific things you still need to do—a little here and a little there, then another month or two or three goes by and then you have it. Because you have offered what the Lord required, he can now respond. Of course, we must remember that all these principles are subject to the overriding will of the Lord. He will always do what is best for us.

—*Gene R. Cook*

How to Receive an Answer

Moroni put it this way: "And when ye shall receive these things, I would exhort you that ye would ask God, the Eternal Father, in the name of Christ, if these things are not true; and if ye shall ask [now, mark you] with a sincere heart, with real intent, having faith in Christ, he will manifest the truth of it unto you, by the power of the Holy Ghost. And by the power of the Holy Ghost ye may know the truth of all things." (Moroni 10:4–5.)

Ask with a sincere heart, with real intent, desire to know, and faith in the Lord Jesus Christ. But you've got to desire it with all your soul! You've got to have all the intensity of which you are capable and a desire that this is the most prized thing in all the world for which you seek! Then, in faith believing that there is an unseen power to which you can appeal and receive direction, then you will know.

—*Harold B. Lee*

The Lord Won't Give Us What Harms Us

We must be careful not to "ask for that which [we] ought not" (D&C 8:10). Sometimes we ask for things that would not be in our best interest. In such cases the Lord is being very kind when he doesn't grant our requests. But when we want something badly, we often times don't hear any answer other than the answer we want. And since the Lord isn't going to give us something he knows would be harmful for us, we think he isn't answering us at all.

—*Lindsay R. Curtis*

"Thou Didst Hear Me"

It isn't surprising to find our heroes in the scriptures saying things like, "Thou didst hear me." They say this with relief and joy, usually after a long wait. Here is how Alma said it: "And thou didst hear me because of mine afflictions and my sincerity" (Alma 33:11).

He doesn't speak as if the answer came right away. For him and all of us, there is usually this matter of a trial of faith. The trial may be before we pray or it may come after or during, or all of these. But during the trial our Father draws closer to us, and we draw closer to Him.

Notice Alma's words: "because of mine afflictions." Affliction makes a life interesting, to us and even to the Lord. Alma's prayers were interesting to the Lord because there were important things going on. There was some drama. There was a struggle, a battle for good. Things were at stake. Alma was giving his all. People were in need. What kind of story is it where there is no need, no emergency, no problem, no toil, where there is no place for integrity or heroism or courage? The word for that might be "boring." Alma's situation called for divine help, it called for miracles. Now that was interesting. He was heard because of his afflictions.

But he also mentioned another thing: "Thou didst hear me because of mine afflictions and my *sincerity*." You've probably heard teachers encourage their students to ask questions by saying there is no such thing as a stupid question. There may be one exception to that general rule: the *insincere* question, the fake question, the one asked just to get credit or just to make an impression, the question asked by someone who doesn't really care about the answer. Most teachers don't like that kind of question. They don't like pretended questions or pretended sincerity. They love to answer students who care. . . .

Alma wasn't guilty of casual prayers or routine, boring, thoughtless prayers, He was hungry. He pled. He begged. You see this in every case where the faithful say that God heard them.

—*Wayne E. Brickey*

Helaman's Formula for Battling the Adversary

Helaman was leading an army that was "not strong, according to . . . numbers" (Alma 58:15) and had to "contend with an enemy which was innumerable" (Alma 58:8). Viewing the odds, he knew he needed additional strength, but the Nephite government "did not send more strength." (Alma 58:9.) They would have to make their determined stand alone.

"Therefore, *we did pour out our souls in prayer to God, that he would strengthen us and deliver us.*" (Alma 58:10.) It is not always enough to climb to the top of Lehonti's mountain; deep prayer is also required. Notice what four things came as a result of their prayers: "The Lord our God did visit us with *assurances* that he would deliver us; yea, insomuch that he did speak *peace* to our souls, and did grant unto us *great faith,* and did cause us that we should *hope* for our deliverance in him" (Alma 58:11.) When we face innumerable forces that attempt to get us to come down from our places of security in spite of our resoluteness, if we pray deeply for strength, the Lord will bless us, too, with assurances, peace, great faith, and hope. These are especially needed in the latter days, for Nephi "beheld the church of the Lamb of God, and its numbers were few," just like Helaman's army. (1 Nephi 14:12.)

Filled with the comfort of these four things, Helaman's men

"did take *courage.*" With this new infusion of courage, they were now "*fixed with a determination* to conquer [their] enemies, and to *maintain* [their] . . . cause of [their] liberty. And thus [they] did go forth with *all [their] might.*" (Alma 58:12–13.)

Helaman has provided us with an effective formula. Prayer leads to assurance, peace, great faith, and hope, which create the courage necessary for us to remain fixed and determined in maintaining our spiritual liberty. Now we can battle the adversary "with all our might."

—*S. Michael Wilcox*

The Example of Enos

Enos provides a positive model on how and why one receives answers to prayers. . . . Enos had heard the words of his father, Jacob, about eternal life and joy. Enos now hungered for such joy; he prayed all day and into the night. His petition was not because of any serious sins or for selfish motives, but simply because he hungered after the blessings of the Spirit. His request was not granted after a brief prayer, but only after his soul supplicated the Almighty for many hours. . . .

Enos was among those mortals who have received special divine communication through the Holy Spirit. The Holy Ghost serves the Godhead as a revelator, revealing great, new, and important truths. God, with his infinite knowledge and power, has developed a system of communication far superior to anything mortals have yet developed or even conceived. Through the Holy Spirit, he is able to communicate with his children instantly, individually, and personally. However, his spiritual communication is perceived only by certain sensitive individuals. His voice is neither loud nor disturbing, and one might not hear or sense it unless one were in tune with God's soft, still, small voice.

God can communicate with many people simultaneously yet individually. He provides a simultaneous, instant, individual communication. Even more impressive is the fact that he communicates not only messages but a verification of the truthfulness of those messages. . . .

The Holy Ghost is unique. Through the Holy Ghost, we receive a message, a validation of that message, and then comfort, direction, and peace.

—*Victor L. Ludlow*

The Lord Will Show His People Salvation

When Jehoshaphat, king of Judah, faced a strong combination of surrounding armies against which he knew his people could not stand, he called a "fast throughout all Judah," then went up to the temple to pray. Notice the words of his prayer: "O Lord God of our fathers, art not thou God in heaven? . . . Art not thou our God, who didst drive out the inhabitants of this land before thy people Israel, and gavest it to the seed of Abraham thy friend forever? And they dwelt therein, and have built thee a sanctuary therein for thy name, saying, If, when evil cometh upon us, as the sword, judgment, or pestilence, or famine, we stand before this house, and in thy presence, (for thy name is in this house,) and cry unto thee in our affliction, then thou wilt hear and help. . . . O our God, . . . we have no might against this great company that cometh against us; neither know we what to do: but our eyes are upon thee." (2 Chronicles 20:3–12.)

The Lord hearkened to the prayer of Jehoshaphat, telling him to "stand . . . still, and see the salvation of the Lord" (2 Chronicles 20:17), which they did the next day. The "great company" began to fight against themselves, and in their own bitter quarrels they left Judah alone. What the Lord was willing to do for Jehoshaphat's people, he will surely do for us when we face "prevailing, combined" enemies and forces we feel "we have no might against."

—*S. Michael Wilcox*

DAY 183

God Is Limitless and Long-Suffering

I have never felt a moment's hesitation in asking my Heavenly Father for assistance, for clarity, for wisdom, for strength and willpower. It has never even occurred to me that he would be otherwise engaged, put off, offended, or impatient with my requests. I have never sensed that he wished that I would go away, stop asking questions, cease from troubling him with my problems, or end my endless importuning. Even the kindest and most sensitive mortals will reach their limit, identify the last straw, and eventually cry out, "That's it. I just can't take any more. I'm empty. I have no more to give." Our God is limitless and supremely long-suffering. His strength and power are infinite, and his compassion and empathy never fail. As I understand our relationship to Deity, we can never approach the throne of grace and be unwelcome guests.

—*Robert L. Millet*

Exercise Confidence

I believe that many people are confident that the Lord's will will be done and that the Lord can do anything, but they're not confident that he will do it for them or that he wants to do it now.

This lack of confidence in our ability to gain access to the powers of heaven is a major reason why more of our prayers aren't answered. In fact, as I travel around the church I often meet people who say, "My prayer wasn't answered because it just wasn't the will of the Lord." They want to place the responsibility for their unanswered prayer on the Lord. But often the truth is that they just didn't exercise enough faith; they didn't have enough confidence in their ability to receive an answer.

It is true that we must ask according to the will of God. As John wrote:

"This is the confidence that we have in him, that, if we ask any thing according to his will, he heareth us: And if we know that he hear us, whatsoever we ask, we know that we have the petitions that we desired of him." (1 John 5:14–15.)

But too often we use this as an excuse. Instead of trying to place the responsibility on the Lord when we don't get the answers we want ("obviously it wasn't the will of God"), we should learn to have confidence before him so that we can "come boldly unto the throne of grace" (Hebrews 4:16) and receive the desires of our hearts.

—*Gene R. Cook*

We Have to Be Humble

We have to be humble in order to have our prayers answered. Before we can have an answer to our prayers, we have to have a deep feeling of spiritual need; and unless we get to feeling that, we can't just say words and receive an answer. We must pray with real intent, with desire to know, and with faith on the Lord Jesus Christ; then by the power of the Holy Ghost we may know. That is the only way we can have an answer to prayers.

—*Harold B. Lee*

Recognizing an Answer to Prayer

Three little boys were flying a kite in a field away from their homes. It began to rain, and they wanted to save their kite. As they hastily pulled it from the sky, it caught on a tree limb high over their heads.

They found a long stick and tried to pull it down, but they couldn't reach it. They tried everything they could think of to get it down, but the kite just turned and twisted in the storm. One of the boys finally said to the others, "I think we should pray." The other two looked at him, then followed his lead, bowing their heads while he said the words. As they opened their eyes, they saw a car coming toward them down the road that led to the field. As it neared, the boys stood motionless and almost breathless, staring at the lady driving the car.

Their stares fascinated the lady, so she stopped and called to them, "Are you having trouble?"

"Yes," they said. "Our kite is caught on the tree. Will you help us get it down?"

"I'll try," she said. "Stand away while I back up."

She backed her car to position it under the kite, then she got out, climbed on top of the car, and, with the long stick retrieved the kite.

When the boy who had offered the prayer carried his kite into the kitchen, he told his mother about the kite's getting caught in the tree. She asked, "Who helped you get your kite down?"

"Heavenly Father," he replied. The boy, who had prayed with perfect trust, knew the answer to a prayer when he saw it.

—*Dwan J. Young*

We Must Be Still and Listen

The scriptures give us ample instruction about how the Spirit speaks to us, but to hear the still, small voice we must be still and listen. This was forcefully brought to my mind early one morning as I finished my prayers. I admit to being guilty of often jumping to my feet as I conclude a prayer with "amen." But on this particular morning I simply stayed on my knees and listened.

I had been praying, as I always did, for my father. He had suffered for many years from the effects of Parkinson's disease. As the disease progressed, he gradually lost his ability to speak, to eat, and to control bodily functions. In his prime, Dad had been a superintendent of schools, president of a variety of civic organizations, and a leader in the community and his church. To see him unable to do anything was almost more than I could bear. For years I included in every prayer I offered, "Please, don't let Dad suffer."

That morning when I stayed on my knees and listened, I gained an enormous insight—an eternal perspective. As if the Lord Himself stood beside me, words came clearly into my mind: "My Son suffered."

I recorded in my journal: "It almost took my breath away. I felt as if I had been 'taught from on high.' I began to pray that both Dad and I would be able to endure to the end." . . .

Just as I needed personal revelation to understand my father's suffering, so we all need personal revelation for our own lives.

President Boyd K. Packer told graduating students at Brigham Young University–Hawaii: "These are sobering times. . . . You won't survive spiritually, unless you know how to receive revelation." He, too, acknowledged that we live in a "noisy world" but added, "revelation comes in the quiet times. It will come when the Lord can speak to our feelings. . . . Go quietly," he counseled. "Go quietly into the world. Go quietly about your affairs, and learn that in the still, small hours of the morning the Lord will speak to you. He will never fail to answer your prayers." (Packer, BYU–Hawaii Commencement Address, December 17, 2005.)

—*Carolyn J. Rasmus*

DAY 188

Ways Prayers Can Be Answered

There are many ways prayers may be answered. Joseph Smith often had heavenly visitations. Moses heard a voice from a burning bush. Some people receive dreams. I must confess that I have never seen a vision nor had such a dream, nor have I ever heard an audible voice speak to me from the other side. But I can identify with Enos, who said, "While I was thus struggling in the spirit, behold, the voice of the Lord came into my mind" (Enos 1:10). . . .

He answers others in other ways. He spoke to Oliver Cowdery about a feeling like a burning in the bosom (see D&C 9:8). That feeling comes to different people in different ways, I've learned. For some it's a warm feeling in their chest. For others it's a feeling of exhilaration. For still others it may come in yet another way.

But we must remember that the burning in the bosom is not the method of answering prayers that the Lord mentions the most. In revelations to Joseph Smith, Oliver Cowdery, and Hyrum Smith, the Lord talks about answering prayers by enlightening the mind, speaking peace to the mind, telling the person "in your mind and in your heart," filling the soul with joy (see D&C 6:15, 23; D&C 8:2; D&C 11:13–14). He will speak to us in ways that will be most effective for our own conditions. We must learn to recognize how we feel when the Spirit is with us and when he is communicating to us.

Sometimes the answer to our prayer is no. We can receive that answer in the form of a "stupor of thought" (D&C 9:9); or it may come as a dark feeling, a feeling of disquiet and unrest, a feeling of uneasiness.

—*Lindsay R. Curtis*

DAY 189

Asking and Receiving Answers

A scripture concerning prayer which had always troubled me suddenly became understandable to me. ("The eyes of my understanding were opened"—D&C 138:11.) Christ said to his disciples:

"Ask, and it shall be given unto you; seek, and ye shall find; knock, and it shall be opened unto you." (Luke 11:9.) That instruction seems clear enough, but what follows gives us great insight concerning our Father in Heaven: "If a son shall ask bread of any of you that is a father, will he give him a stone? or if he ask a fish, will he for a fish give him a serpent? Or if he shall ask an egg, will he offer him a scorpion? If ye then, being evil, know how to give good gifts unto your children: how much more shall your heavenly Father give the Holy Spirit to them that ask him?" (Luke 11:11–13.)

These scriptures relate a father responding to a son to our Heavenly Father responding to us. Often a child asks for something, but either because of experience or knowledge or understanding (of the child and/or the situation), the parent does not give the child what he asks for. This may occur because the request is not in the child's best interest, or because of the parent's love for the child. Sometimes in being given "bread" the child perceives he is really receiving "a stone."...

All of our prayers *are* answered, though sometimes not in the way we anticipate (and in retrospect, how grateful we can be that they are not).

Even the Savior's prayer in Gethsemane was answered in the negative. In addition to learning that prayers are not always answered as we wish them to be, we learn two other important lessons from the Savior's experience. First, following his prayer we are told that an angel appeared unto him, strengthening him. Sometimes when we wish for a certain situation to be resolved or made right or prevent it from happening, it is in our own best interest to be blessed instead with peace or understanding or additional knowledge or comfort or courage or increased faith or strength to bear up. Our Heavenly Father who is all-knowing, all-wise, and who loves us very much, will always answer our prayers!

—*Carolyn J. Rasmus*

Prayer Heals

I remember one evening when I was an ordained teacher, father said, "Eldon, will you lead in prayer tonight? And remember your sister, Lily, who is ill." (She had had spinal meningitis for some weeks, and the doctors didn't seem to be able to cope with it.) So I prayed to the Lord that she might be made well, that his healing influence would be upon her. I felt so good as I said those words because I felt that I was actually praying to God for blessings which we needed at that particular time. It's always been a testimony to me that the Lord does answer prayers. She, my older sister, began to heal shortly after that prayer was offered and became entirely well, and is a mother and a grandmother today, enjoying life.

—*N. Eldon Tanner*

The Lord's Grace

After we have done all in our power, the grace of the Lord will intervene. The prophet Nephi said it masterfully:

"For we labor diligently to write, to persuade our children, and also our brethren, to believe in Christ, and to be reconciled to God; for we know that it is by grace that we are saved, after all we can do." (2 Nephi 25:23.)

In my judgment, this principle explains why it is that when a little child prays he can so readily receive the blessing. The child doesn't know how to do very much except give all of his heart, but that's enough. Then the Lord puts in the rest. Children have great access to the heavens.

We also can have such access if we will pray with all our hearts and do all we can to qualify for the blessing we seek. Then, through the grace, or enabling power, of Christ, the heavens will intervene and bring us that which we desire.

But I want to stress once again that all of these principles are always subject to the overriding will of the Lord. Because of his great love for us, he will always do what is best for us in the short term as well as in the long run.

—*Gene R. Cook*

Praying for Extra Help

A few years ago, a university student related to his elders' quorum an event he had experienced just after being ordained a deacon in the Aaronic Priesthood. He lived on a farm, and his father had promised him that an expected new calf would be his very own to raise. One summer morning when his parents were away, he was working in the barn when the pregnant cow began to calve prematurely. He watched in great amazement as the little calf was born, and then, without warning, the mother cow suddenly rolled over the calf. She was trying to kill it. In his heart he cried out to the Lord for help. Not thinking about how much more the cow weighed than he did, he pushed on her with all his strength and somehow moved her away.

He picked up the lifeless calf in his arms and, brokenhearted, looked at it, the tears running down his cheeks. Then he remembered that he now held the priesthood, and he felt he had every right to pray for additional help. So he prayed from the depths of his boyish, believing heart. Before long the little animal began breathing again. The young deacon knew his prayer had been heard.

After he finished telling this story, the tears welled up in his eyes and he said, "Brethren, I shared that experience because I don't think I would do now what I did then. Now that I am older, less naive, and more experienced, I 'know better' than to expect help in that kind of situation. I am not sure I would believe now, even if I relived that experience, that the calf's survival was anything more than a coincidence. I don't understand what has happened to me since that time, but I wonder if something is missing now."

—*Bruce C. Hafen*

DAY 193

Prayer Combined with Gospel Living

Prayer alone is not to satisfy the soul. It is not enough to seek one's own welfare through prayer. Nor is it enough to ask God to bless the sick and afflicted and those who mourn. No, prayer should motivate us to get up and help those in need.

"And now behold, my beloved brethren, I say unto you, do not suppose that this is all; for after ye have done all these things, if ye turn away the needy, and the naked, and visit not the sick and afflicted , and impart of your substance, if ye have, to those who stand in need—I say unto you, if ye do not any of these things, behold, your prayer is vain, and availeth you nothing, and ye are as hypocrites who do deny the faith. Therefore, if ye do not remember to be charitable, ye are as dross, which the refiners do cast out, (it being of no worth) and is trodden under foot of men." (Alma 34:28–29.)

Very typically, we ask the Lord to bless the missionaries, the leaders of the Church, those who mourn, and those who are sick and afflicted. I am quite sure that this has value and meaning. It is in God's interest to inspire missionaries and leaders of the Church. As our Father of mercy and compassion, he is surely concerned with those who are in pain.

Why not, following the suggestion of Amulek, use prayer to motivate ourselves to help the Lord achieve his purposes? "Father, help me to write and encourage missionaries, to accept callings from the bishop and carry them out cheerfully and wholeheartedly. Father, help me to turn off the television and visit the sick, afflicted, and lonely of my acquaintance. Help me to find the right things to say to the Smith family who have lost a son." Prayer should not be a substitute for gospel living but a motivation to live it.

—*Lowell L. Bennion*

Prepare for Opposition

Be Prepared for Increased Opposition

If you're praying for something that really matters, you can count on the fact that the devil will get involved. He's eager to do what he can to thwart you. He will do his best to dissuade you from going forward. He'll give you such thoughts as "You can't do it. You're not worthy enough. Your family's got too many problems. You can't do what the Lord requires." He'll engineer whatever he can to try to make you doubt. So you may as well know up front that he is going to tempt you.

When you attract the devil's attention and he starts to give you more opposition that you normally have, that's a great sign that you're on a course that pleases God and displeases Satan.

I've found that when you begin to pray for something that really matters, many times things get worse, not better. Often the cause is Satan and his helpers, who are doing their best to make sure you don't succeed. That ought to be a signal to a man or woman of faith: "I'm on the right track. I'm doing something that's making a difference and I will double my faith." If you can increase your faith in that moment, you will have won most of the battle.

—*Gene R. Cook*

About Doubts and Prayer

It is said, "I don't pray because I have doubts. I doubt things about myself, about the gospel, and even about God." It is truly said that doubt and faith do not coexist in the same person at the same time, but they can exist within a second of each other. Witness Heber C. Kimball's standing by the door while Brigham Young was lying on what appeared to be his deathbed. Said Heber, "I doubt very much if Brigham ever rises from that bed."

However, "he had no sooner uttered the words, than he spoke up, as with another voice, and said, 'He shall live, and shall start upon this mission with me tomorrow morning.' And they did start the very next morning, on their mission to England." (Orson F. Whitney, *Life of Heber C. Kimball* [Salt Lake City: Bookcraft, 1967], p. 434.) He was right the second time. From doubt to faith.

On another occasion he stood in the Bowery in Salt Lake City and announced to threadbare and barely surviving people, "States goods will soon sell in Salt Lake City for less than they sell for in New York. In the name of the Lord. Amen." And as he returned to his seat from the pulpit, he said he "had missed it this time." Someone on the stand said, "I don't believe a word of it." And Brigham Young said, "Let it stand." It did stand. When the California gold rush came, the prophecy was actually and completely fulfilled.

Elder Kimball was right the first time and he went from faith to doubt. (See *Life of Heber C. Kimball,* pp. 389–90.)

It is an honest prayer to say: "Lord, I believe. Help thou mine unbelief." And it was, after all, a prophet of God, Joseph Smith who said—and he was a man of faith—"If I had not experienced what I have, I could not have believed it myself" (*Teachings of the Prophet Joseph Smith,* comp. Joseph Fielding Smith [Salt Lake City: Deseret Book Co., 1976], p. 361).

—*Truman G. Madsen*

Satan Hates When We Pray

"The evil spirit teacheth not a man to pray, but teacheth him that he must not pray" (2 Ne. 32:8). Satan desires to block our communication with God. He does all he can to cause us to forget or forego our prayers, lulling some away through complacency. He convinces others that they cannot pray because they have committed serious transgressions.

—*Clyde J. Williams*

Too Busy to Pray

In my judgment, all of our excuses and reasons for not praying can be resolved if we will just:

1. Decide that we ought to be praying,
2. Believe that it really will work, and
3. Decide when, where, and how we'll do it.

With respect to schedules, *if we're too busy to pray, we're just too busy*. We may have to get up a little earlier in the morning, or we may have to stay up a little later in the evening. We may have to adjust the time we are giving to a hobby or the time we spend watching television or going out for recreation. We may need to make an adjustment here or an adjustment there. But whatever we decide, we need to realize that choosing not to pray should not be an alternative.

If you are not in the habit, it is time to get in the habit. . . . If you don't believe prayer will work, it is time to put it to the test anew. I promise you that if you will follow the Lord and seek him with all your heart, he will surely bless you—and he will surely give you answers to your prayers.

—*Gene R. Cook*

When We Need It the Most

As a young mother, I was inspired by Chieko N. Okazaki (one of my heroes). There is one specific address she gave called "Lighten Up!" that really changed me. She talked about how as mothers we tend to compartmentalize our lives. We have different cubbyholes for different things: family, church, gardening, and so on. She said instead of thinking of our spiritual lives as one of our cubbies, it should be more like the scent in the air that drifts through all the rooms. She relates this story:

"Suppose the Savior comes to visit you. You've rushed around and vacuumed the guest room, put the best sheets on the bed, even got some tulips in a vase on the dresser. Jesus looks around the room, then says, 'Oh, thank you for inviting me into your home. Please tell me about your life.'

"You say, 'I will in just a minute, but something's boiling over on the stove, and I need to let the cat out.'

"Jesus says, 'I know a lot about cats and stoves. I'll come with you.'

"'Oh, no,' you say. 'I couldn't let you do that.' And you rush out, carefully closing the door behind you.

"And while you're turning down the stove, the phone rings, and then Jason comes in with a scrape on his elbow, and the visiting teacher supervisor calls for your report, and then it's suppertime, and you couldn't possibly have Jesus see that you don't even have placemats, for Pete's sake, and someone forgot to turn on the dishwasher so that you're eating off paper plates, and then you have to drive Lynne to her basketball game. So by the time you get back to the room where Jesus is still patiently waiting for you, you're so tired that you can barely keep your eyes open—let alone sit worshipfully at Jesus' feet to wait for those words of profound wisdom and spiritual power to wash over you, to make you different, to make everything else different—and you fall asleep whispering, 'I'm sorry. I'll try to do better. I'm so sorry'" (in *Women and Christ: Living the Abundant Life,* 6).

Isn't this how we are as mothers? When we really need the Savior's guidance the most, sometimes we tend to shut it out. The secret is to use prayer to our advantage. Let the Savior "follow" us around and help us out when we're at the end of our ropes. That is when prayer really works!

—*Shawni Eyre Pothier*

DAY 199

Finding Time to Pray

Time must be budgeted so that enough time is balanced between secular and spiritual interests.

Devotion and prayer will be an integral part of lives charted on a true spiritual course. There will *always* be time for prayer. There will *always* be the moments of blessed solitude, of closeness to the Heavenly Father, of freedom from worldly things and cares.

—*Spencer W. Kimball*

Why Don't We Pray?

I have often asked myself and tried to answer this question: Why do some people refuse to pray? Is it because they feel they have not the time? . . .

Do people not pray because they feel too independent, too smart, and think they can go it alone? Or are they ashamed to call upon God? Do they think it shows a weakness? Or do they not believe in or have faith in God? Or is it that they do not appreciate their many blessings? Or do they not feel worthy? If one does not feel worthy, he should acknowledge his weaknesses, express regret, repent, covenant to do right, and ask for guidance.

Is it because some do not know how to pray? If that is true, I suggest that you go to your Heavenly Father in secret. Pour out your heart to him. Pray regularly so that you can feel at home and comfortable while communicating with him. All one needs to do is express his feelings, which the Lord understands. He has invited all of us to call on him regularly and has promised that he will hear our supplication.

—*N. Eldon Tanner*

Barriers and Roadblocks

Surely no roadblock could be more prevalent than distraction and preoccupation. Sometimes we don't pray well because our minds and hearts are focused on other things. We are too prone to think of prayer as something within the spiritual realm and of religion as just another department of life. Communion with the Infinite requires discipline, and discipline requires making priorities. Obviously we need to chase wickedness out of our lives if we are to draw close to God in prayer. But, in addition, when it is time to pray, we must put aside the things of the world, even good things, in order to engage the greatest good. . . .

Another roadblock to an effective prayer life is duplicity, or trying to lead two lives. James explained that "a double minded man is unstable in all his ways." (James 1:8.) Thus we would suppose that a person who is worldly throughout the day would have great difficulty praying intently at night. Elder Howard W. Hunter observed: "Henry Ward Beecher once said: '*It is not well for a man to pray cream and live skim milk.*' . . . That was a century ago. There is now before us a danger that many may pray skim milk and live *that* not at all." (In Conference Report, October 1977, 79; italics in original.) Just as our lives are only as good as our prayers, so our prayers are only as good as our lives. That is, the more faithful we become in keeping the Lord's commandments and putting first things first in our lives, the more we open the doors of communication with the heavens and the more comfortable we feel with holy things and holy beings.

—*Robert L. Millet*

Sacrifice for Prayer

We may say that our work drives us and that we have not time to pray, hardly time to eat our breakfasts. Then let the breakfasts go, and pray; get down upon our knees and pray until we are filled with the spirit of peace.

—*Brigham Young*

DAY 203

Overcoming Obstacles to Prayer

When I've asked people why they don't pray more consistently, I've heard a number of reasons:

- I don't have enough time.
- I just haven't gotten in the habit.

PREPARE FOR OPPOSITION 225

- My family just never did it, so I'm not in the praying mode.

- I believe I should. I guess I just haven't made a firm decision yet to do it.

- I hate to admit it, but sometimes I don't believe that prayer really makes that much difference.

Whatever your reason, I hope you'll remember that it is the devil who teaches us not to pray. (See 2 Nephi 32:8–9.) I believe the devil has some of his most elite emissaries trained in how to cause men not to pray. He says simple things like, "You're too tired." "You can do it tomorrow." "You can't take the time now—you have too many other priorities." "Think of your sins—surely you don't think you're worthy to pray!" "Prayer doesn't work. Don't you remember the time you prayed and nothing happened?" Thus, on and on he goes in trying to convince people that prayer does not work, or is not worth the effort. Of course, all of these whisperings are lies.

I hope you'll make up your mind not to listen to the devil but to listen to the Lord, who consistently invites us to pray unto our Father in Heaven, that he may bless us.

—*Gene R. Cook*

The Great Tragedy of Life

What does one do when he feels, as Lorenzo Snow put it, "that the heavens are as brass over his head" (see *Juvenile Instructor* 22:22). That though he ought to pray, he doesn't feel like praying. And when he does feel like praying, he is so ashamed that he hardly can. What then? My response is this glimpse from the Prophet.

The period just prior to the dedication of the Kirtland Temple saw an outpouring of the Spirit. Many of the brethren saw glorious visions, and the Prophet himself had a manifestation in which he saw, in panoramic vision, the lives of the Brethren of the Twelve— saw them in their strugglings, their flounderings, saw them preaching the gospel, saw them eventually brought back into the celestial kingdom. . . . He saw them, standing in a circle, beaten, tattered, their feet swollen, and clearly discouraged. Now, there are different levels of discouragement; we can be disturbed a bit, we can be worried, we can then be despondent, and there are moments in life for some of us when we ask, "What is the use?" And when we sink that far, we're almost to the point of wishing we could cease to be.

Well, the Prophet didn't indicate that it had gone that far with the Twelve, but they were looking down in their discouragement. Yet standing above them in the air was the Lord Jesus Christ. And it was made known to the Prophet that He yearned to show himself to them—to reach down and lift them—but they did not see Him. And the Savior looked upon them and wept. (See *History of the Church* 2:381.) . . . The great tragedy of life is that, loving us and having paid that awful price of suffering, in the moment when He is prepared to reach down and help us we won't let Him. We look down instead of up, accepting the adversary's promptings that we must not pray; we cannot pray; we are not worth to pray. But says Nephi in response to that, "I say to you that ye must pray always, and not faint." (2 Nephi 32:8–9.)

—*Truman G. Madsen*

DAY 205

Prayer Strengthens Us

It has been said that prayer keeps man from sin, and sin keeps man from prayer. Powerful talks have been given and beautiful stories shared about the power of prayer in our lives. I have learned that there is no more faith-promoting and discouragement-chasing experience than to kneel before God and, through the Holy Ghost and in the name of Jesus Christ, pour out our hearts to a loving God who knows us, understands our needs, and desires to bless us.

—*Jack H. Goaslind*

Cast Out Doubt and Fear

I'm always impressed as I think of the negative power of doubt and fear on the power of faith. Joseph Smith said, in essence, "Doubt and fear cannot reside in the mind of man at the same time as faith. One or the other will leave." (See N. B. Lundwall, comp., *Lectures on Faith* [Salt Lake City, n.d.], lecture 4, paragraph 13.)

One of the greatest difficulties of trying to accomplish something through faith and prayer is to really believe it will happen. Doubt and fear are so powerful that they can sometimes dissuade you from starting the endeavor in the first place, or when you get started they can motivate you to quit.

We all know the story of Peter walking on the water. He saw Jesus approaching them on the surface of the sea, and, in a great act of faith, said, "Bid me come unto thee." (Matthew 14:28.) Jesus bade him to come, and Peter stepped out of the boat. . . . Then it appears the devil moved into the picture. The wind stirred up, and waves lifted higher, and Peter began to doubt; he was filled with fear; and down he went into that dark, frightening water.

Then Jesus reached out and saved him, saying, "O thou of little faith, wherefore didst thou doubt?" (Matthew 14:31.) Jesus could also have added, "Peter, you were tied to my power, as long as you were believing and walking and having faith. But the moment you let doubt in, see what happens?"

What a great lesson! And how essential! I'd have to say that as my wife and I have tried over the years to increase our own faith and our family's faith, the greatest challenge we've faced is to really believe with all our hearts, to believe beforehand, to not doubt or fear, and to not give up. If you can do that and have an unshakable faith, you'll receive the blessings you seek—assuming, of course, that what you seek is in harmony with the will of the Lord.

I've heard some people say, "I'll try it, but I'm sure it won't work." And they're right. They're filled with doubt. And I've heard others say, "I don't know how this will work, but the Lord has promised, and I have confidence it will." And they're right, because they're filled with faith.

—*Gene R. Cook*

What If I'm Not Good with Words?

It is said: "I don't pray because I am not good with words. I would rather someone else would do the talking." Fair enough, but our history is filled with instances of people who had mind-boggling verbal gifts and of others who did not. There have been many, like Moses, who needed an Aaron. And there are in our midst today those who are both deaf and dumb, whose lips are sealed but who yet may pray from their core wordlessly. Joseph Smith offered a better rendering of the King James Version's line by Paul that says

"the Spirit maketh intercession for us with groanings which can
be uttered" (Romans 8:26). The Prophet's version is "with striv
which cannot be expressed"—meaning, in words (see *Teachings*,
278). But if a person does have trust in the living God, he can fro
his core reach upward, put an arrow on those imprisoned needs
and they will be carried by the Spirit, perfectly communicated and
responded to. And what relief when we do it!

—*Truman G. Madsen*

DAY 208

What Gets In Our Way

What then might be said of the . . . common blocks, that get
in our way when we struggle over what to pray for? First, there is
a lack of realization on our part that we can actually be guided in
terms of what we should pray for. We tend to pour out petitions
without letting inspiration pour in. God can truly prompt us in
our prayers to ask for that which is right, to not ask amiss. God can
educate our desires.

We also sometimes fail to study things out in our mind before
praying so that we do not fully frame our questions and petitions.
Our petitions are often skimpy on the "whereas" and move too
quickly to the "be it resolved" portion of prayer. Further, we sometimes deflect the promptings that come when we petition; these

may be faint beginnings of our apprenticeship in prayer and in revelation.

We may sometimes inappropriately pray, in effect, to be taken out of the world rather than praying that we will be kept from evil and prevail.

We too often pray in generalities to bring before the Lord specific weaknesses we have, yet he knows of them anyway. We thus prevent ourselves from gathering and gaining the strength we might need to overcome them. Admitting aloud (though in private) our weaknesses and stating our promises is sometimes better than just thinking of them. Dealing with our specific weaknesses is far better than simply praying that we will be more righteous.

Fatigue tends to produce prayers that are hasty generalities. This suggests that to pray only just before retirement at the end of a taxing day is to adversely affect the content of our prayers.

Our unwillingness to deal boldly with our problems tends to produce prayers in which the objects of the petitions are couched again in generalities.

—*Neal A. Maxwell*

"Disregard Previous Memo"

It is said, "I do not pray because my prayers have not been answered." Answered, we mean, do we, not heard? Ah, but they have been heard and recorded. We are taught that one day we will have a perfect, bright recollection of all that has been in our lives here, but what of all that has been before that? The historian B. H. Roberts thought long and hard on the record, and he pursued this subject so often and so deeply, trying to account for the radical differences he perceived among those who have received the gospel in this dispensation. Seeing that some seemed almost to be born with it, and had responses to the gospel and its powers far beyond anything they could have learned in the short space of mortality, he concluded that they did bring it with them. Thus his summary was "Faith is trust in what the spirit learned eons ago." We do come here bringing, though they are locked under amnesia, the residual powers, the distillation of a long experience. And to those of us who see the hand of the Lord everywhere and to those who see it nowhere the same promise is made: The day will come when we shall know that we have seen Him, and that He is the light that is in us, without which we could not abound (see D&C 88:50). There is locked in all of us as there was in Enos—and I understand Enos to say he was surprised that it was there—more faith than we presently know. We are heard, but the response of God may not be what we would here and now wish. Yet haven't we lived long enough to say to the Lord, "Disregard previous memo," to thank him that He answered no, and to ask that He erase some of the requests that we now realize were foolish or hasty or even perverse?

—*Truman G. Madsen*

DAY 210

Perseverance and Prayer

Righteous goals are never easy. There are always obstacles. And it seems that as soon as we set a goal to really improve or to accomplish something worthwhile, not only do we face the expected obstacles, but we also begin to get all kinds of new opposition. The best answers to opposition and other obstacles are perseverance and prayer. . . .

The Lord desires that we be people who help make things happen. He doesn't want us to be thwarted by obstacles or opposition. He desires that we draw upon the all-powerful arm of God and add it to the power that resides in each of us. If we will do that, learning to do things in the Lord's own way, asking for help, the help will come.

—*Gene R. Cook*

Learning to Listen

Listening after We Pray

Isn't it interesting that we always talk about "saying our prayers" and seldom, if ever, about "listening our prayers"? When we pray we communicate with our Heavenly Father. Often, we act as though prayer is a one-way communication. Praying to our Father should include listening. To *commune* is the root of *communicate* and *communion*. To commune with another means to *talk together* intimately; to be in close rapport. (*Webster's New World Dictionary*, s.v. "commune.")

Prayer should not be a one-sided experience in which we do all the talking and then walk away. We need to learn to listen—to take note of thoughts and impressions that come into our minds and of the feelings we experience (see D&C 8:2). As we listen, He will speak to us, teach us, reassure us, and bless us.

—*Carolyn J. Rasmus*

Choosing the Spirit

We sometimes think that the hard part of listening to the Spirit is to persuade the Spirit to talk to us. That's absolutely not true.

The Spirit is on call and fully available twenty-four hours a day. It whispers continuously as the "still small voice, which whispereth through and pierceth all things" (D&C 85:6). It's a persistent voice. It is always available either for a direct question or a thorough, open-ended exploration. But because it is both small and still, it can be drowned out by the hiss and buzz and static of our hurried, distracted lives. The problem isn't that the Spirit isn't talking. The problem is that we aren't listening.

This is why I make the point about choosing. The Spirit is always speaking, but we must choose to listen. The Savior promises that "the Holy Ghost shall be thy constant companion, and thy scepter an unchanging scepter of righteousness and truth" (D&C 121:46). But this isn't the same thing as saying that we're the Holy Ghost's constant companion, is it? We must choose to notice who our companions are. This isn't mysterious or complicated or hard. Would you notice the absence of your three-year-old? Would you notice if your teenager isn't in the house when you wake up in the morning? Would you notice if the secretary isn't in the office or if your spouse isn't present at the supper table? Of course you would.

In the same way, noticing the presence of the Spirit begins with the fervent prayer uttered many times each day, "Please let the Spirit be with me." This prayer is coupled with the equally short, equally fervent prayer of thanksgiving when you feel the Spirit's presence.

—*Chieko N. Okazaki*

Allow His Messages to Get Through

After you have talked to him, listen to him. You must listen carefully, or you are going to miss his answers. Sometimes people will pray for a minute, or two, or five, or fifteen, and then not even listen for a second. Perhaps something different would happen if you continued to kneel at your chair or your bed (after you prayed) for a minute, or two, or five, or fifteen, until you get that good, warm feeling that you have received an answer. Then you know the Lord has heard your prayer, you know he's there, and you know that you have finally found a way to allow him to get his messages through to you. A great experience comes to those who feel the Spirit.

—*H. Burke Peterson*

We Need to Listen to Receive Answers

A second problem is that we don't listen. Our senses are constantly bombarded with other information: we kneel to pray and feel the floor under our knees or our arms folded across our chests;

a truck rambles past the house; rain hits the window pane; the clock ticks loudly in the corner. No wonder it's difficult to find enough spiritual quiet to hear the things the Lord is trying to tell us. But we can make things even worse by failing to make a real effort to listen. We utter our prayers, even with feeling and sincerity, and then immediately rise and jump into bed, rise and run to work, rise and converse with a family member about nonrelated concerns.

How can the Lord get through to us under those conditions? It takes practice and patience to learn how to receive spiritual communications in the best of circumstances. Again, the difficulty is not with the Lord; it is with us. I believe he will give us answers fairly freely, but if we are not listening or if we are not in tune, we may not receive or understand the answer. The result is that we may think the Lord is not even listening, when the real problem is that we're not listening.

We can learn to listen by trying to rid ourselves of outside interference—as well as inside interference—and by taking the time just to feel the Spirit.

—*Lindsay R. Curtis*

Recognize His Promptings

If you still wonder what the Spirit feels like or "sounds" like in your heart and mind, ask. As you begin to pray, ask if the Holy Ghost will come and be with you. Ask to learn what it feels like when He does. Ask if the Lord will help you understand, little by little as you work and pray, to better recognize His promptings and whisperings. Ask.

—*Sheri Dew*

Tuning into the Spirit; Tuning Out Interference

Elder Boyd K. Packer talked about the importance of attuning ourselves to listen to the "quiet voice of inspiration" in our prayers; to illustrate, he described how one of his sons had always been interested in ham radio. Elder Packer cheerfully admits that, as he has sat with this enthusiastic son, speaking to someone in a distant part of the world, he has been amazed and impressed by his son's ability to communicate: "I could hear static and interference and catch a word or two, or sometimes several voices at once. Yet he can understand, for he has trained himself to tune out the interference." ("Prayers and Answers," *Ensign,* Nov. 1979, p. 19.) . . .

We've all had this experience, haven't we? We've scanned the crowd pouring down the concourse at the airport, and our eye has instantly picked out the figure of our husband from the hundreds we're scanning. Or we can hear our own fourth-grader singing in his school chorus. We can hear the voice of the Spirit in the same way, after we have poured out our hearts in prayer, speaking to us in impressions, in promptings, in gentle whispers, in inclinations in one direction and a turning away from another.

—*Chieko N. Okazaki*

DAY 217

Are You Listening?

In our prayers, there must be no glossing over, no hypocrisy, since there can here be no deception. The Lord knows our true condition. Do we tell the Lord how good we are, or how weak? We stand naked before him. Do we offer our supplications in modesty, sincerity, and with a "broken heart and a contrite spirit," or like the Pharisee who prided himself on how well he adhered to the law of Moses? Do we offer a few trite words and worn-out phrases, or do we talk intimately to the Lord for as long as the occasion requires?

Do we pray occasionally when we should be praying regularly, often, constantly? Do we pay the price to get answers to our prayers? Do we ask for things absurd and not for our good? The Lord promised:

> Draw near unto me and I will draw near unto you; seek me diligently and ye shall find me; ask, and ye shall receive; knock, and it shall be opened unto you.
>
> Whatsoever ye ask the Father in my name it shall be given unto you, that is expedient for you;
>
> And if ye ask anything that is not expedient for you, it shall turn unto your condemnation. (D&C 88:63-65.)

When we pray, do we just speak, or do we also listen? Our Savior . . . stands and knocks. If we do not listen, he will not sup with us nor give answer to our prayers. We must learn how to listen, grasp, interpret, understand. The Lord stands knocking. He never retreats. But he will never force himself upon us. If our distance from him increases, it is we who have moved and not the Lord. And should we ever fail to get an answer to our prayers, we must look into our own lives for a reason.

—*Spencer W. Kimball*

Perfect Prayers

In the Book of Mormon we read that the Savior directed, "Whatsoever ye shall ask the Father in my name, *which is right,* believing that ye shall receive, behold it shall be given unto you." (3 Nephi 18:20; emphasis added.)

This is one of the most significant and distinctive insights given to us in all of the scriptures. Even though we may ask in faith for something, unless it is right for us, God reserves the decision-making power to himself. A perfect, loving, and omniscient Father would do just that. Thus, in addition to having faith, we need to ask for that which is right. This same tonal truth appears in modern revelations. The Lord told the Prophet Joseph Smith, "Whatsoever ye ask the Father in my name it shall be given unto you, that is *expedient* for you." (D&C 88:64; emphasis added.)

Clearly, the Lord reserves the right to determine that which is best for us, lest we ask for something in our spiritual naïveté that would not conform to the will of God. Nephi, the prophet, understood the importance of precision and propriety in prayer. He knew from happy experience that God would give liberally to him if he, Nephi, prayed in such a way that he "ask not amiss." (2 Nephi 4:35.)

Thus we see the importance of what a modern prophet has told us. President Joseph F. Smith asserted that spiritual growth includes "the education of our desires." (*Gospel Doctrine,* [Salt Lake City: Deseret Book, 1939], 297.) Our task is to come to that point in our progress where our very desires are right in the sight of God. When we arrive at that point, we will have the "mind of Christ." (1 Corinthians 2:16.) From those with the "mind of Christ" will come perfect prayers.

—*Neal A. Maxwell*

DAY 219

Receiving Spiritual Insights about Ourselves

As we make prayer one of the central parts of our day, God will let us know, feel, and understand things about ourselves. Each day he will strengthen us. We will be filled with the Spirit. Line upon line and precept upon precept, he will let us know who we are in his sight and what we can become. . . .

Many spiritual insights come when a person takes time in meaningful daily prayer. Perhaps each of us could find a quiet spot to retire to someone during a day, during our lunch hour at work or while the children are napping. The location isn't important. It could be on a front or back porch, in a quiet spot on a school campus, in a backyard, on a park bench, in an office, car, or bedroom, or, as the scriptures suggest, in our closets. It can be in any place where we can sit or kneel and truly pour out our hearts in prayer for at least fifteen minutes a day. Prayer is the key to knowing who we are and what God expects of us.

—*Diane Bills Prince*

DAY 220

Asking the Right Questions

If questions play such a primary role in bringing revelation, we ought to give careful thought to the questions we ask of ourselves and of the Lord. As one of my colleagues in the Seventy is fond of saying, "It really doesn't matter what the answer is if you don't ask the right question."

. . . Most of us ask questions of the Lord, but in many cases they may be too general. For example:

- Instead of, "What should I do to be a better person?" we ask, "What things in my life right now are most grievous to the influence of the Spirit?" Or, even more specific, "What should I do differently or better as a father (or mother)?"
- In addition to "Bless the missionaries and help lead them to the honest in heart," we ask, "Wouldst Thou please put someone in my path that I

can talk to about the gospel of Jesus Christ, and wouldst Thou give me the courage to do so?"

• Instead of "Bless me as a bishop," we ask, "Of all the duties and responsibilities I have as a bishop, husband, and father, what should be my highest priority in terms of my efforts right now?"

—*Gerald N. Lund*

DAY 221

Inspiration through Prayer

Inspiration comes from prayer (D&C 63:64). Inspiration is essential to properly lead (D&C 50:13–14). We must have the spirit of inspiration whether we are teaching (D&C 50:13–14) or administering the affairs of the kingdom (D&C 46:2). If we do our part in preparation and work and have the Spirit of the Lord, we can be led, though we do not know beforehand what needs to be done (1 Nephi 4:6; Alma 17:3). Therefore, we should always pray, especially prior to commencing the work of the Lord (2 Nephi 32:9).

—*Ezra Taft Benson*

He Brings Thoughts to Our Minds

There is a whole host of ways in which our Heavenly Father and our Savior may choose to communicate with us and sustain us. One way is certainly through the workings of our minds, through our thoughts. The Prophet Joseph Smith explained that the spirit of revelation may take the form of "sudden strokes of ideas" flowing into us. Enos, son of Jacob, wrote that the voice of the Lord came into his mind, affirming that his sins had been forgiven (Enos 1:5). On many occasions I have pleaded with the Lord for direction in preparation of a lesson or a sermon. Often I have been for a time unsure, unclear about the course I should pursue, only to sense, at a certain point in my preparation, that ideas in the form of scriptural passages, prophetic or apostolic statements, and even overall organization have begun to flow into my mind. Similarly, it has been my experience scores of times to be speaking of teaching in a certain avenue, only to have a related idea, experience, or unusual insight make its way onto the stage of my mind. I have never been disappointed when I have responded positively and actively to such promptings, and I have come away from such experiences knowing more surely that God is God, that he knows his children and their individual needs far better than I, and that it is in my best interest as his servant to follow where he leads.

—*Robert L. Millet*

We Will Find Him If We Call Out to Him

It is so easy to *speak* the truth. I often plead with the Lord to help me to *live* the truths that I so easily speak. After the pleading, we must learn to listen. Sometimes, before the "Amen" is said, the answer comes. We start praying, and we pray and pray, and in some of the spaces between, we receive the answer. Sometimes the answer is disguised in the words of the four-year-old who repeats a memorized line in the Primary program, or in a quiet conversation with a friend, or in the words of a faintly remembered patriarch whose blessing has yellowed. Or sometimes it may even come as I drive alone in the car . . . intruding . . . with such power that I cannot deny its source. Sometimes answers may come even before the questions or the pleading.

—*Ann N. Madsen*

Guidance Comes When You Ask and Then Listen

Experience the power of prayer in your daily lives. Talk with our Father in Heaven every night and every morning. Tell Him how it is with you. In your daily prayers you might ask, "Father in Heaven, what can I do today to help in thy work?" You might simply ask, "What should I do or not do to be a better member of my family, a better friend, a better member of the Church, a better student at school?"

If you listen carefully, thoughts will come into your mind, and you will be surprised at the guidance you will receive when you sincerely ask and then listen. It may come as a simple reminder to express appreciation to your parents or an impression not to see a particular movie or listen to a popular song. You may feel the need to resist compromising or making excuses or rationalizing to justify what you want to do, or maybe the whispering will come in the words of a scripture you have read: "A new commandment I give unto you, That ye love one another; as I have loved you, that ye also love one another." (John 13:34.) But when you follow these promptings, a warm, good feeling will come over you, and you will know that what you are doing is right.

—*Ardeth G. Kapp*

God Sets the Conditions

How revelation is given is completely the Lord's prerogative. We don't get to decide whether we will have an angel appear or receive instructions through the still small voice. The Lord chooses. The revelation may come in an audible voice, a dream, or through a sudden flash of insight as we read the scriptures.

Revelation is not a menu from which we get to select what items we find most appealing.

This can be a great test of our faith. For example, a woman bears testimony on fast Sunday of a remarkable way in which the Lord answered her prayers. Someone in the audience may have been searching for months for a similar answer and has received nothing.

Another example is seen in healings. Why does one person see a miraculous healing after a priesthood blessing while someone of equal worthiness and faith receives a blessing and no deliverance from suffering comes? Those kinds of circumstances are commonly seen and are part of life. Again and again, there is only one answer. God sets all of the conditions for the giving of revelation, and we must learn to trust His wisdom and timing.

This is at the very heart of learning to develop faith or, as the Lord said to Abraham, to see how we will respond as He "proves" us (Abraham 3:25). In this process, we must take care that we don't compare ourselves to others and conclude that we are more or less righteous and faithful than someone else because of what has happened to us.

—*Gerald N. Lund*

Unexpected Answers

The Most Difficult Part of Prayer

The peace God speaks to our minds will let us know when decisions we have made are right, when our course is true. It can come as personal inspiration and guidance to assist us in our daily life—in our homes, in our work. It can provide us with courage and hope to meet the challenges of life. The miracle of prayer, to me, is that in the private, quiet chambers of our mind and heart, God both hears *and* answers prayers.

Perhaps the greatest test of our faith and the most difficult part of prayer may be to recognize the answer that comes to us in a thought or a feeling, and then to accept or to act upon the answer God chooses to give. Consistency in prayer, along with searching the scriptures and following the counsel of living prophets, keeps us in tune with the Lord and enables us to interpret the promptings of the Spirit more easily.

—*Rex D. Pinegar*

Sometimes the Answer Is Unclear

When I was younger and prayed fervently for answers to prayers, sometimes I didn't feel I received an answer—and then I wondered if the Lord really did love me. I had prayed earnestly and put my trust in the Lord, exercised faith, fasted, and seemingly received no response from the heavens.

I have realized in later years that in many instances the Lord does not give a direct answer to our prayers, since that would destroy our opportunity to exercise faith. Sometimes he knows an unclear answer or a delayed answer is exactly what we need, for a time, so we will learn to exercise greater faith.

But my experience has been that, even if an answer doesn't seem to come, the Lord will still communicate with you. I believe that if you will watch carefully, he will somehow express his love to you, telling you that you are okay in some other way, independent perhaps of that for which you are praying. In this way he will give you comfort and yet not defeat his purpose of causing you to have more faith. . . .

That sweet whispering of assurance will give you confidence that he has heard your prayer, that he knows the situation, and that, if you will be patient, he will handle the whole matter. I have particularly seen this to be the case when, because of my ineptness or inability, I have tied myself or my circumstances up in knots. If I then will be patient and express my love to the Lord, letting him know I trust him even when there seemingly is no answer, he will gradually untie all the knots I have so neatly tied up in my life. And, as those knots are untied, he will give me the final peace and assurance that I am okay.

—*Gene R. Cook*

DAY 228

We Must Be Prepared to Hear

The pattern of our lives determines our eligibility to receive the promptings of the Spirit and to hear the answers to our prayers. Again, let there be no misunderstanding. Heavenly Father does answer our prayers, but often we aren't prepared to hear him. Some are answered immediately, but some do take longer, and that's where we may become discouraged.

—*H. Burke Peterson*

What Happens When We Receive No Answer?

To better understand why the Lord has asked that we pray always and not faint, let us walk through what happens to a person of faith when he or she (1) faces a major crisis or turning point in life, (2) begins to pray earnestly for help from God, but (3) receives no answer from the Lord.

When nothing seems to be happening, a natural reaction is to ask ourselves why. There are at least three possible answers:

• *The answer is no.* In a way that is not a comforting answer, but it is understandable and therefore more easily accepted. We decide that the Lord simply isn't going to grant us our request for whatever reason, and so we just have to accept it. We conclude that no answer means the answer is "no."

• *The problem is with God.* When nothing happens and the situation has great urgency, some individuals get highly frustrated. They turn bitter or angry and conclude, "Either God doesn't hear me or, if He does, He doesn't care." Being weak in the faith, they turn a little bitter. "Well, that's fine. I'll show Him! I'll just stop believing in Him. I don't need Him." *Thus they harden their hearts, locking the gate against any spiritual influences.*

• *I must be the problem here.* This reaction most often comes from people of faith, people who not only deeply believe in God but also have a solid understanding of His attributes. They know that He is perfect. Therefore they have to conclude that He cannot be the source of the problem. That leaves only one other possible conclusion. If God is not the problem, then *I* must be the problem.

If we come to this last significant conclusion, interesting things begin to happen. We begin to ask questions of ourselves, question like "What am I doing wrong? What is there in my life that is blocking the Spirit?" This triggers an inward search, a spiritual inventory, as it were. We begin to assess and evaluate where we are in our relationship to God. More important, we begin to change.

We move from questioning the situation to self-examination. Self-examination brings remorse and a resolve to do better. This humility softens our heart and opens it even more to the influence of the Spirit. With that change of heart, the very nature of our prayers begins to change as well. Our prayers will begin to fill with greater power, deeper yearnings, and more righteous petitions.

—*Gerald N. Lund*

DAY 230

Unexpected Answers

There are times in my life when I think He answers, but I misunderstand the message. . . . I expected one answer and got another. In the Gospel of Luke the Lord urges us to come to him for answers. "Ask," he says, "and it shall be given you; seek, and ye shall find; knock, and it shall be opened unto you." (He is always telling us that. It's one of those principles he repeats many, many times because he does not want us to miss it.) "For every one that asketh receiveth; and he that seeketh findeth; and to him that knocketh it shall be opened" (Luke 11:9–10).

He then illustrates that truth: "If a son shall ask bread of any of you that is a father, will he give him a stone? Or if he ask a fish, will he for a fish give him a serpent? Or if he shall ask an egg, will he offer him a scorpion? If ye then, being evil [meaning being human—imperfect], know how to give good gifts unto your children: how much more shall your heavenly Father give [good gifts through] the Holy Spirit to them that ask him?" (Luke 11:11–13).

There are times in our lives when I think the Lord says, *I gave you bread, but it wasn't the kind of bread you wanted and because you keep thinking about the kind of bread you wanted you've turned my bread into a stone. I gave you a fish, but it wasn't the flavor of fish that you wanted, and you've turned the fish into a serpent. Or I gave you an egg, but I cooked it differently from how you ordered it, and you think I've given you a scorpion.*

—S. Michael Wilcox

We May Already Have an Answer but Just Don't Recognize It

One [aspect] of personal revelation is recognizing it when it comes. Some forms of revelation are so subtle, so indirect, and so hard to define that when they come we may not recognize them at all. Sometimes the answer may have already come, but it didn't come in a way that we were expecting, or it came in a way that we didn't recognize it as coming from the Lord.

This may also happen in cases where we have been earnestly seeking for help and the answer comes in small incremental changes (line upon line). They are so small that we don't at first recognize that something is happening. In other cases an event occurs that seems totally unrelated to the issue about which we were praying. We may even give up and assume the Lord's answer is no or that we didn't get an answer. Only some time later—months perhaps, sometimes even years—do we look back and see that the event was a turning point.

—*Gerald N. Lund*

The Answer We Need

Acts 12 relates the time when Peter was in Herod's custody, awaiting an almost certain death. "Prayer was made *without ceasing* of the church unto God for him" (Acts 12:5; emphasis added). An angel delivered Peter, who went to the house of Mary, where the Saints were praying for him. When Rhoda discovered Peter at the gate, she was so overcome with joy that she left him there and ran to tell the others that he was alive and outside the gate.

When Rhoda ran to tell the other Saints that Peter was on the porch, they did not believe her. They told her she was mad. They didn't have time for her distraction; they were busy praying for Peter's release. But Rhoda would not back down from what she knew. So the Saints decided that Peter must have already been killed and that it was his angel standing on the porch. I find it interesting that within that very moment the Lord had already answered their prayers—they just didn't realize it.

Meanwhile, Peter stood waiting and knocking at the door.

Finally they opened the door, and when they saw him there they were astonished. Great worry turned immediately into great rejoicing. I imagine this is a story the Saints laughed about for many years after the experience. How, in the darkness of the night, Rhoda had listened to hear the voice of the one who approached the gate. How, in her gladness, she had forgotten to let Peter in. How all of them had discerned that it couldn't possibly be Peter, but must after all be an angel. And how, in unexpected and unanticipated ways, their prayer had been answered—but they hadn't recognized it until they opened the door and saw Peter standing there. Suddenly, after all, it was a good day (see Acts 12:1–16).

This story teaches an interesting lesson on prayer. Sometimes we are so busy praying for the answer we want, in the way we envision it will happen, that we almost miss the answer the Lord is sending us. Although we are praying without ceasing, the answer almost goes unnoticed.

—*Emily Freeman*

Divine Tutorials

We may not get an answer to our prayers because the Lord is about something much greater in our lives than we can see at the moment.

Years ago I was in a Church history class at Brigham Young University. We had studied the Missouri persecutions, the exile from Nauvoo, the sacrifices of the Saints as they made the arduous journey across the plains to the Rocky Mountains—especially of the Willie and Martin handcart companies.

After we rehearsed that catalog of adversity and suffering, one of the students asked this question: "Why was the way so hard? I know they were being tested, but did it have to be so relentless, so intense?" The professor's answer showed tremendous insight into the purposes of God. He said: "What you have to realize is this. There was a great work to be done, and these people were just common folk. They weren't great crusaders or proven heroes. However, by the time they reached the valley, many of the physically weak had died, and almost all of the spiritually weak had apostatized. So what Brigham Young had left to work with was pure steel."

. . . What may appear to be indifference on God's part may actually be one of the great evidences of his love for us. Like so many other Saints before us, we may simply be in the midst of an intense divine tutorial.

—*Gerald N. Lund*

DAY 234

Clarity through Prayer

In the early stages of work to achieve my doctoral degree, I had what I thought was a brilliant idea for a dissertation and was anxious to talk it over with my advisor. I made an appointment, arrived at her office at the appointed hour, and told her my purpose in coming. She asked to see my written proposal and an outline of what research I wanted to do.

"I don't have anything in writing yet," I responded. She

dismissed me from her office and told me she would be glad to talk with me when I had something in writing.

I perceived her actions to be inappropriate and cruel. Yet, in the days that followed I discovered, as I struggled to put my thoughts into words, that I had not carefully thought through what I wanted to do. In fact, as a result of this exercise, I determined on my own that my idea would not be appropriate for a dissertation.

Often it is as we commune with our Heavenly Father through prayer that things become clear in our own minds. As we commune with him and seek to have his will done in our lives, we take time to reflect on the counsel and instruction he has already given us through the scriptures. In fact, Christ tells us that when "my words abide in you, ye shall ask what ye will, and it shall be done unto you." (John 15:7.)

The Lord told Nephi, son of Helaman, that because "thou . . . hast not sought thine own life, but has sought my will," whatever he asked would be done. Nephi knew the Lord's will and the Lord knew Nephi. He knew that Nephi would "not ask that which is contrary to my will." (Helaman 10:4–5.)

It is incumbent upon us to learn the will of the Father. Perhaps that is why Nephi told us to "feast upon the words of Christ; for behold, the words of Christ will tell you all things what ye should do." He also taught us that the Spirit can teach us to pray. (See 2 Nephi 32:3, 8.) This idea is reinforced in a revelation given through the Prophet Joseph Smith: "He that asketh in the Spirit asketh according to the will of God." (D&C 46:30.) Likewise, the Spirit helps us to pray. Paul taught, "We know not what we should pray for as we ought: but the Spirit itself maketh intercession for us with groanings which cannot be uttered." (Romans 8:26.)

—Carolyn J. Rasmus

DAY 235

Are We Accepting What the Lord Gives Us?

Another possible answer to our question of why God doesn't seem to be answering our prayers may stem from our unwillingness to accept what the Lord gives us.

I had this experience as a bishop. A returned missionary in the ward had been home about a year. He came to me one day and said that he was struggling to know what to do with his life. He felt that he was going nowhere. He had a construction job and was making good money, but he felt that construction wasn't what he wanted to do as a career. After a couple of counseling sessions, I said: "I feel impressed to say to you that what the Lord wants you to do is sell that new pickup truck you recently bought, break off the relationship with the girl you are currently dating, and go to college."

For a moment, he just looked at me, clearly shocked. Then he shook his head sadly. "I couldn't do that, Bishop," he said. "If I sell my truck, I'll lose a lot of money on it. And I really love this girl.

And besides, why should I go to college? I've got a good job. Isn't there something else I can do?"

Some years ago Elder Boyd K. Packer gave a talk in general conference about the need to develop spiritual self-reliance. In that talk he made an observation that seems to apply here:

> We seem to be developing an epidemic of "counselitis" which drains spiritual strength from the Church much like the common cold drains more strength out of humanity than any other disease. . . .
>
> There are many chronic cases—individuals who endlessly seek counsel but do not follow the counsel that is given.
>
> I have, on occasions, included in an interview this question:
>
> "You have come to me for advice. After we have carefully considered your problem, is it your intention to follow the counsel that I will give you?"
>
> This comes as a considerable surprise to them. They had never thought of that. (Boyd K. Packer, "Solving Emotional Problems in the Lord's Own Way," 91–92.)

In the model on learning by faith and increasing our ability to receive revelation, we noted that one of the key steps was to *do*. Part of doing is *responding* appropriately to what the Lord counsels us to do. If we don't, the flow of further inspiration and revelation will be significantly restricted.

—*Gerald N. Lund*

Follow Through with What You Are Told

President [David O.] McKay said, "I want to tell you one thing: When the Lord tells you what to do, you've got to have the courage to do it or you had better not ask Him again." I've learned that lesson, too. Sometimes in the middle of the night I've been awakened and am unable to sleep until I've gotten out of bed and put down on paper the thing that I have been wrestling with. But it takes a lot of courage to act when directed as an answer to prayers.

—*Harold B. Lee*

Sparrow Prayers

We're commanded to pray, urged to pray, encouraged to pray, and promised absolutely that prayer will give us what we seek. The scriptures are full of miracles about answered prayers; but our personal lives, even though they contain examples of answered prayers, often give us painful examples of seemingly unanswered prayers or postponed prayers. Are we being told two things when only one of them can be true? I think one of the answers may lie in what I call sparrow prayers.

Sparrow prayers are the little prayers that the Lord can answer when granting our request to the great prayers is not possible. Despite our faithfulness, the Lord may not reverse the course of a crippling cancer that is slowly taking the life of a beloved mother or brother. But he may be able to grant a prayer for a good night's sleep or a pain-free afternoon. He may not grant the prayer of a righteous woman for marriage, but he may teach her the very real pleasures of solitude and give her other companions who are also valiant and honorable.

—*Chieko N. Okazaki*

Whatever He Gives Is Good

When I was young I wanted to go on a mission. I dreamed of that mission. I thought I should learn a language, so I took French starting in the eighth grade. I took it in the ninth grade, the tenth grade, and the eleventh grade. I quit after the eleventh grade because I didn't like the French teacher. She was from Paris, was very proud of her language, and if you mispronounced a word (for instance the French *R,* which is rather difficult for an American to get right), she would throw chalk at you. She would literally pelt you with chalk. If you really insulted her ears by butchering her language, she would throw an eraser at you. And I got pelted quite a bit. I thought, *If this is what the French are like, the last place on earth I want to go on a mission is France.* Besides, I loved all things Danish— I'm half Danish. My mother would say the good half of me is the Danish half. My grandfather went to Denmark, my uncles went to Denmark, my cousins went to Denmark. . . . I prayed I would go to Denmark. But I had the feeling of impending doom that I was not going to go to Denmark—I was going to go to France. So I began to plead with the Lord that he would send me to Denmark. I prayed night after night for a Danish mission.

As the bishop and I began to fill out the missionary papers, I had a feeling it probably was not appropriate to tell the Lord to which country he should send you on your mission, but I didn't think it was inappropriate to eliminate one country out of the hundreds in the world. I changed my prayers. I began to pray he would send me anywhere but France.

I remember vividly the day my call arrived. I was at work. . . . I knew my call was in the mailbox, and I knew it said France. Don't ask me how I knew, I just did. I did not want to go home and open it. . . . I pulled to the side of the road, parked the car, bowed my head, and said, "Father in Heaven, I know my call is at home; I know it says France. Thou art all-powerful! Thou canst do all things! Please change it in the envelope. I will go anywhere, I don't need to go to Denmark, I will go anywhere, just please, please don't send me to France!"

I ended my prayer, drove home with a spark of hope, and opened the envelope. What did it say? France. . . . It didn't take me very long in France to love the French people. I love the French people—wonderful people. They have a beautiful language. Their culture went right to the center of my heart. I had a marvelous mission. . . .

I repeat: All things given of God are good. He doesn't give scorpions; he only gives eggs. He does not give stones; he only gives bread. Whatever he gives is good!

—*S. Michael Wilcox*

Prayer Is Not Just about Us, God Sees All People's Needs

I remember several lessons I was taught by those faithful people [in Tonga]. We would always pray for protection, success, and good seas and wind to take us to our destination. Once I asked the Lord to bless us with a good tail wind so we could get to Foa quickly. As we got under way, one of the older men said, "Elder Groberg, you need to modify your prayers a little."

"How's that?" I replied.

"You asked the Lord for a tail wind to take us rapidly to Foa. If you pray for a tail wind to Foa, what about the people who are trying to come from Foa to Pangai? They are good people, and you are praying against them. Just pray for a good wind, not a tail wind."

That taught me something important. Sometimes we pray for things that will benefit us but may hurt others. We may pray for a particular type of weather, or to preserve someone's life, when that answer to our prayer may hurt someone else. That's why we must always pray in faith, because we can't have true, God-given faith in something that is not according to His will. If it's according to His will, all parties will benefit. I learned to pray for a good wind and the ability to get there safely, not necessarily a tail wind.

—*John H. Groberg*

The Lord Will Not Limit
Someone Else's Agency

God, even in His infinite power and knowledge, will not force the human heart. This principle often brings sorrow and suffering into the world because many choose to do evil, and that almost always directly affects others.

Sometimes to get an answer to our prayers, what we pray for would require the Lord to force another person to do something against his or her will. He will not do that. He may intervene in ways that soften the heart or change the mind, but He will not force or coerce us in any way. We have to remember that *life isn't just about us.*

Many faithful, righteous parents have undergone the bitter sorrow of seeing a child turn away from the gospel and fall away "into forbidden paths" (1 Nephi 8:28). The parents may offer years of fervent, heart-wrenching prayers. They may remain faithful and true to their covenants. With little or no change in their child, they may wonder if their faith is strong enough.

We must always factor in agency. Considering the heartbreak Lehi and Sariah faced with some of their children, Lehi's counsel takes on special meaning: "Wherefore, men are free according to the flesh. . . . And they are free to choose liberty and eternal life, through the great Mediator of all men, or to choose captivity and death, according to the captivity and power of the devil" (2 Nephi 2:27).

—*Gerald N. Lund*

Examining Our Desires

If God so honors the principle of agency and free will that He allows the fulfillment of our desires, even if they run counter to the plan of happiness, then we must carefully examine our desires. What if what we hope and long and work for is not for our long-range good? What if we are so "in love" with a person that we are not willing to consider if he or she will have a long-term destructive effect on our lives? What if we desire a comfortable and safe calling in the Church that doesn't take us out of our comfort zone?

If we are not careful, even those striving to be faithful disciples of the Father and Son may close our hearts to any guidance or counsel from the Lord and thus lose out on great opportunities. The Lord will not force anything upon us, even if it is the absolutely best thing for us.

Elder Erastus Snow, an early member of the Quorum of the Twelve, stated it this way:

> If our spirits are inclined to be stiff and refractory and we desire continually the gratification of our own will . . . , the Spirit of the Lord is held at a distance from us. . . . The Father withholds his Spirit from us in proportion as we desire the gratification of our own will. We interpose a barrier between us and our Father, that he cannot,

consistently with himself, move upon us so as to control our actions. (Erastus Snow in Neal A. Maxwell, *That Ye May Believe,* 137.)

A deep and abiding desire to surrender our will to God's will, to put our lives in harmony with the Father and the Son, is the open latch on the gateway to our hearts, as it were. Until we truly desire to let the Father and the Son take a hand in our lives, our hearts may remain closed to some things, and we will miss out on the marvelous blessings They have to give.

—*Gerald N. Lund*

DAY 242

One of "All These Things"

The time will come when we will thank Him for saying no to us with regard to some of our petitions. Happily, God in his omniscience can distinguish between our surface needs (over which we often pray most fervently) and our deep and eternal needs. He can distinguish what we ask for today and place it in relationship to what we need for all eternity. He will bless us, according to our everlasting good, if we are righteous.

Perhaps the parable about the gospel seed falling on different kinds of soil and not flourishing in one type of soil because there was "no deepness of earth" also describes the shallowness of those

UNEXPECTED ANSWERS 275

who do not ponder and pursue the basic doctrines—of which true petitionary prayer is surely one! (Matthew 13:5)

Thus is a very real way, one of "all these things" through which we must pass (the experiences that we must have that are for our good) is *growing and learning by praying*. Most often this learning will occur in personal and secret prayer rather than in public prayer.

—*Neal A. Maxwell*

"Because of Thy Faith in Christ"

Enos wrote only one chapter in the Book of Mormon, but his message is vital. Enos began, "I will tell you of the wrestle which I had before God, before I received a remission of my sins" (Enos 1:2). Because all of us must receive a remission of our sins, Enos chose to write about something important to all of us. It's as if Enos were saying, "This *must* happen in your life. Here's how it happened in mine."

Initially, Enos went to hunt beasts in the forest, but he later began to reflect on the words his father had taught him. As they "sunk deep into [his] heart," he apparently lost all interest in hunting. He began to pray and continued praying all day and into the night, until finally a voice declared, "Enos, thy sins are forgiven thee, and thou shalt be blessed." Enos responded in gratitude and amazement:

"Lord, how is it done?" The answer came, "Because of *thy faith in Christ*" (Enos 1:3–7; emphasis added).

I like this scripture because of how easily we can apply the question "How is it done?" to our own lives. It really doesn't matter what "it" is; the formula is always the same—faith in Christ.

—John Bytheway

You Have Prayers to Give

You also have an unlimited number of prayers to offer during this season. You can pray for the people in the hospital as you drive by. You can pray for the policeman directing traffic after the basketball game. You can pray for the person you see on the news whose face and plight touch you, even if you see her face only in a crowd. You can pray for the clerk in the shoe store, for the Salvation Army bell ringer, for the grandchild in Florida, for the president of the United States, for the person standing in the detergent aisle trying to make up her mind what soap to buy. And this doesn't even begin to touch the hundreds of people you know personally for whom you can pray.

Think of the power of that prayer. It's as if you lift someone with loving hands and hold him or her up in remembrance before God. That person is in your memory, in your heart, in your thoughts. And now you have brought his or her name before God in joyous, sympathetic remembrance. What a wonderful gift of plenitude!

Now, perhaps you're thinking, "But some of these people are strangers. I don't even know them. I don't know if they need my prayers. I don't know if my prayers will do them any good." That's not the point. You're not praying for them because they need it. You're praying for them because you have a prayer to give. The prayer does not exist because of their poverty. It exists because of your richness.

—*Chieko N. Okazaki*

DAY 245

Praying for Others

I will never forget the first time I spoke from the Tabernacle pulpit in a general meeting. I had prepared for weeks. I had fasted and prayed. But as my turn to speak approached, I began to have what could only be described as a meltdown. I had expected to be nervous, but the "terror of the Tabernacle" was far worse than anything I had imagined. At one point, I literally couldn't breathe. As I pleaded silently with the Lord for help, I mentioned that it would be important to be able to get air into my lungs when I stepped to the pulpit.

And then, just moments before I stood to speak, an unexpected image came to mind. It was of a group of sisters in Montreal, Canada, where I had visited a few weeks earlier. They had promised to pray for me at this meeting, and I knew they were keeping their promise, for a feeling of total and immediate calm washed over me.

Not long thereafter when a friend visited Montreal, I asked her to tell the Relief Society president of the Montreal French-speaking stake that she and her sisters had made all the difference for me that night. Upon hearing the story this woman exclaimed, "We just knew she knew that we were praying for her!"

—*Sheri Dew*

DAY 246

You May Be Somebody's Answer

Have you ever thought that someone somewhere may be pleading with Heavenly Father for help and you may be the one chosen to help answer that prayer? The Good Samaritan may have been on his way to a prayer meeting or some other important appointment, but he was willing to stop and fill a need. If we're willing, God will use us.

—*Mary Ellen Edmunds*

Helping Each Other Along the Way

"Therefore, care not for the body, neither the life of the body; but care for the soul, and for the life of the soul.

"And seek the face of the Lord always, that in patience ye may possess your souls, and ye shall have eternal life" (D&C 101:37–38).

I have thought about these words, to "seek the face of the Lord *always* that in *patience* ye may possess your souls, and have eternal life." (Emphasis added.) For me this translates into striving each day to become better, to be worthy to seek the face of the Lord. Each new day gives us many opportunities; how wonderful it would be to live so that we could be the answer to someone's prayer. I am glad that we are taught weekly in our meetings and are reminded continually of the things that will help us in our life, such as daily prayer and daily study, for I believe that it is through our daily actions that we are seeking "the face of the Lord." Another key word in that scripture for me is "patience," since perfection is built slowly as we go on from grace to grace. We are all striving to be on the straight and narrow path that leads to eternal life, but we each are in different places along the route. As we help each other along the way, we also help ourselves, for we really cannot be exalted alone.

—*Carlfred Broderick*

Answers Can Come through Others

When we plead with the Lord for help, *the answer to our prayers often comes through another individual.* It has been said that answers to prayer usually don't come down through the roof but they do come knocking on the door! The corollary is that we should strive to be spiritually in tune so that, should he choose, the Lord can use us to bless the lives of others.

—Anne Osborn Poelman

DAY 249

Friends Can Be Answers to Prayers

The compassion of Christlike friends deeply touches and changes our lives. We should well remember that the Lord often sends "blessings from above, thru words and deeds of those who love." Love is the very essence of the gospel of Christ. In this Church, prayers for help are often answered by the Lord through the simple, daily service of caring brothers and sisters. In the goodness of genuine friends, I have seen the reflected mercy of the Lord

Himself. I have always been humbled by the knowledge that the Savior regards us as His friends when we choose to follow Him and keep His commandments

—*Joseph B. Wirthlin*

DAY 250

"Is Anyone in Need of My Help Today?"

One morning several years ago I was driving with my family to Disney World in Florida. Our four young daughters were excited as we approached the turnoff to that famous park. The laughter and happy chatter stopped suddenly, however, as our rented station wagon sputtered and chugged to an unexpected stop on the exit ramp. Many cars sped by us in the rush-hour traffic as I tried unsuccessfully to get the car running again. Finally, realizing there was nothing more we could do, we got out of the stalled car and huddled together off the road for a word of prayer.

As we looked up from our prayer we saw a smiling, handsome man and his son maneuver their bright red sports car through the lanes of traffic and pull off the road beside us. For the remainder of the morning and into the afternoon these men assisted us and cared for our needs in many kind and helpful ways. They took us and our belongings to the receiving area at the park. In their small car, it took several trips. They helped me locate a tow truck for the stranded car; they drove me to the rental agency to get a replacement vehicle. Then, because there was some delay, they drove back to where my family waited to let them know where I was. They bought refreshments for them and then waited with my family until I returned several hours later.

We felt that these men were truly an answer to our prayer, and we told them so as we said good-bye and tried to thank them. The father responded, "Every morning I tell the good Lord that if there is anyone in need of my help today, please guide me to them."

—*Rex D. Pinegar*

DAY 251

Mite Moments

When I was twelve years old the stake president called me into his office. I was a brand-new deacon. He said, "Michael, I want you to give the opening prayer in stake conference."

I was terrified, but I said, "Okay." I was a tiny little short kid. I looked about eight. I didn't grow until I started eating pastries during my mission in France. I looked like I was just a little kid, even though I was twelve. They had to lower the pulpit all the way down (and when you're a deacon, you don't want to have to use the little stepstool). I remember standing there, giving the prayer, and being barely able to look over the top of the pulpit. I'm sure I gave just an ordinary, normal prayer. Ten years later—ten years!—I had recently returned from my mission and a sister came up to me and said, "Mike, I need to thank you. You changed my life and I've never told you."

I said, "I can't remember having ever done anything for you."

"Well, you probably won't remember this," she said, "but when you were a little boy you gave an opening prayer in a stake conference."

I said, "I remember that."

She said, "I was struggling with my testimony at the time. I did not think God listened to my prayers, but I came to stake conference and saw a boy pray. It wasn't anything you said, it was just the image of a boy praying and the sense I had inside that the boy believed someone was listening to him. It reawakened all my belief in God, the belief that I had as a little girl. The crisis was over and I never thanked you. You changed my life."

Now, did *I* change that woman's life? No! I said a prayer in stake conference, but it was a "mite moment" for her, and in God's hands these simple things can have profound results. God sees the importance of the smallest acts.

—*S. Michael Wilcox*

What More Can I Do?

Elder Groberg, on his way to a small island to meet a family that was prepared to receive the gospel, found the sailboat he was on stuck in the middle of a calm ocean with no wind.

Many beautiful, pleading, faithful prayers ascended to heaven. But when the last one finished and everyone opened their eyes, the sun was still burning down with greater intensity than before. The ocean was like a giant mirror. . . .

I thought, "There is a family at the harbor that wants to hear the gospel. We are here and we want to teach them. The Lord controls the elements. All that stands between getting the family and us together is a little wind. Why won't the Lord send it? It's a righteous desire."

As I was thinking, I noticed this faithful older man move to the rear of the boat. I watched as he unlashed the tiny lifeboat, placed two oars with pins into their places, and carefully lowered the lifeboat over the side.

Then the old man looked at me and softly said, "Get in."

I answered, "What are you doing? There is hardly room for two people in that tiny thing!"

The old man responded, "Don't waste any time or effort. Just get in. I am going to row you to shore, and we need to leave right now to make it by sundown."

I looked at him incredulously, "Row me *where?*"

"To the family that wants to hear the gospel. We have an assignment from the Lord. Get in."

I was dumbfounded. It was miles and miles to shore. The sun was hot and this man was old. But as I looked into the face of that faithful brother, I sensed an intensity in his gaze, an iron will in his very being, and a fixed determination in his voice as he said, "Before the sun sets this day, you will be teaching the gospel and bearing testimony to a family who wants to listen."

I objected, "Look, you're over three times my age. If we're going to do it this way, fine, but let me row."

With that same look of determination and faith-induced will, the old man replied, "No. Leave it to me. Get in the boat. . . ." We got into the boat with me in the front and the old man in the middle with his feet stretching to the rear of the boat, his back to me. . . .

The old man bent his back and began to row—dip, pull, lift, dip, pull, lift. . . . The old man did not look up, rest, or talk. But hour after hour he rowed and rowed and rowed. . . . The old man concentrated his efforts and energy on fulfilling the calling he had from the Lord—to get the missionary to the family that wanted to hear the gospel. He was the Lord's wind that day.

. . . . No matter what our trials, we should never say, "It is enough." Only God is entitled to say that. Our responsibility, if we are faithful, is to ask, "What more can I do?" then listen for the answer and do it!

I'll never forget the example of that old man.

—*John H. Groberg*

Prayer in Adversity

The Enabling Power of God

How many of us sometimes try to resolve life's challenges ourselves, without seeking the intervention of the Lord in our lives? We try to carry the burden alone.

How many times, likewise, as we have prayed for assistance or help with our problems, have we severed ourselves from the power of God because of doubt or fear and thus could not obtain the blessings he would give us? (See D&C 6:36; 67:3.)

As some are faced with trials and afflictions, they say, "Why won't God help me?" Some have even struggled with doubts about their prayers and their personal worthiness and say, "Perhaps prayer doesn't work."

I bear testimony that prayer does work, and that the Lord stands ready to help us. One of the keys seems to be to learn better from the Lord how to engage the powers of heaven to intervene in our behalf, which we do when we receive his grace.

The best definition I know of the word *grace* is found in the dictionary of the LDS edition of the Bible. It says:

"The main idea of the word is divine means of help or strength, given through the bounteous mercy and love of Jesus Christ. . . . Grace is an enabling power." (*Holy Bible* [Salt Lake City: The Church of Jesus Christ of Latter-day Saints, 1979], Appendix, 697.)

Grace, then, is the enabling power of God. In fact, we could replace the word "grace" with "God's divine enabling power" every time we see it in the scriptures, and we'd have a great insight.

—*Gene R. Cook*

Dealing with Problems

If you are the one who is experiencing the problem, you can pray for an easing of the burden, even if you cannot be delivered from it. And this step is particularly applicable if you know about a problem someone else is experiencing. You may not know how to solve someone's problem. You may not know how to help that person solve her own problem. There may not be a way for the problem to be solved. There may not even be a way to talk about the problem and to share your sympathy directly with that person. But you can pray for her deliverance. You can remember her in your morning and evening prayers and lift your heart to the Lord during the day, in love and compassion and the desire that she will be delivered.

Being able to pray with sincerity of heart about a problem breaks down the walls of denial and evasion. When you're praying on the inside about, say, an addiction to a prescription drug, you can't very well maintain the illusion on the outside that you don't have a problem. Another important effect is that such a sincere prayer is an invitation for intervention. You are much less likely to reject help when it comes, even in an odd disguise. And if you are praying about the needs of someone else, then I think you are much more open to the whisperings of the Spirit about something that would help . . .

—*Chieko N. Okazaki*

DAY 255

God Bless the Sick and Afflicted

Across the pulpits, beside the beds, around the tables at mealtime, from the kneeling circles of families beginning a day, in holy temples, in busy hospitals, and in private places, countless good people offer the universal plea at prayer time, "O God, bless the sick and afflicted."

What a comforting thought that is, because sooner or later we all qualify to be counted among the sick and the afflicted. How good it is then, to be included in somebody's prayer! . . .

Until this current sickness or affliction is resolved or has run its course, you seek comfort, patience, strength to endure, and sustaining support. You want God's blessings. While you may know the sweet uses of adversity when it is your turn to be among the poor, the sick, or the afflicted, prayers are a powerful force in helping you get through the siege.

There are countless choice reports of the miracles wrought in healing, of resolution and peace resulting from God's goodness as united prayers from the faithful pour out before heaven.

Regarding those prayers for the sick and afflicted, there are some people who when they pray, "O God, bless the sick and afflicted" include a request that they themselves may be directed by heaven to appropriately bring comfort or cure to others in their times of assaulting affliction.

What a refreshing idea!

Doing something for others is still the best way to forget your own troubles. That's when joy can come.

God bless the sick and afflicted?

He does!

—*Elaine Cannon*

DAY 256

Praying When Faced with Obstacles

In our lives each of us must face a mountain to climb. It may be a financial crisis, a great soul-shaking illness of a loved one, or some other great test. During those trying times a prayer might be worded like this: "Heavenly Father, I have come to a mountain I can't climb. I have thought about it, I have studied it, I have read the scriptures. I have counseled with many about it, and I simply cannot solve this problem. The mountain is too big. I can't get over it; I can't climb this one. Please, I am asking for help. No, I am not asking—I am pleading, I'm begging. Please, please, dear God, help me."

In that moment, I promise you that it would be as though he would say, "Take my hand in yours; I will walk with you all the way. I am not going to take away the problem, because I want you to grow. Trust in me and I will take you down streets you would have thought impossible, and I will cause you to speak beautifully, eloquent words of truth. You will serve in places you never would have supposed. I will walk with you all the way to the mountain's top. I will never forsake you. Have faith and trust."

. . . When those times of soul-shaking experiences come, each of us can turn to deep, meaningful, sincere prayer.

I testify that the great being we affectionately call our Father in heaven, that being who is the supreme and all-powerful Almighty God, the Great Elohim, will, with love and tenderness and absolute compassion, give us answer to our prayers.

—*Vaughn J. Featherstone*

Without Prayer, Small Problems Can Become Big

When adversity in any form hits, pray. Usually we think of prayer in the life and death traumas. But small problems can become bigger ones if we haven't made a practice of turning first to Heavenly Father for whatever it takes to solve, survive, and deal appropriately with our challenge at the moment.

Prayer is a great blessing.

... I wonder how people manage life without taking their burdens to the Lord. He may not give us immediate relief from the problem we're struggling with, but we can get a lift in spirit. We can sense direction. We can feel God's love. We can be greatly strengthened. We can be aware of his sustaining influence. We can be heartened to go forward.

If you are burdened, pray. You will feel comforted.

If you are dying, pray. You will have peace.

If your husband goes off with another woman, pray. Pray for comfort, for guidance, for patience, for forgiveness, and the soul will heal.

If your teenager is in desperate trouble with drugs, sex, dishonesty, rebellion, or grades, pray. You'll know that God cares. He'll sustain you in your efforts to help the troubled youth.

If you lose your job and the bills are piled high, pray. Pray until your faith is firm. Then your mind is ready to receive God's will.

If you are depressed and hopeless, pray. Hope is the other side of faith. Pray, and know that God lives. Everything will ultimately be all right.

—*Elaine Cannon*

DAY 258

From Simple Trials to Our Gethsemanes

Prayer in the hour of need is a great boon. From simple trials to our Gethsemanes, prayer can put us in touch with God, our greatest source of comfort and counsel. "Pray always, that you may come off conqueror" (D&C 10:5)—persistent prayer. "Exerting all my powers to call upon God to deliver me" is how the young Joseph Smith describes the method which he used in the Sacred Grove to keep the adversary from destroying him. (JS–H 1:16.) This is also a key to use in keeping depression from destroying us.

—*Ezra Taft Benson*

Faith in the Lord's Will

A note of caution: Faith is not willing our own desires into existence. That would be exercising faith in what *we* want. For example, many of us have experienced the death of a loved one and have concluded that if we'd only had more faith, the loved one could have been healed. But again, that is faith in what *we* want to happen, not faith in Christ and what he, in his wisdom, wants or allows to happen.

Jesus taught, "And again, it shall come to pass that he that hath faith in me to be healed, *and is not appointed unto death,* shall be healed" (D&C 42:48; emphasis added). When our faith in Christ is strong, we can be assured that "all things have been done in the wisdom of him who knoweth all things" (2 Nephi 2:24). This kind of faith allows us to pray with a measure of peace, acknowledging, "Not my will, but thine, be done" (Luke 22:42).

As we all know, even when our faith in Christ is strong, we still have problems. Jacob the brother of Nephi told the people that if they would pray with exceeding faith, God would "console [them] in [their] afflictions" (Jacob 3:1). Jacob didn't say that God would remove their afflictions but that he would comfort them and help them through. But even in our afflictions, if we can keep the faith and maintain the perspective the gospel offers, we'll be able to stay positive. Elder M. Russell Ballard has taught:

"The best thing about living a Christ-centered life, however, is how it makes you feel—inside. It's hard to have a negative attitude about things if and when your life is focused on the Prince of Peace. There will still be problems. Everyone has them. But *faith in the Lord Jesus Christ is a power to be reckoned with in the universe and in individual lives.* It can be a causative force through which miracles are wrought. It can also be a source of inner strength through which we find self-esteem, peace of mind, contentment, and the courage to cope."

—*John Bytheway*

DAY 260

The Prayer of the Faithful

For the faithful, the normal tests and trials of life need not be the enemy of faith. While we don't necessarily look forward to these obstacles and challenges, we accept them, and we build our lives and faith from them. To the faithful, the very obstacles that we overcome draw us closer to our Heavenly Father by helping us develop a humble, submissive spirit and causing us to be grateful and appreciative of those blessings that flow from a loving Father. In short, these experiences can and often do increase our faith. The faithful do not pray to be spared the trials of life but pray that they may have the strength to rise above them. In so doing they come closer to Heavenly Father and to that state of perfection they are seeking.

—*Richard C. Edgley*

Testing Our Faith

When we're seeking answers to prayers, the Lord will surely test us. He wants us to see if we will serve and love him at any cost. He wants us to see if we will continue in faith even if we don't receive the answer we had hoped for. . . .

I honestly believe that that if a family is praying for what is honorable and right, they have every right to assume that the Lord will respond to them. He will either bless them with what they desire, or give them some indication of why they cannot have it, or indicate that they ought to quit praying for something they will not receive. . . .

All the Lord wants from us is to know where our hearts are. If our hearts are right we may receive the trials, but it won't diminish our faith. Or we may not be required even to receive the trials if the Lord feels that we have already gained the benefit that would come from them. Sometimes the Lord will "pull the rug out from under you" in order to be sure of your heart. He may let you pass through difficult circumstances, contrary to what you may have prayed for, just to help you prove to yourself that you really will do anything he might ask you to submit to.

—*Gene R. Cook*

What We *Really* Are and What We *Really* Yearn For

The Lord reminded us that our prayers will be granted if our lives are righteous and if we ask in faith for that which is expedient. (D&C 88:64–65, 78.) He attached the same condition in his visit to the Nephites when he said the prayers of the faithful will be granted if they ask for that "which is right." (3 Nephi 18:20.)

We are also given a vision of becoming sufficiently spiritual so that our very petitions are inspired beforehand (D&C 50:30), and thus they can be granted even as we ask (D&C 46:30).

The Lord has spoken of temptations "to prove thee, to know what was in thine heart." (Deuteronomy 8:2.) If we link that scripture up with one in Jeremiah in which the Lord says, "I the Lord search the heart, I try the reins, even to give every man according to his ways" (Jeremiah 11:20, 17:10), we see the ultimate expression of agency and divine justice. If each of us really finally receives that which has been really wanted, none could quarrel with the justice of God. Trials and tribulations tend to squeeze the artificiality out of us, leaving the essence of what we *really* are and clarifying what we *really* yearn for. Therefore, the record will be clear.

—*Neal A. Maxwell*

Humble Supplication

It is often in the valleys with our afflictions that we are truly humbled and better prepared to remember the gift of eternal life for which he paid the price—those times when we feel least worthy, least comfortable about carrying his holy name, and have a keener sense of our imperfections, those moments when the flesh is weak and our spirits suffer disappointment for our errors and our sins. We might feel a sense of withdrawal, a pulling away, a feeling of needing to set aside a time at least for that divine relationship with the Savior until we are more worthy, But at that very moment, even in our unworthiness, the offer is again given to us to accept the great gift of the Atonement—even before we change. When we feel the need to pull away, let us reach out to him. Instead of feeling the need to resist, let us submit to his will. Let us bend our will as well as our knees in humble supplication.

—*Ardeth G. Kapp*

Fasting and Prayer Help When Facing Adversity

How, then, shall we respond to undeserved adversity in our own lives? How may our responses to affliction and suffering draw us closer to the Savior, to our Heavenly Father, and to the realization of our own celestial potential? May I suggest some examples and role models found in the scriptures.

The sons of Mosiah, in the course of their missionary labors, "had many afflictions . . . both in body and in mind . . . and also much labor in the spirit." (Alma 17:5.) Partly because of such experiences, they became "strong in the knowledge of the truth; . . . men of a sound understanding . . . [who] searched the scriptures diligently, that they might know the word of God. . . .

"They had given themselves to much prayer, and fasting; therefore they had the spirit of prophecy, and the spirit of revelation." (Alma 17:2–3.) Through their positive response to adversity, they grew spiritually.

In the time of Nephi, son of Helaman, "the more humble part of the people . . . [suffered] much affliction"; but they fasted and prayed frequently and became "stronger in their humility, and . . . firmer in the faith of Christ, unto the filling their souls with joy and consolation." (Hel. 3:34–35.)

From their example, we learn some positive responses to our own undeserved adversity.

—Ronald E. Poelman

Why Bad Things Happen to Good People

It is both possible and likely that the closer we come to Christ, the more we will be aware of what we yet need to do. He said, "If men come until me I will show unto them their weakness. . . . *if* they humble themselves before me, . . . then will I make weak things become strong unto them." (Ether 12:27; emphasis added).

So if we are becoming more aware of our weaknesses, that doesn't mean we are drifting away from Him; it may well mean that we are drawing closer. Like a good coach, a good tutor will always help his students see and correct their mistakes. When we understand that, correction is motivation, not discouraging. For because of the Atonement, we can learn from our mistakes without being condemned by them.

The paradox of this divine tutorial is that the Lord will not only correct us but may also lead us into some forms of personal affliction. Because Elder Maxwell was such a faithful student of discipleship, I draw again from his words: "If we are serious about our discipleship, Jesus will eventually request each of us to do those very things which are the most difficult for us to do." Thus, "sometimes the best people have the worst experiences because they are the most ready to learn."

—Bruce C. Hafen

DAY 266

Adversity Can Bring Us Closer to God

When we are in deep need, prayers usually are more fervent and frequent than when we are not.

"Let not your heart be troubled: ye believe in God," said Jesus to his Apostles shortly before he picked up the cross to walk to his crucifixion. Then he prayed for them—out loud—so that they could hear him. "This is life eternal, that they might know thee the only true God, and Jesus Christ, whom thou has sent." (John 14:1; 17:3.)

These promises from God can comfort and sustain us through any kind of demand upon our soul. When we turn to God in prayer—with a needful spirit and a contrite heart and a desire to learn, we will feel the Spirit, the healing.

Sometimes praying is difficult because we haven't developed a close relationship with God. Praying without a relationship with our Father is like trying to have an intimate heart-to-heart talk about your fondest dreams with the ticket-taker at the football game.

With God, it is different, of course. He knows us! He is waiting to be gracious to us, but he does not force his way into our lives. He waits upon us—until our growth and choices make us ready for him.

—*Elaine Cannon*

DAY 267

The Importance of Trials

What if every prayer were instantly answered in the way we wanted it to be? What if a little bit of spiritual due diligence now and again kept us in constant and clear contact with our Heavenly Father? If nothing ever tested our faith or our resolve or our convictions—because we really don't know what we believe or believe *in,* for that matter, until we're tested—then what are the chances we would progress far enough spiritually in this lone and dreary world? Whether we like it or not, our trials and struggles can tend to accelerate our push toward godliness. In fact, it's possible we wouldn't go as far as we're capable of going without them.

—*Sheri Dew*

"Not My Will, but Thine"

Even Jesus Submitted to God's Will

There are three recorded prayers from Gethsemane, or at least three versions of the same prayer. I don't think we have to choose which of the gospel writers is most correct, for they are all poignant and beautiful, yet they teach different truths all of which we can relate to. I favor Mark's version, but all of them tell us something about that moment in the Savior's life. We too pray in each of these ways in our own lives. Matthew records the prayer thus: "And he went a little further, and fell on his face, and prayed, saying, O my Father, if it be possible, let this cup [this bitter cup of trembling] pass from me: nevertheless not as I will, but as thou wilt" (Matthew 26:39). Do we not often pray in a similar vein? "Father if it be possible . . ." When we pray this way, the answer we desire is a matter of possibilities. It may not be possible. If it isn't possible, we will understand, but if it's possible that God can take away this trial or bring the hoped-for blessing, we would want God to do so.

Mark's prayer is more deep and poignant. The idea of possibility is removed. Mark's account is thus: Jesus pleaded, "Abba, Father, all things are possible unto thee; take away this cup from me: nevertheless not what I will, but what thou wilt" (Mark 14:36). *Abba* is a word used especially by a child, a little trusting child, to his father. It means *daddy* or *papa*. Have we not prayed this way also? "Father, thou canst do all things! Give me this blessing. Take away this trial." The question of possibility is removed in the prayer in Mark. All that is left is a cry from the innermost realms of the soul. Can a loving Father refuse such a prayer from his beloved trusting child?

The prayer in Luke doesn't present it as a matter of possibility at all. It's a matter of what God wills: "And he was withdrawn from them about a stone's cast, and kneeled down, and prayed, Saying, Father, if thou be willing, remove this cup from me: nevertheless not my will, but thine, be done" (Luke 22:41–42). This is what we might call, in a certain sense, a hinting prayer or request. We hope that God wants what we want, as a child might come to his parent and say, "If it's all right with you, this is what I desire." Regardless of which version you favor, Christ took the cup of trembling because the answer to his prayer, whichever account you prefer, was, "It is not possible. Too much is necessary for my other children that depends on these intensely painful moments."

—*S. Michael Wilcox*

DAY 269

Strength to Drink from Bitter Cups

All prayers are, indeed, answered, and it is well to remember that sometimes the answer is not in the affirmative. When the Son of God prayed in the Garden of Gethsemane that the bitter cup might pass, an affirmative response to His prayer would have thwarted the entire plan of salvation. But the Only Begotten Son demonstrated His meekness and humility and obedience as He added, "Nevertheless not my will, but thine, be done" (Luke 22:42). The divine answer was no, but "there appeared an angel unto him from heaven, strengthening him" (Luke 22:43). This is certainly a prototype and a promise for each of us as we too are required to drink from bitter cups in our lives.

—*Spencer J. Condie*

DAY 270

Christ's Ultimate Sacrifice: "Thy Will Be Done"

Joseph Smith's translation of Matthew 27:54, provided in the LDS edition of the Bible, gives us the full account of the Savior's sixth statement from the cross: "Jesus, when he had cried again with a loud voice, saying, Father it is finished, *thy will is done"* (emphasis added). This utterance is tremendously significant. It encapsulates the whole plan of salvation; it sums up the whole reason Jesus was sent to earth: to do his Father's will, as he himself had indicated on other occasions (John 6:38; 3 Nephi 27:13–14). The Prophet's translation of Matthew 27:54 brings us full circle to the time in premortality when the Savior volunteered to be our Redeemer, to do the will of the Father, and to let all the honor be his—"Father, thy will be done, and the glory be thine forever" (Moses 4:2).

"NOT MY WILL, BUT THINE" 309

The will of the Son was fully swallowed up in the will of the Father. The unparalleled prayer and desire of the Savior articulated in Gethsemane—"thy will be done"—was now fulfilled in every way, completely satisfying every aim, goal, purpose, and requirement of the plan of salvation.

—*Andrew C. Skinner*

DAY 271

God's "No" as an Affirmative Indication of His Love

In our moments of deep anguish, suffering, and bewilderment, in those moments when we ask in faith for certain outcomes and are refused, because to give them to us would not be right (3 Nephi 18:20), then our faith is either deepened or slackened.

Yes, even in our prayers we can, unintentionally, ask "amiss." (2 Nephi 4:35.) No wonder humility is such an everlasting virtue. For us to accept God's "no" as an affirmative indication of His love rather than a lack thereof and as a signal that we have asked amiss— this is truly humility.

How often have you and I in our provincialism prayed to see ahead and, mercifully, been refused, lest our view of the present be blurred?

How many times have we been blessed by *not* having our

prayers answered, at least according to the specifications set forth in our petitions?

How many times have frustrating, even grueling, experiences from which we have sought relief turned out later to have been part of a necessary preparation that led to much more happiness? "And now when Alma heard this, . . . he beheld that their afflictions had truly humbled them and that they were *in a preparation to hear* the word." (Alma 32:6. Italics added.)

How many times have we impatiently expressed our discontent with seemingly ordinary and routine circumstances that were divinely designed, shaping circumstances for which, later on, we were very grateful? Alas, have there perhaps not also been those times when we have been grumpy with God or, unlike Job, even "charged God foolishly?" (Job 1:22.) How many times, naively and ungraciously, have we vigorously protested while on our way to a blessing?

—*Neal A. Maxwell*

Accept the Lord's Answer with Faith

Prayers are not always answered as we wish them to be. Even the Redeemer's prayer in Gethsemane was answered in the negative. He prayed that the bitter cup of sorrow, pain, and mortal life termination could pass, but the answer was a "no" answer.

Can each youth keep an unbiased mind in prayer as did the Lord and have the personal strength to accept the verdict even though it counters desire?

—*Spencer W. Kimball*

DAY 273

Our Desires Become His Will

Sometimes answers to prayer are quite clear, simple, and direct. But often prayer becomes a long and personal conversation. We continue to pray and work and find that, in inexplicable ways, our problems are gradually resolved or changed. Sometimes even our righteous and heartfelt desires are modified. Gradually, our desires become His will. Our pleading becomes part of the experience.

Elder Neal A. Maxwell taught that the Lord works on us through the very process of prayer:

"Some have difficulty with the reality that prayers are petitions even though God knows all and loves all anyway. True, we are not informing God, but we are informing ourselves by reverently working through our real concerns and our real priorities and by listening to the Spirit. For us merely to say, ritualistically, 'Thy will be done' would not be real petitionary prayer. This would involve no genuine working through of our own feelings. There would be no experience in agonizing in choosing, and also in submitting."

And so the power of praying is more than saying at the end of a prayer, "Thy will be done." It is actually finding that His will has become our will. Often the change in our part of the conversation is almost imperceptible. It is simple and small and occurs over time. It is difficult to talk about because by its very nature it is personal and unique—something that is happening between the Father and the individual. And it is unpredictable. He may answer me so immediately and distinctly at one time and so gradually at another time that I may think that nothing is happening. But if I make the choice to keep believing, and I demonstrate that choice by continuing to pray, I am quite sure His will *will* be made manifest, and it will in the end, seem to me to be just right.

—*Virginia H. Pearce*

DAY 274

It Is a Choice to Come unto Christ and Be Changed

The gospel is intended to regenerate individual human beings and renovate whole societies. It is to make of earth a heaven. To pray "thy will be done" is easy enough, or at least it is easy enough to say the words. But to truly mean it is another matter, with far more serious and long-range implications than we may realize. To pray with earnestness for God's will to be done may well prove inconvenient, unsettling to our self-centered world, and off-putting to those who want to "do their own thing" or "march to a different drummer." This is a call for us to align ourselves with the purposes of heaven. It entails first a serious spiritual search to come to know what God wants done and then a consecrated effort to comply happily. To come unto Christ is a choice; it is a choice to be changed.

—*Robert L. Millet*

Our Desire or God's Will?

One of the most important things we can do is to search our own hearts with scrupulous honesty. We must examine our motives, our desires, our actions, our conclusions. One of the things that should become a standard part of our daily prayers is not only "Thy will be done," but "Heavenly Father, help me to be sensitive to thy voice. Help me to recognize revelation when it comes, and to distinguish it from the false voices of the world or my own emotions."

. . . A young bishop [had] a remarkable experience while giving a priesthood blessing to a young mother who had suddenly fallen unconscious and had been rushed to the hospital.

The feeling that came to him as he was speaking was so positive and so powerful that he was sure it was from the Lord. Convinced of that, he then pronounced some very wonderful and specific promises for her. Yet she passed away a few hours later, contradicting what he had said.

As he shared that with me many years later, he was still agonizing over it. When I asked what conclusions he had come to about the experience, his answer was a wonderful lesson about how we can let our own emotions get in the way. He said:

"I know without question that the feelings I had were from the Lord. But in my great desire to bless this woman and her family I put my own interpretation on what I was feeling. Now I understand that the Lord was saying to me, "It's all right. I am here. I will bless her. I am going to call her home, but this is my will. Be at peace, and let the family be at peace." But I wanted so badly to intervene and stop this husband's suffering that I assumed the Lord was saying, "I am going to heal her, so you can make her promises about staying longer in mortality."

Then came a wonderful reminder for all of us. He said, "I have never again given a blessing without being very conscious that I must speak for the Lord and not just express my own desires."

—*Gerald N. Lund*

Sacrificing Our Desires to Our Needs

Let us never forget, however, that our needs will take us to our knees in agony at times. We too will say, "Father, if it be possible." In those moments we will not be worrying about whether or not God knew beforehand what we then petition for. Indeed, we will actually be glad that He knew before that moment—for we will come to Him in desperation, not to bring Him new information!

In those moments our desires of the day may have to be sacrificed to our needs in our endless tomorrows. A mortal life may need to be "shortened" by twenty years as we might view it—but if so, it may be done in order for special services to be rendered by that individual in the spirit world, services that will benefit thousands of new neighbors with whom that individual will live in all of eternity. Perhaps this reality is yet another reason and reminder why we are urged to pray only for "our daily bread," for disciples must be portable. Our omniloving and omniscient Father will release us when it is best for us to be released. But each such release of a righteous person is also a call to new labors!

—*Neal A. Maxwell*

Truly Believing "Thy Will Be Done"

And in all our prayers we remember our insufficiency, our limitations, our dependence, our lack of wisdom. Like children we do not always know what is best for us, what is expedient. And so in all our prayers we say, "Thy will be done" and mean it. We would not ask a Church leader for advice, then disregard it. We must never ask the Lord for blessings, then ignore the answer.

And so we pray, "Thy will be done, O Lord. Thou knowest best, kind Father. I will conform. I will accept it gratefully."

—*Spencer W. Kimball*

Do Not Pray Away Pain

We may at times, if we are not careful, try to pray away pain or what seems like an impending tragedy, but which is, in reality, an opportunity. We must do as Jesus did in that respect—also preface our prayers by saying, "If it be possible," let the trial pass from us— by saying, "Nevertheless, not as I will, but as thou wilt," and bowing in a sense of serenity to our Father in Heaven's wisdom, because at times God will not be able to let us pass by a trial or a challenge. If we were allowed to bypass certain trials, everything that had gone on up to that moment in our lives would be wiped out. It is because he loves us that at times he will not intercede as we may wish him to. That, too, we learn from Gethsemane and from Calvary.

—*Neal A. Maxwell*

Call Upon the Priesthood

It is customary for the person who is afflicted or someone responsible for that person to request the administration of a blessing. The rest it up to the Lord, for he said, "Whatsoever thing ye shall ask the Father in my name, which is good, in faith believing that ye shall receive, behold, it shall be done unto you" (Moroni 7:26). . . .

There are times when healing doesn't happen in God's Church. The beautiful thing to remember is that when we seek God's will during a healing blessing, there comes a flood of comfort and peace, as well as the witness of God's love for those involved, even if the person is not healed or the affliction resolved according to desire.

It is important that when we are sick and afflicted, we *think* about calling upon the elders as our special link with Heavenly Father. It is part of God's plan to bolster our own faith, I believe. "And the elders of the church, two or more, shall be called, and shall pray for and lay their hands upon them in my name; and if they die they shall die unto me, and if they live they shall live unto me" (D&C 42:44).

—*Elaine Cannon*

DAY 280

"But If Not"

"Our God whom we serve is able to deliver us from the burning fiery furnace, and he will deliver us out of thine hand, O king. *But if not,* be it known unto thee, O king, that we will not serve thy gods, nor worship the golden image which thou hast set up" (Daniel 3:17–18; emphasis added).

Shadrach, Meshach, and Abed-nego faced a fiery execution for refusing to worship idols. They knew that God could deliver them, but would He? Either way, these brave young men determined they would not worship a false god. As a consequence, they were thrown into a fiery furnace. But miraculously, they were not harmed. The Lord intervened! However, as the scriptures and our life experiences reveal, sometimes the Lord does *not* intervene. Sometimes the seagulls don't come, the mysterious envelope containing "just enough" doesn't arrive, and the sick are not healed. Then what? Yes, Shadrach, Meshach, and Abed-nego were saved, but Abinadi burned (see Mosiah 17:13). However, Abinadi's last words were not a complaint of being forsaken, but an expression of hope: "O God, receive my soul" (Mosiah 17:19). Our hope is that the Lord will intervene in our lives, *but if not,* we will discover whether our faith is real, or only something we hold onto when it appears to be working for our benefit.

—*John Bytheway*

The Work of a Lifetime

We cannot expect the blessings of prayer unless we submit sincerely, meekly, and fully to the process of prayer.

Granted, finite minds do not fully understand the infinite mind of God. We are not fully comprehending when our agency brushes against His divinity. Yet we should trust Him as our provincial petitions meet His universal omniscience.

King Lamoni's father, for instance, uncertain whether there actually was a God, used these words: "If there is a God." His was a genuine pleading followed by a genuine offering to "give away all my sins to know thee." (Alma 22:18.)

It is necessary for us thus to place our desires and needs genuinely and unselfishly before God in prayer. It is in this process of placing our desires before Him, to a greater extent than we usually do, that we can listen and learn concerning His will. Such could not be done if we were ritualistically submissive or only partially involved.

Of course, after we place our petitions before Him we are to be submissive: "Thy will be done." But this is the last part of the process of petition, not the first.

Learning to pray is, therefore, the work of a lifetime. If we keep on praying, we will keep on discovering.

—*Neal A. Maxwell*

DAY 282

Jesus' Prayer in Gethsemane

Of all the prayers ever uttered, in time or in eternity—by gods, angels, or mortal men—this one stands supreme, above and apart, preeminent over all others.

In this garden called Gethsemane, outside Jerusalem's wall, the greatest member of Adam's race, the One whose every thought and word were perfect, pleaded with his Father to come off triumphant in the most torturous ordeal ever imposed on man or God. . . .

And it was at this hour that he, who then bought us with his blood, offered the most pleading and poignant personal prayer ever to fall from mortal lips. God the Son prayed to God the Father, that the will of the one might be swallowed up in the will of the other, and that he might fulfill the promise made by him when he was chosen to be the Redeemer: "Father, thy will be done, and the glory be thine forever" (Moses 4:4).

True, as an obedient son whose sole desire was to do the will of the Father who sent him, our Lord prayed always and often during his mortal probation. By natural inheritance, because God was his father, Jesus was endowed with greater powers of intellect and spiritual insight than anyone else has ever possessed. But in spite of his superlative natural powers and endowments—or, shall we not rather say, because of them (for truly the more spiritually perfected and intellectually gifted a person is, the more he recognizes his place in the infinite scheme of things and knows thereby his need for help and guidance from Him who truly is infinite)—and so by virtue of his superlative powers and endowments, Jesus above all men felt the need for constant communion with the source of all power, all intelligence, and all goodness.

—*Bruce R. McConkie*

The Lord's Timetable

The Long, Faithful Wait

This business of getting acquainted with Him—life's main business—is very time-consuming. Which is perfectly all right, of course. From the moment of birth to the moment of death, it is one business worth spending our lives on. And it is this business that helps us understand why we have to wait for answers to our prayers.

Permit me to say something obvious about the long, faithful wait: When His answer seems to be getting further away, it is actually getting closer. Now that is a simple fact, but a very important one that we sometimes forget. I repeat it in different words: The longer we wait, the more ready we are for the best possible answer. And the more ready we are, the more determined He will be to grant an answer that will surpass our greatest hopes. That is not just a fact about prayer and answers. It is a fact about Him. Knowing this can keep our hopes bright during the long wait. Remember what Joseph Smith declared: "Since the beginning of the world have not men heard nor perceived by the ear, neither hath any eye seen, O God, besides thee, how great things thou hast prepared for him that waiteth for thee" (D&C 133:45).

Not only is the long wait worth it, but it makes a difference. By the time the answer finally comes, we have matured in patience. Oh, how patient our Father is. And oh, how vital it is that we become patient, too. We are learning about Him on the inside, you might say. Instead of just learning what He looks like, we are learning what it feels like to be as He is.

—*Wayne E. Brickey*

Sometimes the Answer Comes Later

One of the problems we have is that we want our answers and we want them now. Too often we're like the man who prayed for patience and in his prayer added, "And I want it now." Or, to use another example, we may pray for courage and then be astonished when the Lord sends us a lion. We sometimes want the gift without doing the work to obtain it. Facing up to a "lion" will help us to have courage. But if we are not careful, we will not see the lion as a blessing, as an answer to prayer. Instead, we may misjudge the Lord and think we received the opposite. We wanted courage and now we're filled with fear. But the Lord has answered the prayer: He is providing a means for us to participate in the development of that courage and thus participate in the answer to our own prayer.

The Lord answers our prayers in his own way. Some answers come quickly. Some come many, many years later. Some come as we expected. Some come in disguise. But all honest, sincere prayers are answered.

—*Gene R. Cook*

Blessing Us in His Own Way

When our minds have been illuminated to see as God sees, it becomes a joy to accept his will.

At a time when my oldest son was still single and wanting so much to be married, I was anxiously pleading with the Lord to bless him. My request was very specific; I knew what my son needed. As I was pleading (with an eye fixed on my needs and my anxieties), asking the Lord to please bless him, the words came resoundingly into my mind, "I *am* blessing him. Be patient with my plan." I was stunned—moved to tears. I realized I had been commanding heaven, saying, "Lord, here is your work as I have outlined it. Please notify me when you have bestowed my blessings, pursued my plans, and carried out my will."

In sweet reply comes the mild rebuke, "If you don't mind, Patricia, I prefer to bestow my blessings and to do it in my way." When we can feel sure that God has not forgotten us—nor will he ever—and that he is blessing us in his own way, then the world seems a better, safer place. If we can be patient with his process—which simply means having faith—if we can commune personally and often with him, we can spare ourselves the emptiness and frenzy we feel if we are "conformed to the world": fainthearted, impatient, troubled by envy or greed or pride of a thousand kinds.

We can keep our minds fixed enough on eternity to remember that God's ways are not our ways (see Isaiah 55:8–9).

—*Patricia T. Holland*

The Lord's Time Is Not Our Time

One . . . principle in the prayer process is patience. The Lord's time is not our time. A young adult, disabled by a bicycle accident at age eighteen, struggled to live a life of service while in constant pain. She often carried with her the thought: "God does not always come when we call him, but he always comes on time." This helped her grow in patience and saintliness. Those who prayed with her through her forty operations learned that man proposes, but God disposes; we only petition, we cannot control.

—*Joanne B. Doxey*

Listen for Peace

If we, like the Savior, have the faith to put our trust in our Father in Heaven, to submit to His will, the true spirit of peace will come as a witness and strength that He *has* heard and answered our prayers.

If we resist the inspiration of God and turn from His promptings, we are left to our own confusion and lack of peace.

Sometimes, when our prayers are not answered as we desire, we may feel the Lord has rejected us or that our prayer was in vain. We may begin to doubt our worthiness before God, or even the reality and power of prayer. That is when we must continue to pray with patience and faith and to listen for that peace.

—*Rex D. Pinegar*

The Lord's Timing

Sometimes answers to our prayers do not come as quickly as we would like. We try and try again, too often concluding that God must not love us, must not hear us, or must have chosen not to answer. "The answers to our prayers come in the Lord's due time," President Dieter F. Uchtdorf explained. "Sometimes we may become frustrated that the Lord has delayed answering our prayers. In such times we need to understand that He knows what we do not know. He sees what we do not see. Trust in Him. He knows what is best for His child, and being a perfect God, He will answer our prayers perfectly and in the perfect time."

—*Robert L. Millet*

DAY 289

Setting Our Own Timetable

The timing of revelation or answers to prayers is also completely determined by the Lord. We can do things that enhance our readiness to receive revelation. We can facilitate things so revelation comes more quickly than it might otherwise. But when it comes is still the Lord's decision. We may *influence* the timing, but we cannot *determine* it.

In many cases, setting our own timetable, and then asking the Lord to meet our timetable, comes from our own sense of urgency in a matter. For example, we may have two job offers, one of which will soon be withdrawn if we don't answer. We may be inclined to say, "Lord, I have to know by Friday."

Another common mistake we make that is related to the timing of revelation is that we blithely move along with our lives, comfortable and content when things are going well. During such a period, we have somewhat of a casual relationship with the Lord and His Spirit. Then a crisis hits. Suddenly we are desperate for help and drop to our knees to begin pleading for God's intervention in our behalf. Because it is a crisis, there is usually great urgency involved, and we press the Lord for immediate help or guidance.

Because He is our Heavenly Father and because He loves us, there are times when He may answer those urgent pleas for help, even though we have not kept ourselves as ready or as worthy as we should have done. However, we are here to learn to walk by faith, and sometimes the only way we learn faith is to have a blessing withheld. Though we may be tempted to view this as a punishment or decide that God doesn't care, it is simply another manifestation of the principle that God, in all His wisdom and knowledge, decides when a revelation or answer to prayers should be given.

—*Gerald N. Lund*

The Lord Doesn't Always Answer Immediately

What are some common problems that may be holding us back from receiving answers? One is that we ask impatiently. We sometimes expect the Lord to give us immediate answers. But he hasn't promised that—and sometimes it's for our good that he wait. Sometimes when the Lord doesn't answer our questions on the spot—or within a day, or a week, or a month—we assume that he isn't going to answer them at all. That, of course, is a serious mistake. As long as we continue in our prayers we have the promise of an answer. But we've never been promised an answer to questions that we don't ask and we've never been promised an immediate answer.

—*Lindsay R. Curtis*

DAY 291

How Long?

"And Alma cried, saying: *How long* shall we suffer these great afflictions, O Lord? O Lord, give us strength according to our faith which is in Christ, even unto deliverance" (Alma 14:26; emphasis added).

Part of trusting in God is trusting in His timing. Patience is hard. Waiting for the Lord to intervene can be excruciating. Job cried out "how long?" and so did David (see Job 7:19; Psalm 6:3). John the Revelator saw the martyrs throughout the ages who "cried with a loud voice, saying, How long, O Lord, holy and true, dost thou not judge and avenge our blood on them that dwell on the earth?" (Revelation 6:10). In our day, the Prophet Joseph Smith cried out from Liberty Jail, "How long shall thy hand be stayed," and, "How long shall they suffer these wrongs and unlawful oppressions . . . ?" (D&C 121:2–3). The Lord responds to all of these petitions, and to each of us who has ever asked the same question, out of His infinite perspective: "My son, peace be unto thy soul; thine adversity and thine afflictions shall be but a small moment" (D&C 121:7). Incredible as it may seem in the middle of our adversity, the Lord's promise is that one day, all of our current "how longs" will be remembered as "small moments."

—*John Bytheway*

DAY 292

The Blessings of Patience

Some years ago, President Roy A. Welker of the German-Austrian Mission, one of the outstanding mission presidents of the Church, needed to assign a missionary to labor in Salzburg, Austria, to solve a problem in the branch there. Eight new missionaries were soon to arrive in the mission. He prayed that one of them would have the proper visa and currency to labor in Austria. He continued to pray and waited two weeks for an answer. The night before the eight arrived, the Spirit of the Lord whispered to the president the name of the missionary who should be assigned to Salzburg. The one whose name he received was the one who had the proper credentials to go to Austria. I was that elder.

The president's patience not only helped solve a problem in the branch, but it also blessed me and our family in a way that I never could have foreseen. Shortly after I arrived in Salzburg, that part of the German-Austrian Mission was changed into the Swiss-Austrian Mission. Later, I was transferred to Zurich, Switzerland, where I met Brother Julius Billeter, a warm and friendly member who was a genealogist. He was acquainted with the genealogical records of my progenitors. He researched the names of 6,000 of my ancestors for whom temple work later was completed.

—*Joseph B. Wirthlin*

DAY 293

Some Prayers Take a Long Time to Be Answered

There are . . . times when you wonder if he is ever going to answer. About twenty-two years ago our fourth daughter was born. After she was born, the doctor told my wife that she shouldn't have any more children. We talked about it, and she said, "I feel that there is another child for us." So we decided, of course, that we were going to have another baby.

Well, a year went by, and the baby didn't come; and two years went by. Finally one of the girls said to me, "Are you sure we're supposed to have another baby?" My wife had said that she knew we could have one, so we went and collectively asked her, "Are you sure we're going to have a baby?" She said, "Yes, but we haven't prayed long enough or hard enough." So we prayed for another year, and still no baby came. Then we asked the question again: "Are you sure you know what you're talking about?" "Yes," was her reply. So we prayed and prayed and prayed for one and two and three and four and five and six and seven and eight years! And then one day at the table she said, "Guess what? We're going to have a baby." Prayers, you see, are sometimes answered quickly, but other times you pray a long, long time before you get what you want.

—*H. Burke Peterson*

DAY 294

God Will Answer When We're Ready

When I was just a baby, my father, because of concerns in his own life and challenges that he was having, left our family. Our mother alone, therefore, raised my sisters and me, and as I was growing up, my father had very little to do with us as children. I realize he was working with things in his own life, but his decisions created certain challenges and hardships for my mother, my sisters, and me. At age fourteen or fifteen, if you were in my situation, and you knelt down and said: "Father in Heaven, help me find peace concerning my father leaving us and really having nothing to do with us for all these years. Help me forgive my father," would you not think that was an appropriate prayer, one that deserved an answer? But no answer came at age fourteen and fifteen. Twenty, twenty-one comes, same prayers, still no answer. Twenty-five, twenty-six passes, same prayers, yet still no answer. Thirty, thirty-one, thirty-three, thirty-four all come and go. . . .

Then one day I was asked to prepare a talk on families. I thought I would speak about my mother. My mother was a saint. In my eyes she could do no wrong. . . . But the Spirit seemed to whisper, *Speak about your father.* And I thought, *What am I going to say about my father? I have hardly had anything to do with my father growing up.* Yet the Spirit seemed to urge that I think about him.

Just at that moment, my two sons came into the room where I was working. I looked at my boys and all at once the Spirit literally flooded my mind with wonderful memories of things that I had shared with them.

And then the Spirit said: I am now ready to answer your question. Now that you are a father, now that you know a father's love, would you be the son who lost his father, or the father who lost his son? When I heard those words, I just began to weep. . . . Not for *me!* For *my father!* Because I knew what he had missed. . . . I knew it was a greater tragedy to be the father who lost his son than to be the son who lost his father.

Why didn't my Father in Heaven give me that answer at fifteen, or twenty-one, or twenty-five, or when I was married, or when my daughters were born? He needed to wait until I was a father of sons and had enough experiences with my boys to understand what a sweet thing it is to be a father and share memories with sons. The holding place had to be carved in my heart, and as soon as I could really receive and comprehend the answer, the Lord gave it to me.

—*S. Michael Wilcox*

DAY 295

Pray for Blessings *and* Understanding

I want to give you an additional thought on what to pray for. We're all alike, and we seem to want the best for ourselves, but sometimes what we consider to be the best isn't right for us, especially when the Lord doesn't think we're ready for it. May I suggest that when you pray for something very special, you pray for two things. First, pray for the blessing that you want, whether it's a new baby, or a job, or whatever; and second, ask the Lord for the blessing of understanding. Then, if he feels for some reason that the blessing isn't appropriate for that time, the blessing of understanding will come—and the frustrations that ofttimes come because we feel our prayers are not answered will blow away in the wind.

—*H. Burke Peterson*

Not This Way

Sometimes the answer we receive is simply: *No, not this way.*
When the Lord gives that kind of answer, our impatience sometimes causes us to say, *Well, then, which way do you want me to go?* I've
always been intrigued with Paul's second missionary journey. If you
look at it on the map, he's crossing Turkey, Asia Minor, in a very
logical, methodical way—east toward west, south toward north. It's
very logical. We read in Acts: "They had gone throughout Phrygia
and the region of Galatia" (Acts 16:6). Now, if you look at the map
the very next logical spot for Paul to preach the gospel would be
Ephesus in Asia; that's logical, and that's where he was headed. But
we read, "[They] were forbidden of the Holy Ghost to preach the
word in Asia" (v. 6). *Okay, you don't want me to preach in Ephesus, so
I'll go to the north instead of the west of Turkey, to a place called Bithynia.*

They tried to go into Bithynia, but the Spirit "suffered them
not. And they passing by Mysia came down to Troas. And a vision
appeared to Paul in the night; There stood a man of Macedonia, and
prayed him, saying, Come over into Macedonia, and help us" (Acts
16:7–9). Responding to his vision, Paul skips Ephesus and jumps
to Greece where he establishes churches in Thessalonica, Philippi,
Athens, and Corinth before the Spirit allows him to go back to
Turkey and preach in Ephesus. Paul does a backward circle, and
the Lord never tells us in the scriptures why he didn't want Paul to
preach in Ephesus at that time.

Notice, however, how the instructions came. The Lord didn't say, *Paul, would you go over to Corinth? I want you there.* It was instead, *No, not this way.* And sometimes the Lord in our lives says, *No, not this way.* Far too often our response is, *Well, then, which way?* but he doesn't always specify it. Then we try another way. *No, not this way,* comes the answer. Eventually we receive the vision and know where we're supposed to go, but there is some trial and error involved in the process. We must be patient. The Lord knows what he is doing.

—*S. Michael Wilcox*

DAY 297

Opening the Vault of Heaven

Petitioning in prayer has taught me that the vault of heaven, with all its blessings, is to be opened only by a combination lock: one tumbler falls when there is faith, a second when there is personal righteousness, and the third and final tumbler falls only when what is sought is (in God's judgment, not ours) "right" for us. Sometimes we pound on the vault door for something we want very much, in faith, in reasonable righteousness, and wonder why the door does not open. We would be very spoiled children if that vault door opened any more easily than it does now. I can tell, looking back, that God truly loves me by the petitions that, in his perfect wisdom and love, he has refused to grant me. Our rejected petitions tell us not only much about ourselves, but also much about our flawless Father.

—*Neal A. Maxwell*

The Lord Is Listening

To all wherever you may be, never give up on the Lord. The answer to your prayers may not be as clear or as timely as you would like, but keep praying. The Lord is listening! As you pray, ask for help in understanding the promptings of the Holy Spirit. And then do your very best to be worthy to receive those promptings. As you recognize or feel the impressions and whisperings of the Spirit, then act on them.

—*Donald L. Staheli*

Prayers for
Home and Family

Jesus Taught the Nephites to Pray in Families

As Jesus after His resurrection administered among the Nephites, He taught them how to pray by giving them the Lord's Prayer as a pattern. And thereafter, He thus instructed His Nephite disciples:

"Behold, verily, verily, I say unto you, ye must watch and pray always lest ye enter into temptation; for Satan desireth to have you, that he may sift you as wheat.

"Therefore ye must always pray unto the Father in my name."

As to promised rewards, He said:

"And whatsoever ye shall ask the Father in my name, which is right, believing that ye shall receive, behold it shall be given unto you.

"Pray in your families unto the Father, always in my name, that your wives and your children may be blessed." (3 Ne. 18:18–21.)

—*Marion G. Romney*

A Stabilizing Influence

The holding of family prayer is a powerful influence for good in every home where it is a regular practice. Morning and evening prayers, as well as the blessing on our food, bring us a sense of unity in our family as well as a closeness to our Father in heaven. Family prayer is indeed a stabilizing influence in our lives.

President John Taylor asked the Saints, "Do you have [family] prayers in your family? . . . And when you do, do you go through the operation like the guiding of a piece of machinery, or do you bow in meekness and with a sincere desire to seek the blessing of God upon you and your household? That is the way that we ought to do, and cultivate a spirit of devotion and trust in God, dedicating ourselves to him, and seeking his blessings."

—Franklin D. Richards

A Return to Virtue through Prayer

All agree that we need a new emphasis on honesty, character, and integrity. All agree that only as we build again into the fiber of our lives the virtues which are the essence of true civilization will the pattern of our times change. The question that confronts us is, *where shall we begin?*

I am satisfied that it must begin with recognition of God as our Eternal Father, of our relationship to him as his children, with communication with him in recognition of his sovereign position, and with daily supplication for his guidance in our affairs.

I submit that a return to the old pattern of prayer, family prayer in the homes of the people, is one of the simple medicines that would check the dread disease that is eroding the fiber of our character. We could not expect a miracle in a day, but in a generation we would have a miracle.

A generation or two ago family prayer in the homes of Christian people throughout the world was as much a part of the day's activity as were the meals. As that practice has diminished, our moral decay has ensued. I fear that as the quality of our housing has improved, the spirit of our homes has deteriorated.

—*Gordon B. Hinckley*

Prayer Will Strengthen the Youth

As parents, we can help create a spiritual climate with prayers, scripture study, and positive environments.

. . . Alma the Elder would be one of the first to remind us that praying for our young people is not a meaningless ritual or another

PRAYERS FOR HOME AND FAMILY   345

item to check off a list. (See Mosiah 27:14.) We must pray *for* our youth and *with* our youth.

—*Brad Wilcox*

The Army of Helaman

I shall never forget, as long as I live, the impression my mother gave me when she told the story of those two thousand sons who went to battle under the leadership of Helaman. Think of those boys. Hold them as a pattern, you priests, teachers, and deacons, yes, and high priests, seventies, and elders. If two thousand men in that ancient time could live such lives, two thousand, nay ten thousand and a hundred thousand, men can live it today. These were their principles, founded upon the principle of faith, inculcated into their hearts by their mothers, who taught them in their youth that if they prayed to God nothing doubting, their prayers would be answered.

—*David O. McKay*

Very Few Pray Too Much

Jesus Christ counsels man to have family prayer. He said, "Pray in your families unto the Father, always in my name, that your wives and your children may be blessed" (3 Ne. 18:21).

Very few pray too much. It is not one of our weaknesses.

Parents have the sacred responsibility to teach their children the importance and value of prayer, and the responsibility to teach their children how pray. In many homes, even some of the best prayers are ignored and neglected. Prayer is sacred and Jesus said: "Trifle not with sacred things" (D&C 6:12).

Another blessing available through prayer is feeling the love of God in your heart and soul. We have in the scriptures this sacred promise: "Wherefore, my beloved brethren, pray unto the Father with all the energy of heart, that ye may be filled with this love, which he hath bestowed upon all who are true followers of his Son, Jesus Christ; that ye may become the sons of God; that when he shall appear we shall be like him, for we shall see him as he is; that we may have this hope; that we may be purified even as he is pure" (Moro. 7:48).

As the sons and daughters of a living God, a living Heavenly Father, we should stay close to him by humble prayer. We should stay close to him with a clean life, that our hearts may find peace in all of life's sacred opportunities and blessings.

—*Bernard P. Brockbank*

Pray Together to the Lord

We will not always see alike; men will not always reason as their wives do and vice versa, but if you will pray together with a real desire to be united, I can say to you, you will agree on all important matters.

. . . I admonish you to pray together to the Lord, and I do not mean by that to just say prayers, I do not mean to be a phonograph and repeat something over and over again, but open your souls to the Lord as husbands and fathers in your home, and have your wives and your children join you. Have them participate. There then comes into the home an influence that you can feel when you go there.

—*George Albert Smith*

Prayer Makes Us Better People

As I think back to when we used to kneel as a family in prayer every morning and every evening, I realize what it meant to us as children to hear our father call upon the Lord and actually talk to him, expressing his gratitude and asking for the blessings of the Lord on his crops and flocks and all of our undertakings. It always gave us greater strength to meet temptation when we remembered that we would be reporting to the Lord at night.

Family prayer in any home will draw the family closer together and result in better feelings between father and mother, between parents and children, and between one child and another. If children pray for their parents, it makes them more appreciative of their parents, and as they pray for one another, they feel closer to one another and part of each other, especially as they realize that they are talking to their Father in heaven while on their knees in family or secret prayer. Then is when we forget our differences and think of the best in others, and pray for their well-being and for strength to overcome our own weaknesses. There is no doubt that we are better people when we try to tune in to the spirit of our Father in heaven so that we might communicate with him and express our desire to do his will as we pray for his blessings.

—*N. Eldon Tanner*

DAY 307

Unselfish Family Prayer

As individuals need armor, so do whole families. No wonder Brigham Young Jr. warned that a certain influence tempts us to skip our family prayer and to thus miss out on the "ten-fold pleasure" he promised.

Each family is entitled to draw heaven into the home, to rejoice in its friendship and nearness. . . . Home need not be a lonely speck; it can be cradled day and night among the hosts of heaven. By prayer we open a curtain.

God doesn't make a show, of course. His closeness is not stark and tangible during the mortal adventure. But by regular family visits to sacred ground, we let the Father fuse his might to the hearts gathered before him. More than any watchful parent, he sees problems before we do. Because of frequent family prayers, he often solves problems without making a fuss. We permit him to lighten burdens and lead us from temptation. Prayer after prayer, we give him our ongoing permission to breathe his peace among us. He is present in his own remarkable way. . . .

Love leads us to care about the fearsome moments our dear ones may face this hour or this day. Faith leads us to plead for them. Those who pray only for themselves have little grasp of the power of prayer. Unselfish prayer is pleasing to the Lord. He answers it! . . .

A ten-fold pleasure is ours in the safety and goodness of our homes, the wonder of answer after answer from God himself to our little families as the years go by.

—*Wayne E. Brickey*

The Blessing of Prayerful Parents

Only about two years ago I learned from my aunt, Arlene Ash Turner, something precious of which I was completely unaware. It occurred back in May of 1945—the Okinawa period, where I was serving as a frightened infantryman in a mortar squad. Arlene told me that one day my mother had told her that the night before she and Dad had had their parental prayers and had prayed over me and my sisters. When abed they were nearly asleep, Mother reportedly said, "Clarence, we need to get out of bed and pray again. Neal is in grave danger!" They did, pleading for me afresh. I do not know the precise date, but the time zones are such that their late-night prayer would match mid-afternoon or early evening on Okinawa. The Japanese had been trying to hit our mortar squad position but were unable to do so because of some low, intervening hills. They must have moved their artillery pieces, because soon a round of artillery came squarely in between two of our foxholes. Shaken, I prayed most earnestly (doubtless along with others), naively promising to pay the Lord back. Relief came! Now, of course, I am much more in His debt.

I do not know the date of the parental prayer, but in the words of some other young men who had special mothers and who also went off to war, I "did not doubt [my mother] knew it" (see Alma 56:48).

Having such prayerful parents was a great inspiration to all of us in the family, and to learn so many years later of that simple but powerful act has been a great source of joy to me; and it has caused me to weep with appreciation more than once.

—*Neal A. Maxwell*

DAY 309

An Answer to Family Prayer

Elder Groberg relates the story of being placed in a dirty metal customs shed in Suva on his way to Tonga. He was supposed to be met by two elders, but because of a mishap, he was left alone in the shed overnight.

"How long will the light last?" I thought. Then I wondered, "What will happen when those last rays disappear and fold into the night? Maybe if I close my eyes, I'll just disappear or at least circumstances will change." I closed my eyes. However, nothing happened, so I opened my eyes and said, "I must have hope. Things must turn out all right."

I closed my eyes again, this time in prayer. Suddenly I felt almost transported. I didn't see anything or hear anything in a physical sense. But in a more real sense, I saw my family in far-off Idaho kneeling together in prayer. I heard one, acting as mouth, say as clearly as anything can be heard, "And bless John on his mission."

As that faithful family called down the powers of heaven to bless their missionary son in a way they could not physically do, the

352   A YEAR OF POWERFUL PRAYER

powers of heaven came down, lifted me up, and in a spiritual way allowed me for a brief moment to once again join my family circle in prayer. I was one with them. I was literally swallowed up in the love and concern of a loving family and sensed for a moment what being taken into the bosom of Abraham might be like (see Luke 16:22). I was given to understand also that there are other circles of love and concern, unbounded by time or space, to which we all belong and from which we can draw strength. God does not leave us entirely alone—ever!

Tears of joy flowed freely as I had restored to me the warmth of family, the light of love, and the strength of hope. When I again felt the hard, uneven cement beneath me, there was no fear, no sorrow, no trepidation, only deep gratitude and assurance.

—*John H. Groberg*

DAY 310

Do Your Children Hear You Pray for Them?

"Love is spoken in prayer. In your home, do children hear their parents pray for them in specific ways? For instance, when Kami is sick, she can hear the family pray she will have the Lord's healing influence. When Cameron needs a job, it will help him to hear the prayers of his family express confidence in him. If in your home children hear their parents pray for each other daily, then your home is a faith-building home. In it, hearts can be changed, and those who live there may become the children of Christ."

—*H. Burke Peterson*

DAY 311

Practical Advice for Busy Families

I heard a speech once by Mrs. Norman Vincent Peale about their family members who had specific worries at certain times of the day. So we followed suit, and some mornings we would all agree to pray for Noah to do well on his math test at 9:20 or for Dad to do well in an important meeting at 1:30. It was a fun way to think and pray for each other during the day.

Initially, all those morning prayers were on our knees around the coffee table or the kitchen table, but as life got more hectic and basketball boys were leaving in the dark of morning and getting home in the dark of the evening, we decided that whoever was leaving on those hectic school mornings should yell "huddle" as they were standing at the door. Whoever was in earshot met at the front door and, with arms around shoulders, we offered a quick prayer of thanksgiving and protection. Sometimes it was just one child and one parent, sometimes two or three or more joined the circle.

Today we have a group e-mail account where every family

member is reached almost instantly at the touch of a button. There are often requests for prayers from one of our children in distress. We assure each other often that we are praying and sometimes fasting for them. Like those cyberspace messages that can't be seen as they fly through space, prayers reach their destination but with even better accuracy. True, prayers are not always answered as we would wish or as soon as we would like, but we believe that they are heard and answered in the Lord's way and time.

—*Linda Eyre*

DAY 312

Pray for Dad

I was attending conference with the six children of Elder Ezra Taft Benson, one of whom was my college roommate. My interest increased when President David O. McKay announced that the next speaker would be Elder Benson. I watched respectfully as Elder Benson, whom I had not yet met, walked toward the microphone. He was a big man, well over 1.8 meters tall. He was a man internationally known as the United States Secretary of Agriculture and a special witness of the Lord, a man who seemed calm and sure, one who had addressed audiences throughout the world. Suddenly a hand touched my arm. One of Elder Benson's young daughters leaned toward me and whispered urgently, "Pray for dad."

Somewhat startled, I thought, "This message is being passed

down the row and I am to pass it on. Shall I say, 'Pray for Elder Benson'? Shall I say, 'You're supposed to say a prayer for your father'?" Sensing the immediate need to act, I leaned over and whispered simply, "Pray for dad."

I watched that whisper move along the row to where Sister Benson sat, her head already bowed in prayer.

—*Elaine S. McKay*

Prayer Is an Umbrella

Prayer is like an umbrella in the storms of life. When I was a busy mom with seven children at home, I was so grateful when one of my children would say, "We forgot to have family prayer." Sometimes we would stand by the back door and pray as the children ran off to school. It always strengthened the spirituality in our home.

"And you can pray for your family. If there is contention, pray for a spirit of peace. No matter what, Heavenly Father will bless you with peace in your heart. Prayer is a miracle; it can help develop the spirituality in your home."

—*Carol B. Thomas*

Prayer Can Bring Peace to Families

One mother told me of a time when she came home and found that her seventeen-year-old daughter had packed her belongings and was ready to move out. The mother, her heart aching for her daughter, went to her room and alone knelt in prayer, pleading to know what to do. When she sought out her daughter, negative comments spilled from the young woman. But instead of getting defensive and upset as she usually did, the mother listened for the feelings behind the words and realized that her daughter was really crying out for help. *How much pain she must be feeling to be acting like this!* she thought. Calmly, the mother said, "Let's go talk in my room." Her daughter not only followed, but she smiled. They shared feelings and, for the first time in a long time, they talked like friends. Finally, they returned to the daughter's room and put her things away. This mother had effectively looked beyond the defensive wall and heard the crying on the other side.

—*Brad Wilcox*

Pray as a Family

Don't start the day without family prayer; don't get so careless that you forget to kneel together before you retire. There may have been some rough edges through the day and a good way to smooth them out is by kneeling together in prayer. Don't neglect to have your little ones taught early to have family prayer.

—*Harold B. Lee*

DAY 316

Prayer Helps Resolve Marital Difficulties

If, as husband and wife, you are having serious misunderstandings or if you feel some strain or tension building up in your marriage, you should humbly get on your knees together and ask God our Father, with a sincere heart and real intent, to lift the darkness that is over your relationship, that you may receive the needed light, see your errors, repent of your wrongs, forgive each other, and receive each unto yourselves as you did in the beginning. I solemnly assure you that God lives and will answer your humble pleas, for he has said, "Ye shall ask whatsoever you will in the name of Jesus and it shall be done." (D&C 50:29.)

—*David B. Haight*

Finding God for Ourselves

Children whose Church experience includes *private* religious behavior are much more likely one day to go on a mission and marry in the temple than are children who engage only in *public* religious behavior. Private religious behavior includes such practices as personal scripture study and prayer—which establish a real relationship with God, the source of a true, internalized testimony. Young people who experience only public religious behavior—such as Church attendance, social participation, or other public activity—are far less likely to develop the internal motivation that will carry them to the temple. Why is that? The short answer is that just sitting in church won't turn you into a Saint any more than sitting in a garage will turn you into a car.

Laman and Lemuel, for example, had plenty of public religious experience. They sacrificed to follow their parents into the wilderness, they went back to Jerusalem for the plates, and they made the entire journey to the promised land. . . . But they never discovered for themselves "the dealings of that God who had created them"

(1 Nephi 2:12). Lehi told them all about God, but all people value what they *discover* far more than what they are simply *told*. Until we find Him for ourselves, we won't have a complete testimony, no matter how strong the testimony of our parents is.

Nephi, on the other hand, discovered a private spiritual world that Laman and Lemuel never chose to find. Nephi wrote that he had "great desires to know of the mysteries of God, wherefore, I did cry unto the Lord; and behold he did visit me, and did soften my heart that I did believe all the words which had been spoken by my father; wherefore, I did not rebel against him like unto my brothers" (1 Nephi 2:16). Nephi and Sam desired and chose to develop their own testimonies, but Laman and Lemuel did not. That one difference among Lehi's sons is the most important distinguishing element in the stories of their lives—and in the lives of their posterity.

—*Bruce C. Hafen*

DAY 318

Righteous Prayers Avail Much

Our prayers are for our children's welfare. Sometimes as children grow up, there comes into their lives a rebellious attitude in spite of all that we can say and do. Alma found his admonitions futile with his sons and he prayed for them, and his prayers were mighty ones. Sometimes that is about all there is left for parents to do. The prayer of a righteous man availeth much, says the scripture, and so it did in this case.

—*Spencer W. Kimball*

DAY 319

Family Prayers of Gratitude

Home is also the right place to practice and teach gratitude. When our children were young, we started a family tradition of having "prayers of gratitude." Once a week we have a family prayer devoted to expressing gratitude for our blessings. As we enumerate the many ways Heavenly Father has blessed us, we recognize the deep love he has for us and we realize how dependent we are upon him. As we acknowledge his blessings, we come to view our lives as miraculous—and our faith increases. "Trust in the Lord with all thine heart," the scriptures say, "and lean not unto thine own understanding. In all thy ways acknowledge him, and he shall direct thy paths." (Prov. 3:5–6.)

—*Joy Webb Rigby*

Strength from Dedicating a Home

My husband was head of our home in a very real and vital way. He asked each of us to take a turn in [our] little dedicatory services. I prayed first. Then in the order of their birth, each child prayed, expressing his or her feelings and commitment about the new home. Then my husband gave the dedicatory prayer.

It was wonderful. We were of one heart and one mind. The sweet spirit of the Lord filled every soul. And it was amazing to us that in prayer the details of our various expectations became clear to all.

Time passed. This house was never really "finished." There was never time enough nor money enough to refurbish it in the manner we had dreamed of when we moved in and prayed our dreams before God. In fact, our finances got worse instead of better. There were other demanding, diverse trials during these years.

But that day of dedication helped us immeasurably. Through our struggles along the way, we kept referring to the dedicatory prayer when dreams were fresh and spirits humble. We were in these circumstances together from the start, with God, and we pulled together.

—*Elaine Cannon*

A Mother's Prayer

America was deep in the economic depression of the 1930s. I was one of several small children in our family, and our father had been unemployed for many months. There was no government assistance for the unemployed, and the Church welfare program was not yet in operation. Our needs were many. Some might have said we were destitute. Though I was only a child, I felt the anxiety and concern of my parents.

Each morning we knelt together as a family, and each one in turn led our prayer. One memorable morning it was Mother's turn. She described some of our immediate needs, and then she thanked our Heavenly Father for the privilege of living the law of tithing. I immediately experienced a feeling of comfort and assurance. Living the law of the tithe was a privilege and would bring blessings. I did not doubt it because my mother knew it. Those feelings have remained and intensified throughout my life.

—Ronald E. Poelman

The Prayers of Faithful Mothers

Our mothers, and the mothers of our children, whose hearts are filled with solicitude for the welfare of their children, having had conferred upon them the gift of the Holy Spirit, by the laying on of hands, can go to their secret chambers and bow down before God and commune with Him as no other mothers on earth can do, if they will only observe the principles they have embraced and will live up to their privileges.

—*Joseph F. Smith*

Someone Is Looking Out for You

As a mother, there are times I find myself pleading with Heavenly Father throughout the day: "*Please* help me be more patient," or "*Please* bless my kids who forgot their bike helmets to get to school safely," of "*Please, please, please* help me find my toddler in this crowded public place." I never really understood the admonition to pray all day, in public and in private, until I became a mother: until I held my first newborn in my arms night after night, pleading with Heavenly Father to help him sleep so I could sleep, too. I always knew prayer worked, but I never felt that I needed it as much as I did once I hit the trenches of motherhood. I know that prayer works, because I've become infinitely more in tune to it since I need so much help daily. It's the most comforting thing in the world to know that someone is up there looking out for you. The secret is realizing that, and letting Him in.

—*Shawni Eyre Pothier*

DAY 324

The Power of Family Prayer

Think of the power of the thousands of prayers of parents and grandparents and back and back even to Jacob and Isaac and Abraham and beyond, all requesting essentially the same thing: "Bless my children. Bless my children. Bless my children." Can you hear it as it rolls and echoes throughout all eternity?

Let us all be part of that great power for good.

I testify that time and space are no barriers to these righteous influences, and no matter where we are or what our situation is— even in the depths of discouragement, far from our loved ones—we too can feel and be strengthened by those soul-stirring words, "and bless John or Jane or whomever on his or her mission," for indeed life is a mission. We are all here on assignment to learn to love and serve one another; and we can't do this as well as we should unless we have consistent, fervent family prayer.

—*John H. Groberg*

Prayer Helps Fathers Be Righteous

A man who holds the priesthood leads his family in Church participation so they will know the gospel and be under the protection of the covenants and ordinances. If you are to enjoy the blessings of the Lord, you must set your own homes in order. Together with your wife, you determine the spiritual climate of your home. Your first obligation is to get your own spiritual life in order through regular scriptural study and daily prayer. Secure and honor your priesthood and temple covenants; encourage your family to do the same.

Take seriously your responsibility to teach the gospel to your family through regular family home evening, family prayer, devotional and scripture-reading time, and other teaching moments.

—*Howard W. Hunter*

United in Faith

A father of three young sons and an infant daughter, Scott arrived home to find his toddler, Jason, flat on the bed, white and still. He had fallen backwards from a Big Wheel and he wasn't breathing. His wife had called 911 but feared he might die before they arrived. The baby kicked and screamed, and the other two sons shouted questions at their father, fearing for their brother.

Then there was a chorus of, "Pray over him, Dad."

Scott ran to the top of the medicine cabinet and took the consecrated oil from its special box. Without really knowing any details of the problem, he asked the boys to fold their arms for prayer. He directed his weeping wife to kneel down beside the bed. He put his hands on the ailing boy's head, but for a few moments he couldn't speak. His thoughts raced. Jason threatened? Lose Jason? Could he demand of God that Jason rise and walk? Scott, silently, fervently cried out to heaven for faith instead of fear as he performed the ritual of a father's blessing for Heavenly Father's spirit child. In moments his spirits calmed, and he felt the warm confirmation surge through his body as he blessed Jason to awaken and be healed, by the power of the holy priesthood of God vested in him. He had battled with even saying the words "Thy will be done" before he closed the blessing, but then he knew his prayer had been heard. There was a murmured "amen!" from Jason as Scott lifted his hands from his injured son's head. He felt a new lump well up in his own chest to see his little sons still in the reverent mood of prayer with their arms folded, their eyes scrunched shut. Of course Heavenly Father couldn't resist such pleadings from such devoted boys.

Suddenly Scott knelt down next to his wife beside the bed and guided the boys to do the same. Again he addressed Heavenly Father in prayer. This time he spoke as a father of a family grateful beyond expression to *be* a family, grateful for abundant blessings, including trust in a loving Heavenly Father. Especially, they took time for a formal thanks to God for rousing Jason. *If I feel as I do about Jason,* thought Scott, *how much more must a good and perfect being like God love him!*

—Elaine Cannon

DAY 327

Praying for Generations Unborn

The Lord has promised to remember the unselfishness of faithful parents, whether it be their prayers or their travails, whether they be Jewish faithful or Nephite, whether faithful little girls or faithful old men.

. . . Eight-year-old Sarah was always a bright and spiritual little girl. But even her parents were not prepared for the announcement she made one morning before family prayer. "I had a dream about my children."

The father was just picking up the two-year-old to prevent a crafty escape but set him back down and looked at Sarah. "Children you're going to have someday?" he asked.

"I guess so. I had a husband in the dream, and we had four children."

The mother sat down next to Sarah. "So go on. What about these children of yours?"

"Well, in the dream I could sort of tell there was a lot of noise and bad outside our house, like way out in the world." Sarah looked at the floor, thinking back as if the dream were a real experience. She looked up at her mother. "Could we pray for my children today?"

Most of us take a little longer than Sarah . . . to start praying for generations unborn. But those feelings, like the feelings of the ancient Saints, are heaven-sent. They finally come. We come to feel that our grandchildren of the distant future are just as real as our living family. We come to love them and pray for them. The Lord doesn't forget those prayers.

—*Wayne E. Brickey*

Prayer Happens on Both Sides of the Veil

President George Albert Smith likewise emphasized that "those who are on the other side (of the veil) are . . . anxious about us. They are praying for us and for our success. They are pleading, in their own way, for their descendants, for their posterity who live upon the earth."

What could possibly be more important to me when I die than whether my children and grandchildren come unto Christ and walk in his covenants blamelessly? "I have no greater joy," John wrote as a very old man, "than to hear that my children walk in truth" (3 John 1:4). Elder Russell M. Nelson explained, "Salvation is an individual matter; exaltation is a family matter." We cannot be perfect, or fully happy, for that matter, without being joined with our family members in the exalted state, a welding link having been established between the parents and the children (Hebrews 11:40; D&C 128:15,18). Consequently, we pray with all our hearts here for our family to be united in the gospel covenant. Those prayers will continue in the postmortal world of spirits, with at least the same intensity, when we finish our work on this earth. The work of the Lord goes forward on both sides of the veil.

—*Robert L. Millet*

A Prophet's Prayer

Fathers and mothers, pray over your children. Pray that they may be shielded from the evils of the world. Pray that they may grow in faith and knowledge. Pray that they may be directed toward lives that will be profitable and good. Husbands, pray for your wives. Express unto the Lord your gratitude for them, and plead with Him in their behalf. Wives, pray for your husbands. Many of them walk a very difficult road with countless problems and great perplexities. Plead with the Almighty that they may be guided, blessed, protected, inspired in their righteous endeavors.

Pray for peace in the earth, that the Almighty, who governs the universe, will stretch forth His hand and let His Spirit brood upon the people, that the nations may not rage one against another.

Pray for the weather. We have floods in one area and drought in another. I am satisfied that if enough prayers ascend to heaven for moisture upon the land, the Lord will answer those prayers for the sake of the righteous. . . .

Pray for wisdom and understanding as you walk the difficult paths of your lives. If you are determined to do foolish and imprudent things, I think the Lord will not prevent you. But if you seek His wisdom and follow the counsel of the impressions that come to you, I am confident that you will be blessed.

—*Gordon B. Hinckley*

God Is Always More Powerful Than Satan

God will comfort our souls in the storms of life. The greater the good we set out to accomplish, the greater the opposition. Having a family and teaching them properly is of the greatest eternal value. Thus, we can expect great trials, as well as great joys, in our families. This should not surprise us. Satan wants to claim our souls and those of our children. He wants our marriages and our families to fail. He wants darkness to reign. Despite this, we needn't worry or back away from our duty to our family (present or future), our community, or others, for God will always support and bless us in our honest efforts to do His will. He wants us to succeed more than Satan wants us to fail—and God is always more powerful.

—*John H. Groberg*

How Prayer Helps Us

The Power of a Child's Prayer

One morning a good many years ago, a member of the Council of the Twelve came to my office and told me of a beautiful, touching experience that had happened to him that day. He had gone to the old Deseret Gym to enjoy the steam bath for a while. As he sat there in the heavy steam, he heard the door open and looked upward toward the door to see who was entering. He could not see anyone, but he had a feeling someone else was there in the room with him. After a few minutes he saw a young Primary-age boy about eight or nine years old who had seated himself two or three feet away. The boy gradually slid closer to the Apostle, and they finally said "hello" to each other. Then the boy moved even closer until he could look up into the face of the Church leader. The little boy said, "Mister, I think I know who you are." The Apostle said, "Who am I?" The boy said, "I think you are one of the Apostles of the Church. I think you are the one who travels all over the ocean on big boats and little boats and all kinds of airplanes—and you are the one who never gets sick or hurt in any wrecks." The Apostle acknowledged that he was the one who was having those great experiences. The boy then said to him, "Do you know why it is you don't ever get killed or get hurt?" The Apostle said, "No, why is that?" The little Primary boy said, "That's because I pray for you."

What a touching, lovely expression of faith in a simple,

wonderful way! This experience happened forty years ago, but I think of it frequently. There is far more power in simple prayer than many of us think possible.

—*Glen L. Rudd*

DAY 332

Prayer Helps Us to *Know*

Prayer helps us to *know*—not the practical knowledge of this world, but the more enduring knowledge of eternal worlds: the knowledge that God is our Father; that He feels our pain; that, in the darkest nights when no light may come, He knows us and loves us and pities us for the darkness we endure.

. . . Prayer can see us through the failures, help us persevere past the pain. There is no way to avoid the trouble and disappointment of living. Part of the reason we are here is to suffer the pains of life, to experience the trouble and travail of this world.

What gives us the will to survive is not necessarily solutions to our problems but companionship for our grief: the sharing of loved ones, the love of God. And, when there is no other comfort strong enough, God is strong. And, where there is no other love long enough, God's love is long—eternal. The world is easier to see, more confident to touch; but God is the giver whose gifts endure. He is our Father. And, even when He seems so far away, He is near—hoping to help us, eager to touch us, longing to comfort us with His love.

—*Lloyd D. Newell*

A Praying People

Brethren and sisters, I know that you are a praying people. That is a wonderful thing in this day and time when the practice of prayer has slipped from many lives. To call upon the Lord for wisdom beyond our own, for strength to do what we ought to do, for comfort and consolation, and for the expression of gratitude is a significant and wonderful thing. We know that you pray for us, and we appreciate your prayers. They sustain us; they remind us of the great trust which you have placed in us. I want you to know that we pray for you always. We pray for you that you may be happy, and that in living the gospel there may be love and peace in your homes and growing goodness in your lives.

—*Gordon B. Hinckley*

We Can Pray for Others

As Church members read accounts or see graphic pictures of human suffering, they are touched and ask, "What can we do?" Most of us will not be in a position to help on a person-to-person basis when the need is many miles away. However, every member of the Church can pray for peace throughout the world and for the well-being of all its inhabitants. Also, members may fast and increase their fast offerings when they are able and thus enable the Church to do more.

—*Glenn L. Pace*

We Become Like Him

As we pray with all the energy we can muster to be filled with His love, our natures will gradually change, we will slowly become more and more like Him, and our actions and feelings will increasingly be *manifestations* of pure charity. Thus, charity is a healing, transforming balm—bestowed by the Father, applied by the Holy Ghost, to true followers of the Son—that will change our very nature as it purifies us.

—*Sheri Dew*

Prayer Brings Reverence

May I take you who are older back in memory to the homes of your childhood. I think that in many cases there was prayer in those homes; families knelt together in the morning and invoked the watchful care of God. At night they joined again in prayer. Something wonderful came of this. It is difficult to describe, but it did something for children. The very act of expressing gratitude to God, our Eternal Father, brought with it a feeling of respect, reverence, and appreciation. The sick were remembered in those prayers, as were the poor and the needy. The leaders in government were remembered in those prayers. This cultivated a spirit of respect for those in public office. Where is that respect today?

—*Gordon B. Hinckley*

Prayer Fosters Love for Country

One cannot ask God to help a neighbor in distress, without feeling motivated to do something oneself. What miracles would happen in the lives of the children of America if they would lay aside their selfishness and lose themselves in the service of others. The seed from which this sheltering and fruitful tree may grow is best planted and nurtured in the daily supplications of the family.

I know of no better way to inculcate love for country than for parents to pray before their children for the land in which we live, invoking the blessings of the Almighty upon it that it may be preserved in liberty and in peace. I know of no better way to build within the hearts of our children a much-needed respect for authority than remembering in the daily supplications of the family the President and the Congress and others who carry the burdens of government.

—*Gordon B. Hinckley*

DAY 338

A Nation on Its Knees

Never before in this gospel dispensation has there been a greater need for prayer, and never in history has there been a greater threat to our God-given right to pray when, how, or where we wish. How timely and appropriate for the true Church of Christ to emphasize this basic right and all-important need!

I think there would be great safety in a nation on its knees. What assurance it would give of the blessings of the Almighty if the American people could all be found daily—night and morning—on their knees expressing gratitude for blessings already received, acknowledging dependence upon Him, and seeking for His divine guidance. . . .

I am convinced in my heart that the spectacle of a nation praying is more awe-inspiring, more powerful, than the explosion of an atomic bomb. The force of prayer is greater than any possible combination of man-controlled powers because, "prayer is man's greatest means of tapping the resources of God." I would like to see this nation on its knees in humble prayer.

—Ezra Taft Benson

DAY 339

Love Thine Enemy

Of course it is always proper to pray for ourselves, our families, and our friends. But the Savior challenges us to expand our borders of concern: "Ye have heard that it hath been said, Thou shalt love thy neighbour, and hate thine enemy. But I say unto you, Love your enemies, bless them that curse you, do good to them that hate you, and pray for them which despitefully use you, and persecute you" (Matthew 5:44–45; see also 3 Nephi 12:43–44).

Whoa! That's a different matter entirely. Does Jesus really expect me to pray for those who dislike me? Who slander me, who knowingly hurt my reputation? Does he think that I should pray for those who would rather our family had never moved into the neighborhood? Does he believe I should pray for that man who always insults me, even when I try to be kind to him? I can still remember hearing Nikita Krushchev, the premier of the Soviet Union, declare to the people of the United States: "We will bury you." Am I supposed to pray for that kind of person? What about those who continue to state that the Latter-day Saints are members of a cult, that we are not Christian, that we worship a different Jesus and follow a different gospel?

Yes, perplexing and ponderous and painful as it may seem, you and I have been commissioned to stand on higher ground, to turn the other cheek, to forgive and to desire the best for those who hurt us, and even to pray for them. Further, as the Master said, we are to love them! Boy, this Christianity business is tough. . . .

God and Christ are in the business of people, and we are called to labor with them. They do not love me more than they love Buddhists or Hindus or even radical Islamic Jihaddists. And while I tend to think most often and feel most fondly about those within my immediate sphere, the call to Christian discipleship is a call to broaden out, to expand my spiritual horizons, to come to think more often of those I do not know as well and of those I am not as inclined to love and bless and serve, and yes, to pray for.

—*Robert L. Millet*

Praying for Those Who Despitefully Use You

I was late in learning the value of the principle of praying for those who despitefully use us. As a young lawyer, I was handling a matter for the office forwarded by a lawyer from Texas. The matter was successfully concluded, and the settlement check came payable to the client and to our office as joint payees to satisfy the attorneys' lien. As was the custom in our office, I endorsed the check and sent it down to the corresponding attorney, having full confidence that he would promptly remit the agreed-upon portion of the recovery. It did not come.

I wrote many letters. Months passed, and still there was no response. My associates were understanding, but it was not my money to forget or forgive. I felt I was being despitefully used. I thought about referring him to the Texas Bar Association for disciplinary action.

Then a thought hit me. I had not done what my mother had taught me as a child at her knee. I said to myself, "A fine Christian you are!" My conscience was pricked also because I was a bishop.

That night I got down on my knees and prayed earnestly for this person who I thought had despitefully used me.

Then, in the time that it takes for an airmail letter to come from Texas, a letter came with the explanation that this man had become very ill, had been in the hospital, had to close his office, and was ill for many months. He asked my forgiveness and advised that the check was enclosed.

—*James E. Faust*

DAY 341

Prayer Reveals Truth

Pray to have truth- and light-filled thoughts about [others] brought to you by the Spirit. One woman simply prayed: "Please fill my mind with truths about my brother." She discovered that when she added fasting to her prayers, truths about her brother started to lodge in her heart. She experienced a change of mind *and* a change of heart about her brother.

It's quite possible that the thoughts that come to your mind as and after you pray may be the most accurate thoughts you've had about the other person in a long time. When we are drawn to think something marvelous, amazing, or wonderful about someone else, we are probably closer to acknowledging his or her true self than at any other time. So, pray to be influenced by the Spirit, to have eyes to truly see, and a mind to conceive the wonderful things about this other person. Ask yourself, "When I'm with him or her, in whose presence am I really?" Notice what additional truths come to your mind.

—*Wendy Watson Nelson*

"Help Me See What You See"

If we want the best result for our day, we need to start by praying.

And one of the things I pray for often is "that heaven will show [me] the joys of today." What I like to do is pray to be able to see things the way Heavenly Father sees them. I think He sees the joys of today, every day. Wouldn't it be great to have that perspective?

I like to say, for example, "Heavenly Father, help me to see my seventeen-year-old son the way you see him today. Because what I see is a kid who never says more than three consecutive words to me, who can down six bucks' worth of Cocoa Puffs in five minutes flat, and whose room looks like a poster for tsunami relief. Help me see what you see."

And He says, "Remember what the three consecutive words were when he walked out the door this morning? 'Love you, Mom.' Remember how last night when you and your husband got home late, he had already walked the dog without even being asked, so you didn't have to? Remember how many times, on Sundays when you've staggered home after three hours of church, he has just gotten saddled up to help collect fast offerings, or to take the sacrament to somebody who was shut in, to share with them the emblems of the Lord's flesh and blood so they could renew their covenants the same as if they'd been able to be in sacrament meeting? That's who

I see when I look at your seventeen-year-old son." Quite a different picture, isn't it? Prayer really can change the night to day!

—*Emily Watts*

DAY 343

Looking for a Happier New Year?

I love titles. I notice titles. Several years ago I noticed an article in the newspaper because the title intrigued me: "Try Praying This Year." I knew I wanted to read this article. It started out this way: "Looking for a happier new year? A recent university study examining what contributes to a greater sense of well being found a curious factor. Certain types of prayer. They found that frequent prayer heightens happiness, general life satisfaction and religious satisfaction."

What a great study! I can imagine people in white lab coats with 12,000 rats—6,000 of them pray and 6,000 don't pray, and these fellows are there taking notes. "Oh, they're frowning over here—they seem happier on this side." They could have saved a lot of money, a lot of rats, and a lot of time if they had just consulted the scriptures. For example D&C 19:38 records a message Joseph Smith received for Martin Harris in which the Lord taught, "Pray always, and I will pour out my spirit upon you, and great shall be your blessing." In 2 Nephi 32:8, toward the end of his great ministry, Nephi taught, "If ye would hearken unto the Spirit which teacheth a man to pray ye would know that ye must pray; for the evil spirit teacheth not a man to pray, but teacheth him that he must not pray."

The evil one is not just leaving us alone, hoping we won't pray. He is trying to *stop* us from praying. I think about this sometimes when I don't feel that I want to pray. I can easily guess who is trying to convince me that I should not pray. President Brigham Young said, "Were I to draw a distinction in all the duties that are required of the children of men from first to last I would place first and foremost the duty of seeking unto the Lord our God until we open the path of communication from heaven to earth, from God to our own souls. Keep every avenue of your hearts clean and pure before him." (*Discourses of Brigham Young* [Salt Lake City: Deseret Book, 1954], 44.)

—*Mary Ellen Edmunds*

DAY 344

Inspiration and Avoiding Temptation

Pray. There is no temptation placed before you which you cannot shun. Do not allow yourself to get in positions where it is easy to fall. Listen to the promptings of the Spirit. If you are engaged in things where you do not feel you can pray and ask the

Lord's blessings on what you are doing, then you are engaged in the wrong kind of activity.

—*Ezra Taft Benson*

Joseph Smith and Prayer

All of us need deeper understanding in prayer. All of us reach. All of us speak. But none of us have perfected the process and all of us need encouragement. . . .

There is a letter in the Prophet's [Joseph Smith's] handwriting written in 1832—only a few months after one of the most remarkable revelations he received. The record of that revelation is now section 46 of the Doctrine and Covenants. Joseph is writing to his wife, Emma.

"My situation is a very unpleasant one, although I will endeavor to be contented, the Lord assisting me. I have visited a grove which is just back of the town, almost every day, where I can be secluded from the eyes of any mortal, and there give vent to all the feelings of my heart in meditation and prayers. I have called to mind all the past moments of my life, and am left to mourn and shed tears of sorrow for my folly in suffering the adversary of my soul to have so much power over me, as he has had in times past. But God is merciful and has forgiven my sins, and I rejoice that he sendeth forth His Comforter unto as many as believe and humble themselves before Him" (Jessee, *Personal Writings,* 238. Spelling and punctuation standardized).

Now, that one paragraph is enough to tell us that he was struggling—blessed and magnified though he was—just as we are struggling with the weight of life, with the difficulties and weaknesses that are in us, and with the constant desire to receive of the Lord.

—*Truman G. Madsen*

DAY 346

All Blessings Are Available through Prayer

In a stirring plea, Amulek calls upon the saints to pray always for all their needs, both temporal and spiritual. Above all, we are to call upon the Lord for mercy lest, being sinners, we remain subject to the demands of justice and be required with a relentless certainty to pay the penalty for all our evil deeds. Prayer confers upon us the merciful goodness of a gracious Lord who bore our sins and who seeks to wash us clean in his blood. "Cry unto him for mercy," Amulek exhorts, "for he is mighty to save." All of the great and eternal spiritual blessings that prepare mortals for eternal life are available through prayer.

—*Bruce R. McConkie*

Prayer Can Reduce Anxiety

Through years of counseling with people afflicted with anxieties of many different origins, it has struck me as strange that so few of them ever admit to having fervently prayed about the cause of their anxieties, fears, worries, concerns, anger, disappointments, and emotionally upsetting experiences. For those whose unhappiness is lodged largely in impaired interpersonal relationships, Mormon refers to charity as "the pure love of Christ" and he urges "Pray unto the Father with all the energy of heart, that ye may be filled with his love" (Moroni 7:47–48). Prayer is an indispensable means of engendering more tender feelings toward those within our immediate families, of cultivating much greater charity among those with whom we labor, and of reducing untold anxieties about matters which, in an eternal sense, are generally of fleeting importance.

—*Spencer J. Condie*

Finding Balance through Prayer and Scripture Study

Perhaps we might begin each day as President Spencer W. Kimball suggested: "The breaking of the day has found me on my knees" ("Breaking of the Day," 52). Perhaps we could pray for guidance as we struggle to balance our roles as caretakers, nurturers, or providers. Ours might be a prayer for strength as we consider the burdens that will be balanced within our carefully constructed pile. Perhaps we might pray for an increase in charity, or for opportunities to act as instruments in the Lord's hands. The Lord will open our eyes to recognize the good that lies within the day ahead of us if we just take the time to ask.

Always, within each day we must turn to the scriptures. The stories contained therein hold keys to discovering balance. If we search the scriptures for ideas to create balance in our lives, we will find answers to our prayers.

Sometimes when I am overwhelmed with my responsibilities and the tasks on my to-do list seem destined to remain forever unaccomplished, I try to remember a scripture in the book of Isaiah. Speaking of the Savior, it asks, "Who hath measured the waters in the hollow of his hand, and meted out heaven with the span, and comprehended the dust of the earth in a measure, and weighed the mountains in scales, and the hills in a balance? Who hath directed the Spirit of the Lord?" (Isaiah 40:12–13).

I love to picture the Savior with the water of the earth cupped in one hand while the other hand spans the expanse of heaven. He knows instantly how to measure out the dust and to balance the mountains and hills. If the Savior can handle all of that, I know that He can help me balance the details of my life. If I turn to Him for help, the Spirit will direct me, and through Him answers will come.

Balance will become easier to achieve as we approach the day with prayer as our foundation and with scripture study placed carefully above it. If we start there, we will not be working alone. The Lord will be our partner. He will help us to choose the best stones; He will steady our hands; He will guide our progress.

—*Emily Freeman*

DAY 349

Reassurance through Prayer

It is soul-satisfying to know that God is mindful of us and ready to respond when we place our trust in Him and do that which is right. There is no place for fear among men and women who place their trust in the Almighty, who do not hesitate to humble themselves in seeking divine guidance through prayer. Though persecutions arise, though reverses come, in prayer we can find reassurance, for God will speak peace to the soul. That peace, that spirit of serenity, is life's greatest blessing.

—*Ezra Taft Benson*

DAY 350

Prayer Brings Hope

A good friend shared with me an experience she had one day in the temple. Her life had not progressed as she had planned or as she had hoped. She had lost most of her drive to go on, and she had gone to the temple searching for enlightenment. Through the whole temple session she prayed for help, but nothing came. And then these words rushed into her soul, "For those who have come to the temple with heavy hearts, may their hope sustain them in these difficult days." Hope is what she needed, and the Lord had spoken to her clearly.

—*Elaine L. Jack*

Peace in Prayer

Several years ago ... I was a produce supervisor for a large grocery chain. One day I dropped by home and picked up my young son Lawrence, who was three at the time. We went out to visit a farm to see if we could procure produce for that company. I went into the sheds and examined the produce; then I was told that Jack, the farmer, was in the house. I went to the front door and rang the bell. A little lady, probably eighty-five years old, white-haired, frail, stood in the doorway.

"Is Jack here?" I asked.

"No, he isn't. His father just passed away, and he went to the hospital," she said, and then she began to weep.

I said, "Are you Jack's mother?"

She replied, "Yes."

"I'm terribly sorry about your husband." And then I was no longer a produce buyer; I was a high priest in the Church, and I said to her, "Do you believe in the resurrection?"

"I guess so."

And I said, "The Savior said, 'I am the resurrection, and the life: he that believeth in me, though he were dead, yet shall he live.'" [John 11:25.] ... And I went on with several scriptures about the resurrection.

Then finally, as I concluded I said, "Your husband will live again. He will be resurrected. Do you believe that?" I couldn't tell whether she did or not; I just knew she wasn't comforted. So I asked her, "Do you believe in prayer?"

She said, "I used to pray, but lately if I get down on my knees I can't get back up again. When I do pray, I forget what I'm supposed to pray about. And then when I'm down on my knees and no one comes, I just have to wait until someone does come."

"Would you like Lawrence and me to pray for you?"

"Yes."

We entered her home, and I helped this sweet soul down onto her knees. Then we began to pray. I poured out my soul to the Lord to let a sweet blessing of comfort come to her. About halfway through the prayer I felt a warmth and a peace come into my heart that I knew our prayers were being answered.

At the close of the prayer, I stood up and lifted her again from her knees. Peace radiated from her face. I held her hands for a moment and looked into her eyes. There was peace there.

—*Vaughn J. Featherstone*

DAY 352

Receiving the Spirit through Prayer

One morning . . . in the Philippines, my companion . . . and I were tracting. We realized we weren't in the right frame of mind. We'd had trouble getting a bus, and it was a very hot day. We stopped on the dirt road and prayed a silent prayer, asking that God would change our hearts and help us proceed with the right spirit. We came to an orange gate with the number 15 painted on it. We had a good feeling about knocking on that gate.

An older Filipino man with a kind and gentle face answered. We made our usual introduction. He hesitated, apparently reluctant to have us come in. A strong impression came over us that he was meant to receive our message. We explained the best we could (without knowing his language, Tagalog) that we had a wonderful message about God. He told us that many missionaries had knocked at his gate, but he had not invited them in. He hesitated again, but then finally invited us to enter.

We felt impressed to share with him the experience the Prophet Joseph Smith had in the Sacred Grove. Being aware that he was not fluent in English, we spoke slowly and simply. As we finished, he was deep in thought.

"Sisters," he asked gently, "could you please tell me this beautiful story again?"

This time we felt the power of the story more deeply, too. As we finished, he again seemed deeply touched. He hesitated, then asked once more, almost apologetically, "Just once more, please?" And we did a third time. He listened carefully.

This time all three of us felt even more strongly and sweetly the witness of the Holy Ghost that Joseph Smith was a prophet and had literally seen the Father and the Son.

—*Mary Ellen Edmunds*

Prayers Sustain Our Family Members

I recall a story of a Latter-day Saint boy in military service. He was the only Latter-day Saint in his barracks, and he soon wearied of the jibes of his associates. One day when the going was particularly rough, he finally agreed to go into town with the crowd. But as they entered the town, there came before his mind's eye a picture. He saw the kitchen of his home. It was supper time. There was his family, kneeling at the kitchen chairs—his father, mother, two sisters, and a small brother. The little brother was praying, and he was asking our Heavenly Father to look after his brother in the military.

That mental picture did it. The young man turned away from the crowd. The prayer of that little brother, of that family, brought clarity of mind and courage to that Latter-day Saint youth.

—*Gordon B. Hinckley*

Prayer Can Free Us from Addiction

I have a longtime friend who owned a very successful business. Occasionally, to find relief from the stress of his responsibilities, he would partake of substances forbidden by the Word of Wisdom. As the stress in his life increased, so did his consumption of alcohol. Indeed, he was becoming a prisoner to alcohol.

One afternoon he felt the enticings of the Spirit prompting him to overcome this addiction, which had begun to impair his moral agency. He left his office for several hours and drove to a very secluded spot far removed from the city. There he knelt in humble prayer and pled with the Lord with all the energy of his heart for added strength to overcome this addiction, which robbed his spirituality and threatened to destroy his very soul. He remained on his knees for a very long time, and eventually a sweet, purifying spirit began to distill upon his soul, cleansing him from any desire to drink and fortifying him with a firm resolve to keep the commandments.

—*Spencer J. Condie*

Lean on Him

Someone asked a great surgeon, "How does it feel to have the power of life and death in your hands as you operate?" The surgeon answered, "I never feel that way. When I was a young, cocksure surgeon, I was proud of my ability and my record. Then one day I had to make a hair-breadth decision. I wasn't correct. For some time, I wouldn't operate. As I sat depressed, thinking of my failure, it suddenly came to me, in all humility that God had given me these hands, had given me these brains, not to be wasted. I prayed to him then to let me have another chance. I still do. I pray each time I take a scalpel in hand, 'Guide my hands, O Lord, and give me of thy knowledge.' You see *he* is the famous surgeon, I am only his servant."

He is also the famous architect. He is also the greatest of all teachers. Did you ever think that scientists have discovered anything that God didn't already know? Think of it. He has given you and me hands. He has given you and me brains, and he hasn't given them to us to waste. He expects us to lean on him and exercise to the best of our ability in order to use them righteously in righteous purposes.

—*Harold B. Lee*

DAY 356

In Defense of Prayer

President Faust recalls being questioned for Officer's Candidate School in 1942.

The questions asked of me at the officers' Board of Inquiry took a very surprising turn. Nearly all of them centered upon my ... beliefs. "Do you smoke?" "Do you drink?" "What do you think of others who smoke and drink?" I had no trouble answering these questions.

"Do you pray?" "Do you believe that an officer should pray?" The officer asking these questions was a hard-bitten career soldier. He did not look like he had prayed very often. I pondered. Would I give him offense if I answered how I truly believed? I wanted to be an officer very much so that I would not have to do all-night guard duty and KP, but mostly so my sweetheart and I could afford to be married.

I decided not to equivocate and responded that I did pray and that I felt that officers might seek divine guidance as some truly great generals had done. I added that I thought that officers should be prepared to lead their men in all appropriate activities, if the occasion requires, including prayer.

. . . I left the hearing resigned to the fact that these hard-bitten officers would not like the answers I had given to their questions and would surely score me very low. A few days later when the scores were posted, to my astonishment I had passed. I was in the first group taken for officer's candidate school! I graduated, became a second lieutenant, married my sweetheart, and we "lived together happily ever after."

This was one of the critical crossroads of my life. Not all of the experiences in my life turned out the way I wanted them to, but they have always strengthened my faith.

—*James E. Faust*

Confidence in God

Joseph Smith had much to say about confidence in his *Lectures on Faith,* but he spoke of confidence in God, not confidence in oneself—"that confidence in God without which no person can obtain eternal life." That same confidence is mentioned in another revelation given through the Prophet Joseph: "Let virtue garnish thy thoughts unceasingly; then shall thy *confidence* wax strong in the presence of God; and the doctrine of the priesthood shall distill upon thy soul as the dews from heaven. The Holy Ghost shall be thy constant companion. . . ." (D&C 121:45–46; emphasis added.)

Part of the sacrifice of a broken heart and a contrite spirit is a willingness to sacrifice the love affair so many of us have with our own egos. . . .

But when we place our confidence in God rather than in ourselves, our need for self-esteem takes care of itself—not because of our manipulation of successful experiences but because our fundamental attitude allows us access to the only trustworthy source for knowing that the course of life we pursue is known to and accepted by God. It is not just the mistake-free, no-fault life that pleases God. He has deliberately placed us in a sphere where the most sharply focused purpose is to learn from our experience and to grow in both our desires and our understanding to be like him. Obviously that includes the greatest effort and integrity we can muster as we seek to do his will. But the heart of it all is not *self*-confidence. It is confidence in *him,* and in his power to make us into creatures far beyond the reach of what our goal-setting and goal-achieving can ultimately accomplish in the process of becoming as he is.

—*Bruce C. Hafen*

DAY 358

Sustained and Strengthened

During our son's illness, we saw and felt the spiritual power of prayer! Our ward had never prayed harder than it did then, and I don't think the members had ever been closer to each other. Our family was sustained by the collective faith and prayers of our friends. And even as our hearts were breaking in fear that we might lose our son, we felt closer to our Heavenly Father and more aware of our dependency on Him than at almost any other time in our lives.

While the blessings we ask for and receive through prayer are undeniably magnificent, the greatest blessing and benefit is not the physical or spiritual blessings that may come as answers to our prayers but in the changes to our soul that come as we learn to be dependent on our Heavenly Father for strength.

—*David E. Sorenson*

Talking to a Trusted Friend

In early 2000 a Relief Society assignment took me to Africa, and the images of our beautiful African sisters are still vivid in my heart and mind. Their countenances reflect the image of Christ. When they pray, they pray. It's as though they reach right through the veil and talk to a trusted Friend. And despite severe temporal challenges, they are a happy lot. By the world's measure, they have little—except happiness. By contrast, many of us have everything—except happiness. Their optimism springs from a bedrock faith in Jesus Christ, to Whom they have given their hearts. I've found myself wondering who the Lord is most concerned about—those whose temporal challenges are extreme but whose hearts are fixed on Him, or those who have more things of this world but who haven't offered their whole souls unto Him (see Omni 1:26). Hunger may be a problem in Africa, but our sisters there aren't starving spiritually.

—*Sheri Dew*

The Heart in Tune

If your relationship with the Lord is not all that you would like it to be, I encourage you to spend more time with him in prayer. Sometimes we think that we must meet a long list of specifications before we're worthy to approach him. Or sometimes we think that we must withdraw completely from our daily activities to meet him. Perhaps both of these things are partially true in some circumstances, but I testify to you that he is already with us in those daily circumstances and he stands beside us as we anxiously check off good deeds on our endless lists, patiently waiting for us to notice him. He doesn't call us away from our daily activities; he asks simply that we let him be with us as we carry them out—including the carpooling, the housecleaning, the parent-teacher conferences, the meetings at work, and the meetings at church. Prayer is an endlessly refreshing and delightful dialogue that can be carried on, even without words, between the heart in tune and the Spirit of the Lord.

—*Chieko N. Okazaki*

Popcorn Day

In a fast and testimony meeting, a mother thanked the Lord for a tender mercy that had been given to her son the previous week. His first-grade teacher set aside part of one day each week as "popcorn day." Popcorn was served to a student during recess if all of his or her work had been completed. It was her son's favorite day at school, and he looked forward to it all week.

Because of a doctor's appointment, though, he had been unable to attend school on popcorn day. He was so disappointed, and he asked his mother if she thought they might have popcorn day the next day instead. She said no, explaining that it was always held on the same day of the week. If something came up at school that interfered with the treat, then the teacher simply skipped it for that week.

Nothing she said could dampen her son's hope. As he prepared to leave for school the next day, she warned him again that it likely wouldn't be popcorn day. "It's all right, Mom," he said cheerfully. "I asked Heavenly Father if it could be popcorn day today."

Touched by his faith, she said nothing more, but she worried all day about how he would react when popcorn day didn't happen. When he came home, his mother waited for a few minutes, but he didn't mention anything unusual. Finally, she asked if they had had popcorn day. "Sure," he said, as if it were the most natural thing in the world.

Why would the God of the universe, a deity of infinite power and majesty, concern Himself with something as trivial as popcorn day? I believe there are two answers to that. First, it is because He is not just God, but our Heavenly Father. Any parent will tell you that they find joy in doing small and trivial things for their children if it brings them joy.

But second, and more important, consider that while popcorn day *is* perhaps of little eternal consequence, a child's testimony is not. And that little boy's testimony was strengthened that day. . . .

We worship a God who can move "popcorn day" back twenty-four hours and, at the same time, sweep His hand over national or global events and alter the flow of history.

—*Gerald N. Lund*

DAY 362

Creating a Foundation for Your Life

If you remember nothing more of what I say today, I pray you will hear my own testimony and act upon this one truth. The strongest, firmest, most sure foundation for your life is a personal testimony of the truth that God lives, that he speaks again to us, and that he cares for each of us. This testimony will come to you if you will ask in faith, nothing wavering, and with sincere intent. My dear sisters, millions have a testimony, and it can be yours also if you will but ask the Lord in constant, secret prayer.

—*Barbara B. Smith*

There Must Be Prayer

The marvelous and wonderful thing is that any individual who desires to know the truth may receive that conviction. The Lord Himself gave the formula when He said, "If any man will do [the will of the Father], he shall know of the doctrine, whether it be of God, or whether I speak of myself" (John 7:17).

It will take study of the word of God. It will take prayer and anxious seeking of the source of all truth. It will take living the gospel, an experiment, if you please, in following the teachings. I do not hesitate to promise, because I know from personal experience, that out of all of this will come, by the power of the Holy Ghost, a conviction, a testimony, a certain knowledge.

People of the world seem unable to believe it, so many of them. What they do not realize is that the things of God are understood only by the Spirit of God. There must be effort. There must be humility. There must be prayer. But the results are certain and the testimony is sure.

—*Gordon B. Hinckley*

Communion

What of the risen Lord among the Nephites? Why would a glorified, immortal, and resurrected being, now possessing the fullness of the glory and power of the Father (Matthew 28:18; D&C 93:16), spend so much of his time in prayer among the Nephites? Was there some truth he did not know, some godly attribute he did not possess, some energy or strength he lacked? Was there some approval of the Father, some encouragement or permission he needed? I rather think not. . . . Jesus prayed frequently as an example to the Saints and to all men and women of the need to communicate with God—often, regularly, consistently, intensely, reverently.

Building on these truths, we therefore ask further whether there are not other purposes of prayer, both in time and eternity. Jesus prayed to the Father because he loved the Father. Jesus prayed to the Father because it was a reverential way of speaking to his Father, who is forever worthy of the reverence of his children. Jesus prayed to the Father because they enjoyed *communion*. That word *communion* is an especially meaningful word, one that is worth much reflection. President David O. McKay observed that spirituality is "the consciousness of victory over self, and of communion with the Infinite." (David O. McKay, *Gospel Ideals* [Salt Lake City: Improvement Era, 1953], 390.) Jesus possessed perfect spirituality because he had overcome the world (John 16:33; D&C 101:36) and because he enjoyed perfect communion with the Father. This pattern is a call to you and me, is it not, to live our lives in such a manner that we cultivate the cleansing and revelatory benefits of the Spirit more and more; that we yield our hearts unto God (Helaman 3:35) and have an eye single to his glory (D&C 88:67); that we allow our consciences to be strengthened, our judgment to be refined, and our desires to be educated.

—*Robert L. Millet*

DAY 365

Because You Can't Do It Alone

Prayer unlocks the powers of heaven in our behalf. Prayer is the great gift which our Eternal Father has given us by which we may approach Him and speak with Him in the name of the Lord Jesus Christ. Be prayerful. You cannot make it alone. You cannot reach your potential alone. You need the help of the Lord.

—*Gordon B. Hinckley*